133
JO''

THE OTHER SIDE

THE OTHER SIDE

The True Story
of the Boy Who Sees Ghosts

Denice Jones

New Horizon Press
Far Hills, New Jersey

Jones, Denice
    The Other Side: The True Story of the Boy Who Sees Ghosts

Interior Design: Susan M. Sanderson

Library of Congress Control Number: 00-132569

ISBN: 0-88282-198-9
New Horizon Press

Manufactured in the U.S.A.

2004   2003   2002   2001   2000   /   5   4   3   2   1

Take heed that ye despise
not one of these little ones;
for I say unto you,
That in heaven their angels
do always behold the face
of my Father which is in heaven.

- Matthew 18:10

TABLE OF CONTENTS

AUTHOR'S NOTE

This book is based on my real experiences and those of my family. The personalities, events, actions and conversations portrayed within the story have been largely taken from my diary, letters, memory and personal papers.

Some of the dialogue represented in this book was reconstructed from my memory and/or the memories of the participants. A few of the scenes depicted have been reconfigured and enhanced for clarity and dramatic impact drawing on sometimes differing memories and versions, papers and interviews. The presumed thoughts and imagined words of the participants were written in consonance with the true actions of the people involved.

In order to protect their privacy, some characters have been given fictitious names, addresses and descriptions, and identifying details have been altered. With two exceptions, Kirsten and Amanda, who are composites, all of the people in the book are actual.

My story is all too real and I have written it as faithfully as memory will allow, knowing for those who read and believe no explanation is necessary; for those who do not, no explanation is possible.

ACKNOWLEDGEMENTS

I would like to thank:

My husband, Bruce, for his unconditional love, support, and for always believing in me, our life and our love forever;

Our wonderful children, Michael, Kenny and Crystal, for their ability to be strong;

Our parents, for all their love and support throughout our lives;

The Bishop, for his time, prayers and his devotion to our family;

Our attorney, Stuart Rothenberg, for not only his help when we had nowhere to turn, but his true friendship. His jokes keep us laughing, his guidance keeps us strong and his heart of gold keeps us loving and believing in people;

The people who have come to our houses and tried to help, as we always needed and still need to keep our hope going;

Most of all and from the bottom of my heart and soul, God, for being by our sides, giving His unconditional love and being our highest power.

❧ 1 ❧

THE MAN IN THE ROOM

The horror began on a windy, amber-colored fall Saturday with the scent of winter in the air. It should have been one of the happiest periods in my life. After a traumatic marriage, then a bitter divorce and the difficult struggles of being a single mother trying to support and nurture my two young children, I had recently remarried. Bruce was a tall, good-natured man whose kind heart embraced not only me but my sons: Michael, who was nine, and Kenny, who was twelve.

To help our new family blend, Bruce had just bought us a charming, old colonial house painted the soft, heavenly blue so popular in the early 1900s and looking as if it had emerged from a hundred years before. The place was just about perfect for our family. I loved its layout and features which included oak hardwood floors, a wide front porch which looked like it came from the *Gone with the Wind* era, a back patio and garage. Just off the garage were the ample stone patio and a back door that opened into the large kitchen with its huge oven, a laundry room and a small bathroom. The front door opened into a large foyer next to a formal living room and a parlor which became our family

1

room. This combined with a dining room and became the most frequently used room in the house. A staircase with beautiful mahogany banisters led to the second floor from the family room. Upstairs, there were four bedrooms and a large bathroom. Bruce and I had one of the rooms and the boys each had a room, but often slept together in one or the other. A large bathroom with both a modern shower and an old-fashioned footed tub was located down at the end of the hall, next to the linen closet and the locked door to the attic. The outside of the house was surrounded by undergrowth as if no one had lived there for a long time, but though Bruce was working night and day to make our lives better, in the little spare time he had he assiduously cut the debris away. There emerged shady oak and maple trees for the boys to climb and plenty of space for them to play and grow, as well as room for Bruce's daughter, Crystal, who we hoped would be coming to visit us often.

It was an idyllic time. The years before, when my first husband had walked out on us and we were alone, seemed far behind the boys and me now. It had taken us this long to get settled, but we had finally made it at last. We loved the town and the boys loved their school. I had taken a leave of absence from my job in the geriatric field so that the boys could adjust more readily. Life seemed perfect and, for a short time, it was.

But everything changed with one scream.

I was in the dining room setting the table for dinner when I heard it. From one of the boys' rooms came a shrill keening like the shriek of a night creature. Somehow I recognized the sound as my younger son Michael's voice. I raced up the stairs so fast I did not even feel my feet hitting the steps. Our dog, Katie, followed close behind me. Rushing into the room, I searched for Michael. Then I saw him. He was lying on the floor in the corner, his body curled into a tight ball. His hands were clenched around his knees. His face, which the priest at our church often said shone with the purity of a cherub, was distorted and soaked with tears, but it was his eyes that drew me—wide open and staring as though they had just glimpsed something truly frightening.

"Michael," I whispered, kneeling down beside him. "What is it?"

I stroked his hair and tried to pull him toward my lap. His body was so tense it was like dragging a weight across the floor. "What's wrong?" I asked him again. His lips began to move, although no sound came out of them. Finally, his mouth trembled and words breathed out.

"The m-m-man," he stuttered.

"Michael? What man?" I demanded, probably more sternly than I should have, but Bruce was away this week on a business trip and the thought that an intruder could be in the house sent a chill down my spine.

"There was a man," he replied, his voice shaking with alarm. "He tried to touch my shoulder."

"Maybe you were half asleep and it was Katie nudging you," I offered, motioning to our black Labrador retriever who sat outside the room in the hallway.

"No," Michael cried out.

It took a moment for me to calm down enough to try to soothe my son and decide what to do, but then I gently moved Michael from my lap. "Stay here," I told him. I looked around for some sort of weapon. Finding nothing else, I grabbed a toy truck. I hoped our intruder had a sense of humor. "Stay here," I repeated, giving Michael a hug. "I'll search the house." I left Michael and headed down the hall to my own bedroom. I saw no one, but flung open the closet door and looked under the bed anyway. Then I turned and ran downstairs, searching the living room and the dining room, looking in all the corners, jumping at every sound and shadow. I hunted everywhere I could think of that a man could hide himself. At every moment, with each corner I turned, I was convinced I would encounter the man Michael had seen. Finally, I checked the front and back doors—both were locked. There was no one else in the house.

I felt a stab of irritation, but it quickly passed. Michael must have fallen asleep and had a nightmare. I considered how scared he seemed and hurried back to him.

Michael was still in his room, pressed into the corner like a cowering animal. He had a blanket over his head now and as I neared him, I saw it tremble. Sitting down next to him, I called to him softly and watched him inch out from under the covers and scramble into my lap. He was still crying. Gently, I pulled the blanket away from his face.

"There's no man in the house, honey," I told him.

"Did you look everywhere?" he whispered.

"Yes, but there's nobody here."

"But I saw him," Michael insisted. "He was an old man and he kept following me. He tried to touch me on the shoulder and when I called you, he disappeared."

"What do you mean?" I asked. This was not going the way I had planned. I had wanted to comfort my son and tell him that the whole thing had been a dream. But as he spoke, I could feel myself perspiring.

"He was standing right next to me and he stuck out his hand…like this," Michael answered and reached out to me. His small hand was trembling. "When he just about touched me, I screamed out loud and he left."

"No, Michael. I promise you, no one is here." *It was only a dream,* I told myself, *only a dream. Michael likes to watch television more than he should. He must have had a nightmare, that's all.* There was no doubt that Michael was a bright and sensitive child. This was just proof that he was imaginative, too.

"It was just a dream, Michael," I said, putting my thoughts into words. I didn't want to be annoyed with him, but I felt a pang of irritation anyway. I pushed myself up from the floor. "It's almost time for dinner and I've got to get the cooking finished." I told him to stay in his room and play as I started toward the hallway.

It was a dream, I assured myself one more time, but Michael had really been scared. *I guess nightmares will do that to you though.* From the doorway I glanced back at him one more time. The annoyance I felt vanished when I saw the haunted look in his eyes.

I went back downstairs to the kitchen. I didn't know whether to laugh or cry. No one said that raising two kids on my own would be a picnic and it hadn't been. I thought having Bruce around would make us all secure, but now I was worried about the boys' adjustment to a new father. In fact, like many young mothers in trying circumstances, I was always afraid that I was doing something wrong and the boys would end up having emotional problems. Now, a myriad of self-doubts raced through my mind. *Should I have stayed with Michael longer? Should I have told him to come downstairs? Maybe he needed more time with me.* I bit my lip. Nothing like a little guilt to make you doubt yourself. I called up to Michael, "Honey, why don't you come down here and play near me for a while." That way, I could keep an eye on him. He soon clomped down the stairs and landed on the couch with an armload of toys.

He seems fine now, I thought. *Whatever it was, it's over.* I looked over at my son, his tousled head bent in concentration as he set up a Lego village. Suddenly, I felt better.

When all appeared quiet, I picked up the telephone and tried to call my mother and dad. I hoped my mother, who was determined, calm and beautiful, but with a fine insight when her children or grandchildren might be in trouble, would answer, but the line was busy. Talking to Mom was essentially like talking to my best friend. We were very close and I always knew I could tell her anything. She had always supported me and been there for me. *She will make me feel better about this thing with Michael, and Dad, who adores Michael, will be able to talk to him,* I told myself.

I had just placed the receiver back on the hook when my older son, Kenny, walked into the kitchen. He had been playing in the yard with his friends during the incident with Michael.

"I had the best time outside," he told me, giving me one of his infectious grins. "I wish Michael had been with us."

Kenny was a slight boy, very small for his age with blond hair and blue eyes. There was about him a certain gentleness toward others and especially towards his little brother. He was a good kid, I thought as he walked past me announcing, "Mom, I'm hungry!" and sat down on the couch by his brother. Michael nestled against him and they settled back to watch television. I couldn't help smiling at the sight of the two boys as I picked up the phone to try my parents again, but the line was still busy.

Since Bruce was away, I decided that we would just go over to my parents' house instead of calling again. The kids were hungry and we could pick up some burgers from a fast food place on the way to Mom's so she wouldn't have to be bothered fixing something.

"Okay guys, go get your shoes on," I called, knowing they would be excited at the prospect of a kid's meal and toy. "We'll get hamburgers at McDonald's on the way to Grandma's."

Michael and Kenny cheered, delighted at the thought of having burgers and fries and not being coerced into eating vegetables for dinner, as well as happy to be going to my parent's house. I fed Katie her dinner while Kenny retrieved his shoes from where he had dumped them next to the couch and Michael pounded up the stairs to his room to find his.

Suddenly, Michael began to howl.

Once again, I dashed up the stairs. Michael was standing in the center of his room, one shoe on his foot and the other in his hand. He was shivering and his face was pale.

"Mommy, the man was here again!" he cried. "Around him was this light, so shiny I could hardly see. He reached out to me and smiled, and then he went away."

Standing up there in Michael's room, for a split second I thought I noticed a strange putrid odor in the air. Not only did it reek, but it was a pervasive sort, like a dead animal or burning leather. It was there and then gone so quickly I couldn't be sure it hadn't been my imagination. The thought left my mind as quickly as it had come.

I picked Michael up in my arms and sat on his bed, holding him tightly. What the hell was going on? Michael certainly had not been asleep this time! I gently rocked back and forth, trying to comfort him as I had when he was a baby. A snuffing sound caught my attention. I had forgotten about Kenny. He was standing beside me, crying too, as he always did when Michael cried. Keeping one arm wrapped around Michael, I pulled Kenny down with my other arm to sit beside me.

"What happened, Michael?" I asked him, still holding the two boys.

"It was the man again. He's a ghost," he replied looking up at me, his eyes like saucers.

I started to laugh, but choked it back. There was nothing funny about this. "Why would you say that?" I questioned, thinking that perhaps his television time needed to be cut back.

"He was white—crayon color white. He's an old man and he keeps trying to touch me. He tries to touch me right here," Michael said, pointing to his shoulder.

I shook my head. *A ghost? Where in the world did this come from?* I certainly was not a believer in ghosts and certainly never talked about such things to the kids. I didn't even like scary movies!

To change the topic, I said, "Let's go see Grandma and Grandpa. We'll talk more about this later."

Michael and Kenny brightened immediately.

"Don't forget about the hamburgers!" Kenny reminded me.

"I won't forget," I promised and watched as the kids ran out of the room and down the stairs. As I reached the doorway to the bedroom, I turned and looked back inside. *A ghost?* It was ridiculous. I put the thought out of my mind and hurried downstairs.

We used the drive-through of the closest McDonald's and then continued on to my parents' house. I was relieved to see their car in the driveway. They still lived in the same place in which I had grown up. It was a small but cozy house. When I was a child, my sister and I shared the attic and my brother slept in what was now the dining room.

After he retired, Dad opened a craft shop and Mom helped with the books and selling in the store. Dad had a real talent for making clocks and wooden items. He had slowed down some over the past year or so though. His health had not been good.

I let the kids go play in the backyard while I reheated their dinner. Dad had built a swing-set for them there and I wanted them out of the house for a few minutes while I talked to my parents about the situation with Michael.

Mom and Dad, who were thrilled to see us as always, grew concerned when I told them about the incident with "the man" in Michael's room.

"Did you ever tell the boys about ghosts?" I asked both of them. I knew that Dad liked to tease the boys. Could he have good-naturedly tried to scare them while they were staying over one night?

"No, honey," Dad answered. "I've never said a thing about ghosts. Maybe Michael saw something on television, one of those *X-File* shows or something."

I nodded my head. Maybe that was it. I started to ask something else when the back door burst open. Michael and Kenny came running in.

"Wash your hands! Wash your hands!" Mom shouted over the clamor and the boys disappeared into the bathroom. Michael was first out and ran into the living room, where Mom always keeps a full candy dish for visiting grandchildren.

"Michael!" I called after him. "Dinner first, candy later!"

No sooner were the words out of my mouth than Michael let out a blood-curdling cry! We all ran into the living room and found him there, an overturned candy dish in his hands and a terrified look frozen onto his face.

"Mommy, that's the man! That's the man!" he began to shriek over and over again.

"What man?" Dad asked. With a bear hug, he clasped Michael against his chest for a few seconds trying to calm him down. Then he put the boy on the floor, amidst the scattered remains of the candy. "What man?" Dad asked again, his voice calm but firm.

"The man who keeps trying to touch me," the boy replied, running to hug me.

"Where is he, Michael? Do you still see him," I asked.

He nodded and raised his arm and pointed toward the wall. "He's right there in the picture with that lady, Mom," Michael said.

We all looked over to where my son was pointing and saw a large photograph mounted on wood. In the photo was my grandfather and grandmother. It had been taken years before, when I was about ten years old, just before my grandfather died.

"That's the man who comes in my room," Michael insisted.

Dad had a shocked look on his face as he turned to me. "A few weeks ago Mom found a small picture of my father and mother tucked away in the attic after all these years. It's the only one we ever took of my father when he was older. He didn't like taking them. I enlarged the print and since we're selling woodcrafts at the store, I decided to mount the photograph on wood and display it at the shop. But then it looked so nice and brought back so many good memories, we decided to hang it on the living room wall." Dad shook his head. "This is the damnedest thing. Michael never knew my father. In fact, until now, he has never even seen a picture of him except that wedding picture of him and my mother and he looked entirely different then." Dad paused and cleared his throat. "So how can you explain that Michael says he was the man in his room?"

"Oh, that's ridiculous!" I sputtered.

"Maybe...maybe dear," Mom said softly, her eyes widening, "but perhaps Michael really did see him in his room today."

"Great...now you, too!" I managed a half-hearted laugh. "Mom, you're always so metaphysical. Let's not buy into this...this ghost thing."

She looked into my eyes. "I'm not buying into anything, Denice. But remember the trauma when Michael was born? Did you or did you not ask your grandfather to watch over Michael when the doctors thought he was going to die?"

I dropped my eyes from her gaze. "That was different. I was frightened and..."

Mom interrupted me. "Still, maybe he hasn't stopped watching over Michael."

❧ 2 ❧

PAST HISTORY

As we stood in my parents' living room with the photo of my grandfather—the man my son claimed to have seen in his bedroom—looking down at us, my mind spun back to another scary time in my life...

I was pregnant with Michael and on my own. My husband had left us and I already had Kenny to take care of. To make matters worse, I started developing complications with this pregnancy weeks before I was due to deliver. Though they tried, there was nothing the doctors could do but advise rest (something difficult to accomplish with Kenny to care for), keep an eye on me and allow the pregnancy to go as long as possible. That was long enough. One day, as I loaded some groceries in the car, my fluid started to leak and the pain began. I doubled up with agony. The sharp stabbing sensations were becoming so bad I could hardly stand it. Suddenly, I realized I was having contractions.

I managed to get home and call my mother who lived in the next town.

"Call the doctor, Denice."

"But…"

"Call him right now. I'm on my way."

After hanging up, I called Doctor Harrington, who insisted I come to his office right away.

"I'm alone here with my little boy. I called my mother and she's coming. She'll be able to take me."

Packing some clothes and trying to reassure Kenny, whose face was pinched with fear, I waited anxiously. Mom must have flown to my house because she quickly arrived. We put my bag in the back seat of her car with Kenny and she drove me to the doctor. After a quick examination, Doctor Harrington proclaimed in a dire voice, "We'll have to do an emergency Caesarean section or the baby won't live." This sent me into another panic.

In less than an hour I was a patient in the hospital. Permission for surgery was thrust into my hand. Without reading it, I signed. After being prepped, I was immediately wheeled into the operation room.

That was the last thing I remember before waking up with my father sitting by my bed. I was in tremendous pain, but had a detached feeling as though I was sort of floating inside a body that wasn't mine. Dad was smiling at me, a weary look on his face.

"What did I have, Daddy?" I managed to ask him.

"A handsome little boy," he told me, gently holding onto my hand.

I murmured a sound of contentment and started to drift back off again.

"Denice? Don't go back to sleep yet," Dad said. "I need you to be awake enough so we can talk about the baby."

I struggled to get my eyes back open and Dad's face swam into view. Just then, the door to the room slammed open and a nurse strode in. I snapped awake as she came toward me. She had more papers in her hand and pushed them at me.

"Denice? Are you with us?" my father asked.

"What…what's going on?"

"Denice," the nurse said frantically. "We need you to sign these consent forms right now. Your baby has to be transferred to Children's Hospital. He has some complications and they can take better care of him over there. Just sign these and we can move him immediately." She thrust a pen at me.

Somehow, I scrawled my signature on the papers. I was crying now and Dad was trying to calm me down. "Nurse, what's going on? Please tell me what's happening," I pleaded, but she was moving toward the door. I tried to get up and follow her, but I was too weak and collapsed back onto the bed.

"It'll be okay," my father said, helping me back under the covers. "They know what they're doing."

As the door to the room swung open, I heard someone shouting in the hallway. The voice sounded familiar. It belonged to my brother, Ed. He was shouting at a priest who had come to the nursery where the baby was. The priest planned to administer the Last Rites to my newborn son, but Ed refused to let him.

"This baby is going to live," Ed insisted.

A few moments later, the door to my room opened again and two nurses brought my baby inside. He was in a glass case and looked so small and fragile. I was allowed to touch him briefly before they began to wheel him away and transport him to Children's Hospital.

"What's his name?" one of the nurses called to me. She was trying to be kind and must have known my whole world seemed to be collapsing around me.

"His name is Michael," I said wistfully, tears falling down my cheeks.

It turned out that Michael had an infection that required his entire blood supply to be replaced. Since his lungs were not fully developed, air had to be mechanically pumped into him so that he could breathe. To make matters worse, his body was wracked with almost continuous seizures.

I woke up in my room hours later. I was alone. My parents and brother had gone downstairs to the cafeteria to try and eat something. Not knowing what else to do, I began to pray. I asked God to watch over the baby and at some point, the image of my Grandpa appeared in my mind. My memory must have been playing tricks on me, combined with my fear, stress and medication, for I could have sworn that Grandpa was there in that hospital room.

He was standing at the end of my hospital bed, looking down at me. Grandpa was always such a kind and gentle man. He smiled but said nothing. I suddenly remembered the funniest thing. Grandpa would never shave in the morning if he knew I was coming to visit him. I would never kiss his cheek until he had shaved and put on his minty aftershave. So he would always put me up on the edge of the sink and let me help him shave. Then he would put on his aftershave and give me a big kiss. He was such a good person and since his death, I missed him terribly.

For the moment though, he was right there, standing next to me and when he bent down and rubbed his cheek next to mine, sure enough, it was clean shaven and the scent of mint filled my nostrils. I remember looking up at him. "Please, Grandpa," I begged him. "Please take care of my baby."

He smiled reassuringly and nodded. And then, if he was ever there at all, he simply faded away. But oddly enough, I could swear I still smelled his minty aftershave.

Unfortunately, though I wanted to rush to Michael's side, I too had some kind of infection and had to stay in the hospital. The days that followed seemed like an eternity. Dad stayed with me while Mom and Ed went over to Children's Hospital. They called with updates whenever they could. I kept the telephone next to me on the bed. If there was any news at all about my baby, good or bad, I wanted it. I didn't care what time of day or night it was.

I cried myself to sleep every night. On the fourth night I was awakened by the telephone ringing. It jarred me from sleep and I grabbed the receiver. The glowing numbers on the bedside clock read 2:30 A.M. The voice on the phone told me that Michael could not be kept alive without a special ventilator. They needed my permission to transfer the baby to Children's Hospital in Washington, D.C.

"Do whatever you have to. Just save my baby!" I cried.

"We'll call you back with details," the voice said and the phone went dead.

I called my parent's house and Dad picked up the phone. I explained what was going on. He promised to come right over. I also called my sister and although she and I had never been close, she had always been there whenever I needed her. My parents and sister arrived at the same time. Ed stayed with Kenny.

The telephone in my hospital room rang again. This time, the voice told me that the Pratt-Whitney company in East Hartford had donated a plane to take Michael to Washington. He was on his way.

Over the next two days while I fought off my own infection, I received ongoing calls from the hospital where Michael was as he went through one crisis after another. He stopped breathing five times and the doctors thought he wouldn't make it in each instance. But when he did, we all thought that the worst was over until another life and death struggle occurred. A nurse commented to me, "It is almost as if Michael is being pulled to the other side and yet something or someone is pulling him back." Then the Washington, D.C. doctors called me. Those calls were the worst I had ever received. I was informed that they had to remove Michael's jugular vein and replace it with a tube. Somehow, he managed to make it through all this. It was as if a guiding hand was watching over him. I was sure it was my grandfather's.

I finally went home. Weeks passed before they finally decided that Michael could be discharged. Although I hate to admit it, I was almost afraid to take him. In my nightmares, he would come home and go into convulsions. I would not be able to save him and he would die. I was terrified to go and pick him up, but I did it anyway. Mom and I drove down to Washington and brought him back.

At his baptism, I gave Michael two middle names. One for my brother, who had believed that Michael would live from the beginning, and the other the name of my grandfather, who had watched over him. As time passed, I rationalized that my vision of Grandpa must have been a dream, but I never dismissed the idea that he had somehow been there for my son when Michael needed him the most.

Could it be that he still was?

It's always surprising to me that difficult times seem like they will never end and yet when they are over they soon fade as more immediate concerns fill our minds. Mine was caring for my small family. Once home, Michael grew healthy and chubby. He was a happy baby, but I struggled to give him and his brother the things I felt children should have. Though it was hard going, above all I comforted myself that Michael had the most important thing: my family's love. He seemed to know this and gave much love in return.

Even so, it was both a financial and emotional struggle to keep us going. My parents helped when they could, but I had to work long hours and worried that my children didn't always get the attention or time I could have given them had their father not deserted us. Nevertheless, we were a close family. The boys were growing up with devoted grandparents and were very close to each other.

Even when Michael was a toddler, he and his brother stuck together like glue. Kenny was so small they looked like twins. Whenever Michael got hurt or sick, Kenny cried. Because of Michael's birth crisis, Kenny said he was always afraid his brother might die and so he became Michael's protector. If Michael was sick, his brother stayed nearby and brought him juice or read to him from Michael's favorite book, *Who Am I*. Then, later, when Michael went to pre-school, Kenny made sure no one teased or hurt his little brother's feelings because Michael was so sensitive.

However, it was not long before we found out the protection worked both ways. One night while I was asleep Kenny decided to get up at 5:00 A.M. to wash and dry his hair. He quietly washed his hair in the sink so as not to wake anyone. Then he carried the blow dryer back to the room he shared with Michael, who was only five years old at the time. In the middle of drying his hair, sleep overtook Kenny, who then dropped the still running hair dryer onto the carpet next to his bed. Michael awoke when he smelled smoke and then pulled Kenny out of bed with all his might, dragging him into my room. Michael's voice woke me up.

"Mommy, there's smoke in our room!"

I ran to their room and put out the small fire that had started. To this day, Kenny won't use a blow dryer on his hair.

Watching out for his loved ones became Michael's role in the family. Soon, he also became my mom's protector. One time, my parents took Michael to Rhode Island to visit friends. A homeless man approached them outside the restaurant they were going into, begging my mother for coins.

"No. I'll go get you some food instead," my mom told him.

Suddenly, the man rushed at her shouting obscenities. Michael stepped between them. "Don't you talk that way to my grandmother. I know you're a good person inside, but you need to get some help to get well," he said in the same compassionate way he addressed the sick or hurt. And with that, Michael reached into his pocket and fished out sixty-five cents—all the money he had—and handed it to the man. The man stared at Michael and then at my mother.

"You have a very sweet and wise bodyguard," he said and left.

"I wish I could have helped him more," Michael later told her, sighing heavily, "but I guess he'll have to do the rest himself." It was another sign, my mother said, of Michael's sympathy for those in trouble, sick or dying.

Indeed, Michael's kindness, gentleness and unconditional love for people, even those like the man at the restaurant, manifested itself continually. It was almost like he knew people, even strangers, in the past and trusted them. At church on Sunday, he always dropped all his allowance in the collection for the poor. When I reminded him that he needed to save part of it for treats for himself, Michael smiled that cherubic smile that was so much like his grandmother's. He said, "Being with family is the most important thing and I have all of you. I don't need things that cost money when there are poor people who do."

My mother says Michael is an "old soul." And perhaps he is.

One day my father wanted to take the boys fishing. He had just bought them fishing poles and tackle boxes. Always on the go, Kenny wanted to go roller blading with a friend, but Michael, who loves quiet and peace and being with his grandfather, was happy to go.

On the way, Dad bought buckets for them to sit on and headed for his fishing hole, Foot's Pond. As Michael didn't like to put the worms on the hook, my dad did it for him. At first, nothing happened and Dad was worried Michael wouldn't catch anything. "Don't worry, Grandpa," Michael comforted him. "You just have to believe." Michael sat there for the longest time, my dad said later, "and just as I was about to suggest going somewhere else to fish, Michael got a nibble, then another and another and another. It got to a point I had to reel in my pole just to help Michael get the fish off the line. They were coming so fast."

My father loves to tell how Michael caught thirty-three fish that day and before any died, he put them back. "They have a life, too," he had told my dad.

Though he loves spending time with his grandfather, there is one thing Michael doesn't like and that is thrills or what he calls "the tickle in his belly." Whenever our family goes to Adventure Park near my mother's house, everybody opts for the rides that spin and drop—the ones Michael doesn't like. Instead, Michael and I like to walk around together. Michael always calls us "dates for the day." We play games and eat and window shop. Michael is good at the games and invariably wins a stuffed animal or prize which he always gives to me. "I feel badly that you don't have any fun," he said once, hugging me. I reassured him that I was having the time of my life, because the best thing was spending time with him. But it was as if Michael could see a lonely place inside me and knew the truth.

Of course, I did not admit it to him, but Michael saw rightly. I was lonely. I had been divorced for several years and between working and taking care of my boys, I had little time to think of myself.

One evening when my mom was visiting me at my apartment, Carol, a young woman who worked with me, telephoned.

She had just broken up with her boyfriend and wanted to go out. "But it's been so long," she said. "I just don't want to hit the single scene alone. I was hoping you might come."

My mom asked what Carol wanted and I whispered Carol's request to her.

"Denice, go. You've been sitting home long enough. I'll watch the boys. It will be good for you."

Feeling awkward and self-conscious, I stuttered my agreement. Carol offered to come by to pick me up since I felt none too steady at the prospect of going out.

We went to a singles bar Carol knew for a drink. I was beginning to relax as we watched others play pool when I noticed a man, a very good-looking man, walk in and sit down at a nearby table where another guy was. The man I admired was wearing a pair of tight blue jeans, boots and cowboy hat. I looked closer. He didn't appear to be one of those dime-store cowboys, either. He had the rangy look of the real thing.

The cowboy looked at me and smiled, but his friend, who must have thought I was looking at him, got up and came over. "Want to dance?" the man asked me.

I agreed and he took me out onto the dance floor. Hank was a good dancer, very sweet and actually fairly good-looking, although not as handsome as the cowboy. We talked a little and laughed. He turned out to be a nice guy and kept me from worrying about the children for a few minutes. Unfortunately though, I couldn't help thinking about his friend.

"What's your friend's name?" I finally asked him.

"My friend?"

"The cowboy," I said blushing.

"Bruce."

"Is he married?" I questioned none too subtly, but I wasn't too experienced in trying to strike up acquaintanceships with men I didn't know.

"No," He shook his head. "He just went through a nasty divorce."

We talked for a few more minutes and after the song ended, he went back to where the cowboy was sitting. When I looked around for Carol, I was surprised to see her sitting alone only a few tables from Hank and Bruce.

After I sat down with Carol, the music stopped and we could hear the two men talking. "Look, man, will you ask her to dance? She's been asking about you. If you don't, I'm just going to ask her again. She's very cute."

Bruce chuckled. "Alright, I'll ask her."

He got up and walked in our direction. I noticed him heading my way and tried not to act too silly when he stopped at our table.

"Would you like to dance?" he asked me, tipping the brim of his hat.

"Yes, I would," I replied, trying not to be too eager.

I was excited and nervous when we went out onto the dance floor, but Bruce quickly put me at ease. We talked about all sorts of things. Within a short time I felt like I had known him for years. He had an easy-going, caring manner about him and I soon found myself chattering away. All my awkwardness gone, we talked and danced through several songs. Suddenly a strange thought came to me and I felt my face coloring. *This is a man I could fall in love with*, I thought.

I told him about Michael and Kenny and talked about my parents for awhile. Bruce had a daughter from his previous marriage who was just a little bit older than Kenny. Our conversation continued through one song and into the next, then another and another. I'm not even sure how long we danced or even what songs were played. And then, it was probably on impulse yet it seemed the most natural thing in the world, Bruce bent down and kissed me. I found myself kissing him back.

For a long moment, it was as if there was no one else in the place. We were still kissing when we realized the music had stopped. No one else was on the dance floor and everyone in the place was staring at us. I laughed in embarrassment, but Bruce took my hand and led me away.

We sat down at the table with Carol, but had eyes only for each other. He asked me, "Would you like to leave and go get a cup of coffee?" This wasn't a case of Bruce just trying to get me alone either, he really wanted to buy me a cup of coffee. I looked over at Carol and she smiled. I nodded. Bruce and I left together.

And we've been together ever since...

✑ 3 ✐

WATCHED OVER

Although my dad was as shocked and amazed as Mom at Michael's words about his father's picture, his approach to the problem was somewhat different. "Why don't you two go into the kitchen and let me talk to Michael," he said pensively.

A few minutes later, Michael bounded into the kitchen and began searching for his dinner. He was beaming now, a big smile on his face. I left him with my mom who was hovering over him lovingly and went into the living room.

"He seems so happy. What did you tell him, Dad?" I questioned my father.

"I just told him that if his great grandpa really had come to visit him, he should not be afraid for Grandpa Pierce would never hurt him. I said Great Grandpa surely loved him and had watched over Michael when he was a little baby and very ill," my father explained. "He seemed to like that. Michael asked me if Grandpa was an angel now and I told him I was sure he had become one and would protect his great grandson."

I sighed. "Thanks, Dad. I had no idea what to say to Michael."

Dad put his hand over mine. "That's what grandfathers are for," he replied, "coming up with difficult answers." He smiled, but I knew he was serious.

"Dad, can I have the small picture of Grandma and Grandpa Pierce—the one you made the enlargement from? I don't have any pictures of them of my own."

"Of course you can. Better yet, I'll get a wallet-sized photo made and you can take it wherever you go. I'll mail it to you in a couple of days."

"Thanks, Dad. All this talk of Grandpa Pierce has me feeling nostalgic."

His eyes met mine. "What do you really think about all this—Michael seeing Grandpa Pierce?"

I shrugged. "I have no clue where Michael's ideas are coming from. Even if Grandpa was watching over Michael, why would Michael be seeing him and why now?"

Dad had no more answers to this one than I did. After dinner, I took the boys home. They chattered happily on the way and didn't seem to notice my silence. I was worried about how Bruce would take the news.

Bruce would be away all week and, surprisingly, I was glad. My new husband was understanding, but this story would surely tax his powers of trust. Should I even tell Bruce about Michael when I could not be sure what had really occurred? Perhaps it would be better to keep this to myself. Maybe Michael would forget about it in the days to follow and I could, too.

At any rate, for the time being, I just wanted to watch Michael and see whether this whole thing was a figment of his imagination, would go away on its own or was something more serious. How serious it was, and of what nature, I just didn't know.

After a little television, I put the boys to bed. There were no more disruptions or screams that night. Still, I barely slept as the events of the day spun through my mind.

I assumed that Dad's talk had comforted Michael. However, I was still not sure where the idea of the "man" in his room had come from. I was also not convinced that it was my Grandpa who Michael had seen. Trying to reason it out, I decided it was probably a show he saw on television that spooked him, a show with an older man in it he thought was Grandpa. That's why he thought he recognized the picture at Mom and Dad's.

Yes, that is probably it, I told myself.

Suddenly, other thoughts popped up. *But what about the fact that he wasn't dreaming the second time he cried out? Was he just trying to get attention because of my new marriage or was he truly scared? He seemed pretty frightened to me, though, and what about that weird smell when I walked into his room? Was my imagination playing tricks on me as well?*

Around and around my thoughts churned as I tossed in bed this way and that. *Let's say, just for argument's sake, that Grandpa had really been there when Michael was born and let's say he was protecting him then. Why would Michael be seeing him now?*

Finally, I drifted off to sleep for a short time and awakened to see the misty morning light.

The next two days passed without incident. I was beginning to feel relief. *It had all been Michael's imagination*, I repeated to myself like a mantra. On the third day, I poured Michael a bowl of cereal for breakfast, tossed a sweater over my shoulders and sat down with him. That chill which says winter is coming filled the air. I began idly flipping through a magazine while he ate.

"Grandpa says it's going to snow soon," he said to me, breaking the silence. "Can we get a sled?"

"When did you talk to Grandpa?" I asked absentmindedly, turning another page.

"This morning."

"Did you call him?"

"No, Mom," Michael replied impatiently, "he was in my room."

My hands froze on the magazine and I shivered, but not from the cool autumn air. "What are you talking about Michael?" I whispered. "Who was in your room?"

"Great Grandpa was," he said. "Grandpa's daddy...the angel Grandpa! Now when I see him, he's not scary anymore. He's my friend."

I got up from the table. My stomach flip-flopped. "Finish your breakfast, honey," I said and went out into the living room. *What is going on?* I asked myself. *I thought this was over!* I didn't know what was happening, but one thing I did know: maybe Michael wasn't scared anymore, but I sure as hell was.

Early Thursday evening, Michael walked up to me. I was sitting on the living room couch, a book in my hands. The kids had been playing in the family room and I had come in here to read quietly for a while.

"Mommy? Who's upstairs?" Michael asked me.

I put my book down. "Honey, there's nobody upstairs," I said, a little exasperated. The boys had been driving me crazy since they'd come home from school. It had been raining and I didn't want them to play outdoors as they both had colds the week before this.

"There's somebody whispering up there. I can hear it," he insisted. "It's coming from my room."

"Alright, Michael, I'll go check."

I sighed and got up from the couch. *Michael probably left the radio on in his room,* I thought as I climbed the stairs. Our dog followed me. When I reached the second floor, I paused for a moment to listen. I didn't hear anything. I opened the door and went into Michael's room. It was completely silent, but suddenly Katie, as if spooked, whimpered pitifully and ran downstairs.

That's it; I'm sending them outside to play, I decided. Did Michael really want attention so badly that he was going to start with this stuff again?

A little fresh air never hurt anybody, I told myself, but, of course, as mothers do, I worried that the kids would catch pneumonia and decided to keep them in.

When I got back downstairs, Kenny was waiting for me.

"What's the matter with the dog?" Kenny asked.

Oh God, I thought, *what now?*

I followed him into the kitchen and saw the animal curled up in the corner. She was whimpering and acting very strangely. It wasn't like Katie at all. Normally, she was all over me. I even had to get the boys to take her out when I was cooking dinner, because she always got under foot.

"What's the matter, Katie?" I asked, running a hand over her soft, black coat. She was trembling.

"Maybe she's sick," suggested Kenny.

"I don't know. Why don't you take her in the family room while I start dinner?"

Kenny walked over to the doorway, calling the dog to follow. She looked at him, but continued to whimper. She pressed herself further into the corner. Kenny continued to call, patting his hands on his thighs. What was wrong with her?

"C'mon Katie," I urged her. "Go with Kenny."

The dog scrambled backward and let out a huffing sound. I walked over and took her collar. "C'mon girl." I pulled a little on the dog's collar, but she refused to budge. I pulled harder and her claws clattered on the tile floor. I literally dragged the dog through the kitchen. Finally, I let her go.

"What's going on?" asked Michael. He had appeared in

the doorway behind his brother. Suddenly, Katie huffed once more and let out a bark. She rapidly backed away from Michael and hunkered down onto the floor, retreating once more into the corner.

"Just forget it, guys," I said. "Go turn on the television. I'll call you when dinner is ready."

While we were eating, Katie disappeared into the living room. This was also strange. Normally, she circled the table and prodded the boys with her nose, hoping they would give her table scraps. They weren't supposed to, but I always pretended I didn't see them when they gave in to her. Tonight, the dog was noticeably absent.

After dinner, the boys and I sat down in the family room to watch a movie we had rented. It was a comedy and soon we were all laughing and having a great time—except for Katie, that is. I had managed to coax her into the room, but she sat huddled near one of the chairs, looking like she was afraid to move.

I watched as her head jerked from side to side. She seemed to be following the motion of something around the room. I tried to figure out what she was looking at, but I couldn't see anything. Every once in awhile, she barked quietly at this same something. Suddenly, she let out a yelp and ran out of the room. Running into the kitchen, she slid when she hit the tile floor, fell down, got back up and kept running. I had no idea what had spooked her, but she refused to come back in the family room again.

The kids were oblivious to all this, lost in the movie, but I confess that it bothered me. *Is the dog going crazy?* I asked myself.

Perhaps to have their company and not be alone, I let the boys stay up late. After putting them to bed, I turned in myself. It seemed like my head had just touched the pillow when I heard Michael screaming for me. He sounded terrified.

It was dark in the hallway. I stumbled across it and pushed Michael's bedroom door open. As I did so, something slammed against the wall next to me. I reached for the light switch and something else crashed into the door itself. I flipped the switch and light flooded the room. I looked down and saw one of Michael's toy trucks lying on the floor. There was an indentation in the plaster wall where the truck had hit it. Had he thrown it at me?

I turned around and felt a sharp, cracking pain on the side of my head. I saw a flash of light for a moment and another toy, this time a small car, hit me in the head and landed at my feet. I spun in the opposite direction to confront Michael and saw that his bed was empty.

"Michael!" I yelled, now torn between being angry and being frightened.

I heard a small voice answer me. The voice came from beneath the bed. I got down on the floor and flipped the blankets back. I saw my son pressed back against the wall. He had his pillow over his face. How had he gotten down there so fast after throwing those toys at me?

"Michael? Come out from under there," I said firmly.

"Are they gone?" he asked.

"Are who gone?"

"The lights," he said.

"Michael, I have no idea what you are talking about. What lights?"

He moved the pillow and looked at me. His eyes were round and filled with terror. "There were balls of light flying all over my room…and voices. The blankets on my bed kept being pulled," he answered.

"Come out from under there and talk to me," I said more sternly than I felt.

Michael scooted out from under the bed and we sat

together on the edge of the mattress. "What did the lights look like?" I questioned.

"They looked like little balls, like gumballs, 'cept bigger," he said. His fingers curled to make a circle the size of a golf ball. "They were white and they flew all over the place. It scared me."

I hugged him a little closer. "They were probably just angel lights," I said, having no idea of what to say to reassure the child, "you know, from Great Grandpa Pierce."

But Michael shook his head adamantly. "They weren't from Grandpa Pierce. They were ghost's lights."

I sighed. "There aren't any ghosts, Michael."

"Yes, there are!"

"And let me guess," I said sarcastically, "those were ghosts who threw toys at me when I came into your room!"

Michael's forehead wrinkled in puzzlement. "What toys?" he asked me.

My heart froze when I realized he was serious. *Oh my God*, I thought, *what is going on here?*

"Do you still see Grandpa Pierce?" I asked my son, now very serious and feeling very scared.

"Yes, I see him every day."

"Why didn't you tell me?" I demanded. "You haven't said a word about it!"

"I didn't want to scare you," he said simply.

I started to cry and hugged him again. It was too late for that. I was very frightened now, torn between wondering if my son was crazy and wondering if our new house was haunted. Did I believe in ghosts? I wasn't sure anymore what I believed.

Stunned, I turned and held both of Michael's shoulders with my hands. I looked him in the eye, my face just inches from his. "Michael, swear to me that you are not making this up," I said to him.

"I'm not, Mom."

"When you see Grandpa Pierce is he always dressed the same way?" I asked quietly. "Tell me what he looks like." My stomach was fluttering with fear. I didn't know what to make of what Michael was telling me. How could it be? It was just too bizarre and too terrifying to consider.

"He looks just like people," Michael began, then shrugged. "He looks funny, though. All in white, like the color of a white crayon."

I looked at my son again, trying desperately to figure out what was going on. Why would Michael make something like this up? And if he was, how in the world would he have come up with it?

Michael must have sensed my doubts. "How come you don't believe me?" he asked.

"I want to believe you, honey," I answered and pulled him to me. My tears fell onto the top of his head. "I want to believe you." The truth was I really wanted it all to just go away.

Friday, the storm seemed to have passed. Michael appeared to be happy and laughing at breakfast. The boys were supposed to see their father over the weekend. I wondered if things were settled enough for that, but hated to not let them go. They rarely ever got to see him and I didn't want to cancel the trip and ruin things for them.

Their father and I had not been together for years. Ours had been a difficult relationship and when Kenny was small he had left. We were still not on good terms after a bitter divorce, but I didn't want that to reflect on the way the boys felt about him.

When the boys returned home on Sunday evening, Michael bounced in to see me. "Did you have a good time?" I asked.

"It was great!" He smiled. "We went to Dad's church today. Kenny and I got to watch TV while Dad went down in the basement and prayed."

"Pardon me? What church is this?"

"It's at Dad's girlfriend's house. They have a church in the basement."

"And you watched television at this church?"

"Yep," he answered innocently, "and I got to play with this board, too. I got to ask it questions. It's a Weega board."

"A Ouija board?" I asked. "They let you play with a Ouija board?"

"Mom, don't get mad," Michael said. "A lady there told me that I have a present."

"A gift," Kenny interrupted from the doorway. "She said he had a gift."

"I don't care what she said!" I told them. "I don't want you to play with anything like that again. Those are not toys! I am going to call your dad, but you make sure that I don't hear about you doing that ever again!"

I put the boys to bed and immediately called their father. "What's the matter with you?" I started yelling as soon as he answered the phone. He protested at first, but in my concern for Michael I was near hysteria. "You are not to take the boys to this so-called church—in someone's basement no less—and if you ever let Michael play with a Ouija board again, it will be the last time they come over to your house."

I angrily slammed down the receiver and rubbed my forehead. *What is next?*

❧ 4 ❧

TERROR IN THE NIGHT

I had asked the boys not to say anything about the ghost to Bruce when he came home. "I'll explain it to him when I think the time is right." Was it dishonest? I knew it was. I felt terribly guilty, but I had finally found a wonderful man who I loved and who loved me and my sons. Things had been so hard for the boys and me. I didn't want anything to mess up my new marriage and ruin our new family life. I would tell Bruce about Michael's problem, I promised myself, *just not yet.*

With Bruce back, I desperately hoped things would get better. Perhaps Michael would not see the ghost again. Even if the whole episode was in his mind and the rest came out later, at least we might get a brief respite and a little peace.

Of course, I realized if it did start up again or got worse, I was going to be forced to tell Bruce sooner, rather than later. I prayed it would go away.

I checked on the boys several times after they had gone to sleep. Late that Monday night when my husband returned, I breathed a sigh of relief. They were fine. But after Bruce and I had a joyous reunion and we had both fallen asleep, I was awakened by the barking of Katie, out in the hallway. When I went out, I saw her crouched by the door to Michael's room, growling and snarling. Was she able to sense something that I could not? I stared at her sorrowfully. I was scared enough, I realized, feeling my heart pounding in my chest. Seeing her cowering there was making it worse.

Both Michael and Kenny looked tired the next morning.

Bruce had left early for his office, worried that whenever he went out of town work and mail piled up.

"Did you guys get any sleep?" I asked them.

"No," answered Kenny. He grumpily plopped down in a kitchen chair. "Michael came in my room and got in bed with me. He steals all the covers."

"Why were you in Kenny's room?" I asked Michael.

"Grandpa Pierce kept talking," he answered softly. "I could hear him whisper, but I couldn't understand what he was saying."

After breakfast, I decided to talk to someone at our church. Perhaps I could ask them to come and bless the house. I had been a practicing Catholic my entire life. Both boys had been baptized into the church and I knew that Michael had a deep respect for all things connected to religion. This might settle down whatever it was he was experiencing.

Regardless, it was time to try to find help and I really didn't know where else to go but the church.

I got the kids off to school, then drove over to the church. It was a large and rather imposing-looking gray stone building, but I had always felt at home there. I didn't know the parish priest very well, however I was familiar with the nuns who taught the catechism classes for the boys. I decided to talk with one of them first.

Quietly, I explained to Sister Rose that Michael was

seeing ghosts, or at least he claimed to be. I didn't want the nun to think that any of us were crazy, but I wanted her to understand that we needed some sort of help. She smiled the entire time I spoke, then patted my hand. "You'll need to speak to the priest yourself. However, he is not in right now, so you will have to come back another time." I made an appointment for the following day.

I left the church feeling upset and depressed. I didn't want to go home and be by myself. I went out to the local shopping mall, wandered around for awhile and ended up at the movie theater where I sat by myself through a showing of a film of which I have no memory. I did anything to avoid going home.

Around three o'clock I picked up the boys from school and brought them home. I went through the mail and there was an envelope from my dad. Inside was the photo of my Grandma and Grandpa Pierce. Seeing their loving, smiling faces made me feel a little better. I slid the photo in my wallet, then started dinner. Bruce was once again working late, so I made the boys spaghetti for supper, one of their favorite meals. I wanted everything to be upbeat and happy and I certainly didn't want them to know how upsetting my day had been.

After we ate, I helped them with their homework. Then we watched an hour of television. Afterward, I put the boys to bed. Then I soaked in a hot bath for awhile, trying not to think about things, and went to bed myself. The less time that I was awake, the less time I had to be worried about what was going on with Michael.

Unfortunately, it didn't work out that way. I lay there, my eyes wide open and focused on the ceiling above me. I could not get to sleep, so I waited for Bruce to get there. Occasionally, a car drove past the house and its lights made a pattern of white across the ceiling. I could hear water dripping from the bathtub faucet. I heard Katie growling at something in the kitchen.

Then, I heard Michael begin to scream again.

I ran into his room. No flying toys assaulted me this time, but as I crossed the threshold into his bedroom, a wave of putrid air washed over me. It was just like the smell I had encountered the week before, but worse. The smell made me sick to my stomach. I literally staggered in nausea and surprise. What was it? I promised myself I would call an exterminator to check the house.

Michael was still wailing as I scooped him up in my arms. I didn't know what I was doing, but I just needed to get him out of the room. We ran across the hall into my bedroom. I sat down with him on the bed. He was still shaking but started to settle down.

"What happened?" I asked him.

"It was the lights again, only they were whispering to each other this time. They were also poking at me and pulling the blankets off my bed. Grandpa Pierce tried to push them away, but one mean one called my name," Michael told me and held up two small fingers. "It said it two times. It scared me."

"It's okay," I replied and rocked him a little. "It would have scared me, too."

Somehow, Kenny had managed to sleep through this episode and I was thankful for that. I put Michael back to bed and lay down beside him. He soon drifted off. I got up and waited for Bruce to come home. We cuddled tightly together in bed, which brought me some comfort. Still, I got very little sleep again.

I pulled myself together the next morning. We all ate breakfast together and I got the boys to school on time. Then I drove back to the church, anxious to finally meet with the priest. I arrived twenty minutes early and sat waiting in the sanctuary, staring up toward the elaborate altar. Was God in this room? If He was, I hoped that He would help me. I wasn't sure how much more of this Michael or I could take. I prayed to Him for guidance and hoped He could hear me.

My appointment time came and went. I looked nervously at my watch. The priest was nearly half an hour late I noted. Then he appeared, white-haired and rotund. He introduced himself as Father Joe and, with a deep breath, I began to explain the situation.

"What should I do, Father?" I asked him when I was finished.

He looked at me for a moment with a puzzled expression. I had the feeling that he was going to suggest that I speak to a doctor, preferably one who deals with mental illness. "Everything will be fine," he assured me. "The best thing you can do is to love God. He will take care of you and your children."

"But what about my son? What about the things he has seen?"

"As I said, love God. He will watch over you," the priest repeated, then he politely excused himself and walked away.

"Why won't you help me?" I called at his retreating back. I saw the man flinch, but he continued out the door. It swung shut with a thud behind him. I heard the sound of my words echo inside the shadowy sanctuary. They reverberated and then slowly faded away.

I was left standing there in the silent and empty church, feeling more forsaken than I ever had in my life. If my own church wouldn't help me, then who would?

We ate a quiet dinner that evening and retired early. As had become my custom, I checked on the children several times and they seemed fine. I felt better until shortly after midnight, when there was nearly a repetition of the night before. Luckily, Bruce, who is a sound sleeper, didn't awaken. Once again, I heard Michael screaming in the early morning hours.

"The lights are back," he told me, as I sat down on his bed. Was he dreaming this? I wondered if perhaps I should take him to a doctor. Maybe there was something wrong with him. I remembered reading about children and night terrors. Although Kenny never suffered from them, Michael was at an age when that could be the problem.

But what about the flying toys? The putrid smell? The way Katie acted?

Were those figments of my own imagination? I didn't think so. There was something wrong in this house, but what? I lay down next to Michael until he fell back asleep, but I didn't close my eyes. I was too unnerved.

Watching me the next morning, Bruce remarked, "Honey, you're looking awfully tired."

"It's newlywed jitters," I said, trying to laugh off his remark. The truth was I was mentally and physically exhausted. Trying to keep Michael's problem from Bruce made me even more so.

I got the boys to school and sat wearily down at the kitchen table. Katie curled up on the floor at my feet. I was barely able to function, but managed to write a letter to the church. I was afraid to show my face there after the embarrassing episode with the priest; so I wrote begging someone there to at least come and bless our house. I went out to the mailbox and dropped the letter inside.

Days inched by. Bruce was away again. In a way it was good timing because Michael's spells of terror in the night continued. At times, the lights seemed soothing to him and at other times, terrifying. What made them different? He was unable to tell me. "Some of them just don't seem to like me," he told me grimly.

I wavered between belief and disbelief. Certainly I had seen some things I could not explain, but still, Michael was the only one seeing these lights that seemed to speak to each other, and seeing Grandpa Pierce. Could there be something wrong with him? Maybe I should take him to see a doctor. Was he reacting badly to having to share me with Bruce?

Each day I worried that my new husband would find out. I had only been able to keep the secret this long because Bruce was working such long hours and had taken several business trips. When he was home, he fell asleep as soon as he hit the bed.

We had a few days of peace until one evening when Michael was in his room playing and I was doing some laundry. As I came upstairs to put away the clean clothes, I heard Michael talking to someone. I stuck my head in his room. He was seated cross-legged on his bed. "Who're you talking to?" I asked him.

"The voices," he answered and went back to the book that was open on his lap. I felt an icicle of fear penetrate my heart. *My God, when will this stop?*

"What voices?" I asked slowly, already knowing, already dreading the answer.

"Remember the balls of light I told you about? They used to fly around my head and just talk to each other. Now they talk to me."

I sagged against the door frame. I had naively hoped that a few quiet days meant it had all stopped, but it was apparently still going on. *What is wrong with my son?* I wanted to scream this aloud, but I bit my lip. "Michael, when do they come?"

"All the time," he replied calmly.

I went back to my room and collapsed onto the bed. My chest heaved and I began to cry. What should I do? Should I take Michael to a doctor? Should I tell Bruce? All the loneliness and trouble I had earlier suffered made me fearful and filled with self-doubt. What if, even though we're married, he says we're all crazy, kicks us out and has our marriage annulled? He wouldn't do that, would he?

I felt helpless. Surely Michael had to be mentally ill. But what if he wasn't? Did I dare believe the alternative?

Not yet, I decided.

I still hoped the church would be able to help me. If I could get someone to come and bless the house, it surely would have a positive effect on Michael. If there was something here besides my poor son's hallucinations, a blessing would drive it away, wouldn't it? I was willing to try anything. The church remained my greatest hope.

I decided I would try to schedule it after Bruce went to work. Then I would have someone come over, if they agreed. That way, I wouldn't have to explain to him what was going on. I just prayed they would listen to me. If I could convince the church of how great our need was, they might agree to help us.

Still, I had to search for other help if my plea to the church failed. Each day, my first priority was to get the boys to school. The elementary school and junior high, thank goodness, were side by side, because we usually arrived with only minutes to spare. The boys were always tired and their grades were suffering. Perhaps I could talk to a counselor in Michael's grade school and get some help.

One day, I took the boys to school and ran from building to building to get them signed in. They were late, but I smoothed things over with Kenny's principal, then met with Michael's principal in her office. Mrs. Price was a very nice lady, who, when I told her I needed to talk to someone about Michael's problems—the specifics of which I didn't go into—made an appointment for me to see the school's social worker that morning. Soon I was shown into her office.

"Hello, Mrs. Jones," the tawny haired young woman said with a bright smile. She introduced herself to me, "My name is Kathy Ackerman."

We sat down and talked for a few minutes. She seemed so open and accepting, I was soon explaining the situation to her. I included the late night screaming and the fact that Michael was seeing his great grandfather's ghost and hearing voices. I actually felt comfortable talking about everything. She did not judge me, but listened very patiently until I was finished.

"Something unusual is certainly going on at your house," she said. "I will not say that it has anything to do with ghosts, but it is certainly strange. Have you ever known Michael to lie about anything like this or perhaps to try to get attention?"

"He's a normal little boy, mischievous sometimes but very loving," I answered. "There has never been anything like this before. Though I recently remarried and we moved to a beautiful old house...."

She interrupted me. "Remarriage is a traumatic event for most children. Perhaps there is some sort of jealousy issue."

"Maybe," I said feeling awful. Michael hadn't seemed jealous, but perhaps he'd been hiding it and this was the result. "He doesn't seem jealous, but at this point, I just don't know."

"Well, I will meet with the boys and let you know what comes from that," she told me. "I know Michael and Kenny and they are both bright boys. I'll talk to them today."

"Thank you so much," I responded gratefully.

She opened her desk drawer, removed a card and handed it to me. "This is the number of a child psychologist I know. His name is Alex Holt and he's great with kids. Perhaps it might help if you went to see him. Let him talk with Michael and see if he can determine what factors are at work here. Then, we'll go from there."

She stood up and we shook hands again. "Thank you very much for helping us," I told her again. "I have been at the end of my rope with this. I really appreciate your taking the time to see me on such short notice."

"I'll let you know how my meetings with Michael and Kenny turn out," she promised as I left.

I felt better after seeing her. But that night Michael's voices seemed worse. The next morning I called the office of the child psychologist. Surprisingly, I was able to get an appointment later that same day. Apparently Kathy Ackerman had already called their office and they were able to fit us in. Thankfully, something seemed to be going our way.

In a better mood, I called the church again and asked for the priest. The secretary asked for my name and when I told her who I was, she informed me, "No one is available to take your call. Can I help you with something?"

"I want someone to come and bless my house," I explained.

To my amazement, she stated, "The Catholic Church no longer does blessings of homes."

I hung up the telephone and found myself in tears again. *What had I done wrong? Was it God who would not help me or the church?* And what about my marriage? I was hiding the truth from my new husband, afraid of what he might say or do. My desperate insecurity had come back to plague me, leaving me uncertain of Bruce's love.

I dropped Kenny off at school and took Michael to his appointment with the psychologist. The doctor's office was located on the edge of a residential district, in a restored colonial home that had been turned into elegant offices. We checked in at the front desk and I was asked to fill out some paperwork while we waited.

A little while later, Dr. Holt emerged from his office. He was a well-built man with a large, brown mustache and a kindly face, wearing a cardigan sweater over a flannel shirt and corduroys. He was one of those people who just seemed to exude a feeling of warmth. He smiled at Michael and explained that he would like to see me first and then Michael. He turned to my son. "One of my staff members will stay with you while your mom is in the office with me."

We went into his office and sat down. The room, decorated in shades of brown and gold, had huge, comfortable, beige leather chairs. In one corner was a shelf that was packed full of toys, games and puzzles. Stuffed animals and dolls were clustered next to beanbag chairs where children could happily examine them. A few lamps and a couple of scented burning candles softly lighted the room. It was a place where it was easy to feel comfortable and relaxed.

"Tell me about Michael," Dr. Holt said gently.

I took a deep breath. I told him about the trauma of Michael's birth and his early struggle for life. Then I poured out the story of Michael seeing my grandfather and later seeing balls of light and now hearing voices. I told Dr. Holt everything that I could remember. Then he asked me to send Michael in. "After I have talked with him, I'd like to speak with you again."

The visit took some time. I waited anxiously, idly flipping through magazines in the waiting room. Eventually, the office door opened and Michael came out. He was smiling, which was a relief, and he sat down with some toys while I went back in to talk to Dr. Holt again.

"Denice, let me ask you," he said, "What do you think is going on with Michael?"

I let out a deep breath and shifted in my seat. We were facing each other across a small table, each of us seated in a leather armchair. "Well, I don't really know," I answered truthfully. "His school counselor thought he might just be trying to get attention because of my remarriage or having bad dreams or something. But some of the things that have happened are a little too weird."

Dr. Holt nodded. "Like the stench, the flying toys?"

"Yes," I agreed quickly. "Most of all was his seeing my grandfather. I am not sure how Michael would have known who he was. It's not possible Michael could have seen the picture before, but maybe he thought this man he imagined looked like my...."

The doctor's hand went up, cutting me off. "Sorry, I don't mean to interrupt you, but I really don't think Michael is making this up," he said. "I think we have several possibilities here to deal with, four of them actually."

"What do you mean?"

"Well, one, of course, is that Michael is experiencing problems because of your remarriage. However, Michael does not seem to be lying about what he is experiencing. This does not mean what Michael sees is real, but that he truly believes that he is seeing something. I have no doubts about that. The man he is seeing is very distinctive, although I can't say for sure what is causing his visions. In fact, he has drawn me some pictures of what he sees." Dr. Holt opened a folder on the table between us and handed me several sheets of drawing paper.

"What do you mean 'causing his visions'? Do you think he could be sick?"

I took the drawings Dr. Holt had given me and looked them over. They were drawn in childish lines and portrayed my grandfather, who Michael had been claiming to see for some time, and the lights from which voices seemed to come.

"As you can see," Dr. Holt pointed to the crayon representation of Michael's great grandfather. "He looks kindly, but the lights with the voices are another matter. Some sound rather sinister, I think."

I nodded. "He tells me that his great grandfather is nice, but that sometimes he is scared of the voices," I replied. "But tell me, Doctor, why do you think Michael is seeing ghosts?"

"As I said, one possibility is that Michael is having difficulty adjusting to your remarriage and the move," Dr. Holt told me. "Another could be that Michael has a temporal defect that is causing him to see things that are not there. This could be something in the brain, an electrical signal glitch if you will. He does not show any of the signs of childhood schizophrenia. Except for his seeing these people, he seems to be a very ordinary little boy."

"How serious is this?" I asked him. I didn't like the sound of Holt's words.

"Well, we don't know exactly yet, but usually it can be treated with medication, unless it is something organic in nature, say a tumor pressing on his temporal lobe, and then he might need surgery."

"A tumor? Oh my God!"

Dr. Holt quickly reassured me. "That's highly unlikely. I just wanted to mention the possibility, however slight. I'm not suggesting this is what's going on."

"Well, what are the other possibilities?"

Dr. Holt frowned a little and leaned back in his chair. "Well, I probably shouldn't even mention this, because you certainly aren't going to find it in the textbooks. However, some of the things you have told me have gotten me thinking."

"Don't worry. I won't tell anyone," I smiled.

The doctor smiled back. "Well," he said, leaning forward with his elbows on his knees. "You see a lot of strange things when you are working with disturbed kids...things that aren't supposed to happen. After you told me about the putrid smell, the moving objects, etc., I wondered if it was possible that Michael was manifesting some PK effects."

"You'll have to run that by me again," I said.

"PK, psychokinesis. It's the ability, usually unconscious, to move physical objects with the power of the mind."

I let out a short laugh. "You're saying that Michael's psychic?"

Dr. Holt shook his head. "No, no, not psychic, merely manifesting abilities which might be considered psychic. This kind of phenomena occurs sometimes around children and adolescents who are under some sort of great stress. Physical objects may sometimes be displaced, temperature changes occur...it's really an unexplained power over the nearby environment. No one knows how it works and science can't prove it does. There have been some case studies done, but it's still unproven."

"So, why do you think Michael has it?"

"Because I have seen this sort of thing occur," he replied. "Otherwise, I wouldn't bring it up. I do some volunteer work in group homes and the staff members there agree that odd things do happen. Doors slam, things vanish, objects fly across rooms...you'd have to see it to believe it. All we've discovered is that it seems to be bottled up stress or energy that somehow escapes from the body. No ghosts...but definitely beyond the realm of current science."

"But what about my grandfather and the lights Michael sees and the voices he hears?"

He shrugged. "I really don't know," he said. "The other thought behind the unconscious PK is that it may be organically caused, which brings us back to the previous possibility I mentioned. It may be that Michael is manifesting the effects because of some electrical misfire in his brain. This may be causing the symptoms that you talked about as well."

I didn't know whether to be happy about this information or concerned. "You think he may be having some kind of hallucination?"

"I'm merely saying that it's a possibility," Dr. Holt answered. "I hope to know more after I have seen Michael a few times. Plus, I'd like to get some tests done when I meet with Michael again."

Dr. Holt rose from his chair. I got up from mine and picked up my coat. He put out his hand and I reached out with mine, and saw it was trembling. "I can't thank you enough for seeing us. Hopefully, you'll be able to help Michael."

He nodded. "We'll see if we can get to the bottom of all this."

I told him goodbye and he asked me to make another appointment for Michael to see him the following week. My hand was on the door handle when I remembered something. Dr. Holt had sat down at his desk again and, picking up the drawings that Michael had done, he placed them in a folder. "Dr. Holt?" I said. He looked up. "I almost forgot. You mentioned there was a fourth possibility for Michael's problems?"

He cocked his head a little to the side. "I did say that, didn't I?" he replied, chuckling a little, almost nervously. "I think the fourth possibility is that everything Michael is telling us is true. That the ghost and lights he sees really are spirits. And if that's the case, you and your family may have more to worry about than hallucinations and electrical impulses in Michael's brain."

Hardly able to think, I managed to make another appointment for Michael with Dr. Holt. His receptionist, Janice, gave me the number of a neurologist who would perform the tests on Michael that Dr. Holt wanted done.

I heard Dr. Holt's final words echoing in my head as I drove home. I treated Michael to a drive-through meal for lunch. I had gone to the psychologist for some reassurance, but I had felt more troubled than ever as I walked out the door. Still, I couldn't blame him for being honest with me. I told myself that at least we had taken some steps to find out what was wrong with my young son.

Regardless, I realized the time had come that I had to talk to Bruce about all this.

5

MORE THAN HE
BARGAINED FOR

There was no way to hide it anymore. Bruce had to know. I decided to wait until after the kids went to bed before trying to explain things to him. We had dinner and watched some television and finally the boys turned in. My stomach was in knots all evening. How would Bruce react? Would he think we were crazy? Would he even believe me when I told him?

The problem was, what did I believe? Was Michael in need of extra attention because of my divorce and remarriage? Could all of this be caused by a "glitch in Michael's brain," as Dr. Holt had called it? Or was Michael being "haunted" by real ghosts?

After the kids had gone to bed, I followed to make sure they were tucked in and secure. Both boys were used to having night-lights now. In the first few weeks after we moved in they cried when we turned out the lights. Bruce eventually got them small, plug-in lights. They washed the rooms in faint green glows which were eerie to me but the boys liked them.

Bruce was flipping through channels as I walked back into the living room. "What do you want to watch?" he asked me. "All these channels, still nothing on."

"I need to talk to you," I said.

He looked up at me and saw the tight expression on my face. He switched off the television and scooted over on the couch. "Honey, what's the matter?" he asked. It was obvious that something was bothering me. He looked at me with such compassion that I felt a little braver.

"First," I said, sitting next to him and taking his hands in mine, "I need you to promise me that you aren't going to think I'm crazy. Second of all, I need you to listen to everything that I'm about to say before you talk."

"Okay...," he said slowly. "I can do that. Talk to me."

I began to speak and I told him everything. I told him about Michael's screaming in the night, his claims that the voices were from the balls of light he saw, the flying toys, the putrid smell. I told Bruce about Michael's terrible birth and Grandpa Pierce and what Dr. Holt said.... Everything.

He sat there in stunned silence when I finished. His face was unreadable. What was he thinking? Would he leave us to deal with all this alone?

"Say something, Bruce," I pleaded with him.

He pulled his hands away from mine and I realized that I had been clinging to them the entire time I had been talking. "I can't believe you didn't tell me about any of this," he said.

"I didn't know what you would say. We haven't been married that long and I was afraid. It was just easier to ignore it and hope that it would go away. I hoped it would stop, but...."

"You just didn't trust me," Bruce said, an edge in his voice.

"No, that's not it, I swear. I was afraid that you...."

"That I what?" he snapped. "That I would leave you? That I wouldn't love the kids? Denice, you should have had a little more faith in me. You're telling me some pretty tough things to believe, but do you see me leaving?"

"No," I answered in a small voice. I knew he was right. I should have trusted him from the beginning. But how could I explain something that I didn't understand myself?

"You just didn't trust our love," Bruce stated.

"No, that's not it," I tried again. "I have been raising the boys so long by myself that it's just hard to lean on someone else. That's all... It wasn't you, it's me."

"But that's what love is about. You are supposed to be able to lean on me and I on you when trouble comes," he answered. I began to cry. Bruce held me in his arms as I wept. I don't know how long we sat like that, but eventually, he took a tissue from his pocket and wiped my eyes. Then he smiled at me. "It's alright, Denice. Whatever it is we can handle it together." I felt relief and love wash over me as we sat there together.

"Sit still," he said. "I'm going to make us some coffee. I'll be right back."

He was gone for a few minutes and when he came back, I felt like myself again. It had been awhile since I cried like that. I was drained, but refreshed at the same time.

"What do you think we should do?" I asked him.

"Well, are you still planning on taking Michael back to that doctor?"

"Dr. Holt, you mean?" I asked and he nodded. I told him I did.

"You really think he's a lot of help? What if he tells Michael the same garbage about ghosts that he told you?" Bruce frowned.

"So, are you saying you don't believe Michael is seeing ghosts?"

Bruce snorted in derision. "Do you? I mean, I believe Michael may think he's seeing something, but c'mon Denice, you know that kids can be manipulative."

"Michael isn't lying!" I said forcefully.

"Whoa there!" Bruce held up his hands. "I'm not saying that he is. He's a good kid. I'm not saying he's a liar; I'm saying that I don't believe in ghosts."

"What about the rest of it?" I questioned him. "Do you think he might be sick?"

"How do I know? I'm not a doctor, Denice, but I can believe that a lot easier than I can believe that your Grandpa is hanging around our house," he said. "Don't you think it's strange that the rest of us haven't seen anything?"

"What about the things in Michael's room? The toys and the smell? And what about Katie?"

"Maybe both you and the dog were reacting to the way Michael was acting. Who knows?" Bruce shrugged. "Why don't you get him a medical doctor's appointment and see what he says. Then, we'll go from there. You can take him back to this Dr. Holt, too, if you think it will help."

I nodded. "I do think it will help," I said. "Bruce, I don't know what is going on here either, but I think we shouldn't judge too much until we know more."

Bruce took my hand in his again. "Okay, Denice. I'm sorry if I sound judgmental, but this is a lot for me to swallow at once," he said calmly. "I promise to try and keep an open mind about it, but I want you to try to be objective about Michael's behavior and if he is unconsciously or consciously trying to get attention. Let's deal with it."

Trouble, they say, always comes in batches. Perhaps it's true. The next day, we got a call from Bruce's daughter, Crystal. She called often so this was not unusual, but what was strange was that this was the fifth time that week she had called about visiting us. This time she wanted to come right away. It wasn't that we didn't want to see her, but since she wanted to fly halfway across the country on short notice, the airline ticket was pretty expensive. We tried to put aside a little money for a future ticket purchase each week but with buying a new house, moving expenses and now Michael's doctor bills, our finances were strained.

I talked to her for a few minutes and thought she sounded odd so I handed the phone to Bruce. After he hung up, I told him that she seemed upset. "I have a gut feeling that something is really wrong with her." Surprisingly, Bruce agreed. That afternoon, we scraped together the rest of the money and bought a ticket for Crystal to fly out that coming weekend.

This was the first time that she would be coming to visit since we had gotten married. I wondered if this could be what was bothering her. I guessed we would find out that weekend.

Crystal got off the plane on Saturday, greeting all of us with a bright smile. She was a gorgeous girl at fourteen, tall, thin and good-natured. She seemed thrilled to be there and the boys were glad to see her, too. I hoped things would go as well when we got home. I had overheard one of the boys saying something about being "invaded" before we left for the airport, but boys at that age don't always adapt well to change, especially when it involves a new stepsister. I wanted Crystal to be comfortable at the house and had fixed the guest bedroom up especially for her. This was a big change for her—a new family and someone with whom she was going to have to share her Dad.

As we walked through the airport to the car, the conversation seemed to be going well. I hoped none of Michael's problem would surface during her visit. We went out for pizza and then returned home. The boys fell asleep in the car and Bruce got them inside and to their beds. Crystal was joyous about her room, but otherwise silent. I asked her if everything was okay at home.

"Everything's fine. I just wanted to see everybody here," she answered brightly.

The next day, we discovered that things back in Missouri were not what they seemed. We received a telephone call from a detective at the police station in the Missouri town where Crystal and her mother lived. It was then we discovered that Crystal had been molested by a family member. Her mother had told her not to say anything to Bruce because he would be upset. To make matters worse, her mother claimed that Crystal was lying. When we talked to Crystal she seemed crushed and she blamed herself for what had happened. She was embarrassed about the whole thing and heartbroken. We realized now why there was such urgency in her recent phone calls.

The detective assured us that his office had not dismissed the matter and he wanted us to know about it. He suggested that we might want to take steps toward getting Crystal out of that environment. We agreed, deciding then and there that Crystal would not be returning to Missouri. No fourteen-year-old should ever have to go through such an experience. We wanted to make sure that she would never have to deal with anything like it again!

Taking out a loan on the house, we immediately began legal proceedings and after a court hearing, were awarded full custody of Crystal. Unless or until things changed, Crystal would never have to go back to Missouri.

Everything seemed to be working out. We didn't know it, but another nightmare was not far off.

The impending arrival of Christmas seemed to offer hope and excitement as our new family assembled the tree and Bruce and I tried to begin new traditions. Along with these festivities, we tried to integrate Bruce's family obligations, Crystal's need for space, work and holiday school schedules as well as Michael's appointments with Dr. Holt. Despite our efforts, all of this created a lot of stress in the house. Things had reached a boiling point that even the joy of the holidays could not cool down. Everyone became tense and one night, it finally reached a breaking point.

"Mooooom!!!" Michael screamed.

The sound of his voice pierced the silence of the house. Bruce and I were downstairs in the living room. The lights had been turned down low and a movie was softly playing on the television set. Jimmy Stewart was lamenting his life in black and white, although we weren't paying much attention to him. We were just happy to be spending a few moments together in peace.

The shrill pitch of Michael's cry was followed by a thudding sound, a heavy pounding that I didn't recognize at first. Then it dawned on me; it was the sound of someone beating on a door.

"What the hell is that?" Bruce demanded.

We ran upstairs together. When we reached the hallway at the top of the stairs, Bruce flipped on the light. The dog was huddled in the corner. Crystal and Kenny were standing outside their rooms. Kenny rubbed his eyes and Crystal looked annoyed and frightened. There was no sign of Michael.

"What's that sound?" Crystal asked. I didn't realize it at first, but she had to raise her voice to be heard. The thumping continued to ring out and was even louder on the second floor.

It was coming from the door to Michael's room. As each of the loud thumps sounded, it vibrated the wood of the door. Was Michael beating on the other side of it?

Bruce grabbed the door handle and twisted it, but the door refused to budge. "What the...?" he muttered and then called loudly. "Michael? Unlock this door!"

My hand touched his arm. "There's no lock on it," I said and then Michael screamed for me again. I urged Bruce to force the door open.

He shot me a look over his shoulder and pushed on the door again. It still refused to open. The pounding continued, a steady rhythm of solid blows. I could see the tremors in the wooden panel as another one landed and then another. Bruce shoved on the door again, but it still wouldn't move. Finally, he slammed against it with the side of his body. The door shook, but stayed closed.

Then, as suddenly as it started, the pounding noise stopped. Bruce turned the handle and the door swung open. We rushed inside. The room was dark, illuminated only by Michael's night light. As for Michael, he was nowhere to be seen.

"Mom?" he cried again.

"Over there," I yelled. Bruce and I turned and ran to the closet. Michael's voice echoed from inside. I opened the door and he rushed out at us, colliding with Bruce. Both of them fell backwards, sprawling onto the floor.

Michael was terrified and shaking. Bruce sat upright and reached for Michael, taking him in his arms for a moment before he spoke to him. "What happened, buddy?" he asked the boy. "What were you doing in the closet?"

He let Michael go. Michael wiped at the tears on his face with the sleeve of his pajamas. "They locked me in there," he said.

"Who did? Kenny and Crystal?"

Michael looked at Bruce strangely. It was a look that said his suggestion was the most alien concept Michael had ever heard.

Crystal and Kenny watched the scene from Michael's doorway. They were dark forms against the light in the hallway. "I didn't do anything," Kenny insisted. " I was asleep."

Before Crystal could say anything, Michael said, "No, the bad people did it." He went on, "I was trying to get to sleep when I saw these bright lights in my room. I thought I'd hear the voices, but this time it was different. One of the dark lights had something coming out of it, like lightning. I got scared and there was this noise and then one of them grabbed me and I ended up in the closet."

"A light grabbed you." The look of concern that had been on Bruce's face a few moments before had vanished. It was replaced by an expressionless mask. He got up from the floor and I picked up Michael. Bruce walked over to the door.

"What did you do to the door, Michael?" Bruce asked, his voice sounding both tired and irritated.

"Nothing."

Bruce turned on the light and looked at it. I saw his fingers trace what I discovered later were a series of hairline cracks that traveled from the top to the bottom of the wooden door. "Did you hit it with something?" he asked.

Michael shook his head. "No, the bad people did it, I told you."

Bruce looked at him, then looked at me. "You deal with him," he said. "I'm done for tonight. Come on," he said to the other children. He strode out of the room and took Crystal and Kenny with him. Crystal looked angry. As they walked down the hall, I heard her say, "Michael is some kind of weirdo, Dad. He's scaring Kenny and me and making trouble." I carried Michael back to his bed and sat down with him.

"How come he doesn't believe me?" Michael asked. A single tear trickled down his cheek.

"It's just hard to understand, honey," I said softly.

"And Crystal doesn't like me," Michael went on.

"We have to give her some time," I told him.

"I really did see those things, Mom. I wasn't hitting the door. One of the lights did it," he said to me.

"Michael, I don't know what's happening, but we're going to get to the bottom of this. Don't be frightened."

I was awfully scared myself about what had just happened. Could I explain it? Could Michael have done those things? I was pretty sure that he couldn't have held the door and kept Bruce out. Nor did I think he could have hit the door hard enough to make it crack. And how could he have gotten into the closet that fast even if he had?

But was it some kind of ghost? I thought a lot about what Dr. Holt had told me about psychokinesis. Would that explain what had just happened? It might, I thought, and I became determined to get Michael to the neurologist as soon as possible.

"I want you to lie down now and try to go to sleep," I said. "If anything happens, you can call for me and I'll come."

"Will you come right away?"

I smiled at him. "Yes, I'll drop everything and come as fast as I can."

"Okay," he said. That seemed to make him feel better.

I tucked him into bed and pulled the covers up around his chin. "Will you be okay to sleep in here by yourself?" I asked him.

He rolled over, already starting to drift off. "It doesn't matter where I sleep," he said groggily. "I'll see the people anyway."

That was something new. The light-voices had become people who were following him. *Oh God, what is all this? What kind of people were these; they did not seem to have human shapes?* I left Michael's room, torn between feeling guilty at leaving him alone and being glad that he had fallen asleep. I hoped the night would pass in peace. I remembered back a few months ago to when Michael had first seen Grandpa Pierce and his night terrors with the lights and voices had continued for weeks afterward. I had hoped that it would go away but now it seemed to be getting worse.

I went back downstairs to where Bruce was already sitting. He looked up at me, a puzzled look on his face. "What was that all about?"

"That's what I have been dealing with all this time!" I cried. "Michael is so scared and upset and I just don't know what is happening to him."

"No, I think he was feeding you a line! You let him think he's got ghosts following him around and that's what he's going to tell you every time he pulls another stunt like that!"

"What do you know about it? Why don't you try sitting with him every night while he cries and screams about a man in his room?" I said despairingly.

"This is not going to happen in my house!" he said.

"I don't know what we can do but wait and see."

"No, we won't wait and see. Michael has an overactive imagination and your coddling him about this stuff is just making it worse. I'll handle it if it happens again. And I won't put up with it like you do!"

I think we were both as scared as we were angry, but neither one of us was going to back down. I got into bed and lay there without sleeping the rest of the night. It was the first time we had gone a night without holding each other. Not since Bruce and I had met had I ever felt so alone.

∽ 6 ∽

THE BAD PEOPLE

The next morning, I made up my mind that I had to find out more. First, I needed to know whether there could be a medical cause for the strange events Michael was experiencing. So around 8:00 A.M., when I thought his office might be open, I called the neurologist that Dr. Holt had recommended. "I need an appointment as soon as possible for my son," I said. The receptionist informed me there were no appointments available until early March—almost three months away! I felt dejected but, determined to help Michael, I went to the library and took out all of the books that I could find about ghosts, hauntings, polter-geists and psychic phenomena.

Whatever the cause of Michael's visions, I had to know. For I had become convinced, as Dr. Holt had said, that Michael believed he was seeing ghosts. Unlike Bruce, I didn't think this was about my son trying to get attention.

I drove home from the library with a large bag of books, not so much to read them, but to get the names and addresses of the authors and any experts mentioned in the books. After scanning each one and making a list of anyone I felt could help us, I put together a letter, which explained what Michael said he was experiencing in the house, and I mailed a copy to each name I'd copied down. There may be someone out there, I thought, who has had similar experiences. If there was, I was determined to find them.

A few days later, we were getting the kids ready for school, which on some mornings was a major chore. This was one of them. To add to the commotion, the holidays were getting close and there had been a major snowstorm. In addition, Christmas vacation was about to start and the kids were antsy. They were counting off the last hours before the school break.

"C'mon, Denice," Bruce said impatiently. "We need to go."

I sent Michael and Kenny out to the car. "Crystal, please go make sure they're getting in," I said to her. "Michael tends to dawdle in the snow."

"Michael's a pain," Crystal said and went outside. Bruce had started the car and it was idling in the snow-covered driveway. I grabbed the lunches I had made for the boys and followed Crystal out. Bruce locked the door behind us.

"Wait," Crystal called. "I forgot my history book. It's sitting on the counter."

Bruce sighed. "I'll get it," he said, snapping the car door latch back open. He ran back toward the house and was inside for a moment before coming back outside. His face was flushed and he looked angry. "Everybody! Get in here!" he bellowed and went back inside.

Crystal and I looked at each other in bewilderment and the boys climbed out of the car. "What's going on?" Kenny asked me.

The four of us trudged through the snow to the house and went into the kitchen. "What is it?" I asked Bruce.

He was standing next to the stove. I looked down and

saw that all the electric heating elements on the top of it were bright red, glowing with heat. The dials indicated they had been turned up all the way! A dish towel, its corner near the edge of one of the burners, was already smoldering. I grabbed it and ran to the sink to run water over it.

"Who turned on the stove?" Bruce demanded. "Denice, did you leave it on this morning?"

"No, we didn't even use it, Bruce," I answered. "What's going on?"

"That's what I'd like to know!" He angrily reached over and then flipped the dials on the stove to the OFF position.

"Well, I know I didn't turn it on," Crystal said. "Maybe it was Michael." She snatched up her history book and walked toward the door.

"Stop!" Bruce barked at her. "I want to know who turned this on and who left the dish towel there. We'll stand here all day until someone tells me who it was! The whole house could have burned down while we were gone!"

"Daddy! I didn't do it, I swear!" Crystal said. "I'm going to be late for class!"

"What about you?" Bruce turned to the boys, who looked scared and puzzled. They both shook their heads at him.

"I didn't do it," Kenny said softly.

"Me neither," Michael added.

"Well, they didn't just turn on by themselves! Someone must have turned them on!"

Bruce pushed past all of us and marched out of the house. Silently, we followed him outside, got in the car and left to take the kids to school. No one spoke during the entire trip. When I dropped Bruce off for work, he didn't even bother with a goodbye.

During the next few days, more unexplainable things set Bruce off. They were all small things, like the water being left running in the sink when no one claimed to have been in the bathroom and lights being turned on in the house when all of us were out for the evening—small, minor annoyances that seemed to have no rational explanation.

Ghosts? Or merely forgetfulness? I didn't pretend to have the answers, but I had a feeling that Bruce was beginning to wonder about this house.

He just wasn't going to admit it.

The following week, I picked up the kids on the last day of school before their Christmas vacation. They were all excitedly talking in the car, anxious to begin the winter break and not have to think about schoolwork for awhile. Arriving home, we walked into the house. Katie was waiting for us at the door, but instead of her usual tail wagging and happy barking, she was whimpering nervously and cowering at our feet. I immediately sensed a strange odor—that same one I had experienced in Michael's room many months before!

"Gross! What is that?" Crystal asked, "It smells like a dead animal in here."

I turned and looked at her. She was holding her nose, pinching her nostrils shut. So she was experiencing it, too! It was not my imagination! The smell was real... so real in fact that I felt nauseous. We walked all over the house trying to figure out from where the odor came. We looked in closets and under beds, but found nothing. However, the smell appeared to be everywhere. And then just as suddenly as it had come, by the time we returned downstairs and were back at the front door, it disappeared. Just as we were starting to relax, another problem began.

"What's that noise?" Kenny asked. I bent close to him and heard a combination of steady hissing and roaring, coming from somewhere in the house. Katie began barking and howling before hiding under the family room couch.

"Denice?" Crystal cried out. She had walked into the kitchen. "Look, the water's on!"

The hot water handle on the sink had been twisted all the way on and steaming water was gushing into the basin. The water was scalding, sending clouds of fog into the air.

"It's on in here too!" Kenny yelled from the downstairs bathroom.

I cranked off the water in the kitchen sink and hurried into the bathroom on the first floor. Kenny was turning the handle on the sink, but the shower in the small bathroom was running as well, spraying hot water. The mirror in the room was fogged over.

"Mom!" Michael yelled. His voice sounded far away and I realized he was upstairs alone. Running up the steps, I found him in the bathroom. The water in the sink and in the bathtub had been turned on all the way, splashing scalding water onto the floor. Michael turned off the water in the sink as I twisted the knob on the tub.

Suddenly, the house was silent. I sighed and blew a loose strand of hair off my forehead as I collapsed onto the lid of the toilet seat.

"What in the world?" I asked myself, not even realizing that I said it aloud.

"It's the people," Michael answered. He was standing next to the sink. His heavy coat was still zipped up and he had a stocking cap pulled down on his head. Both of us were now soaked with water.

I stared at him. That was the second time he had mentioned people. "What people?" I asked, my voice trembling.

"The bad ones," he said and walked out of the room.

Bruce worked late again that night. He had been working twelve and thirteen hour days. I felt part of his effort was trying to stay away from home as much as possible. I knew that I had been hard to deal with lately and the kids were on edge, not to mention the recent episode with the stove.

We had already eaten dinner by the time Bruce walked in. The kids were upstairs doing homework. I had saved his dinner for him and took the warm plate from the oven.

"I'm not hungry right now," he said as he passed through the kitchen. "I grabbed a sandwich at the office. Just leave it on the table and I'll eat it in a little while."

"Bruce, are you alright?" I asked.

He didn't answer; so I followed him into the family room. Katie lay curled up in front of the couch.

"Did you stop by home on your lunch hour today?" I asked him.

He sat down on the couch and began taking off his shoes. "What lunch hour? I eat lunch at my desk to save time."

"Did you stop by home earlier today or not?"

"No, I didn't stop by home. Why do you want to know?"

I explained to him the mess we had found when we walked in the door.

He just shook his head. "One of the kids must have turned the water on when you left this morning," he said.

"All over the house? It was steaming hot water. It couldn't have been running all day or it would have been cold by the time we got home. Besides that, don't you think I would have noticed if one of the kids had run around and turned on all of the water faucets as we were leaving the house?"

He shrugged his shoulders and picked up the mail. He started flipping through it. "Is there any beer in the fridge?" he asked.

"Yeah, I picked some up at the store yesterday."

He walked out of the room and Katie followed him. *So much for conversation,* I thought. Then, a whimpering Katie ran back into the family room with her tail between her legs and I heard a sharp intake of breath coming from the kitchen.

"Denice? You better come in here!" I heard Bruce call. His voice sounded very strange, a strangled sort of rasp.

I hurried into the kitchen and stopped dead in my tracks. We had been out of the room for less than three minutes and someone, or something, had wreaked havoc in the moments we had been gone!

All of the kitchen cabinet doors were open. Drawers had been pulled out and hung precariously at the end of each hinge. The door to the refrigerator leaned to one side and a steady stream of multi-colored liquid, the combined contents of several containers, dripped onto the floor. In the center of the kitchen table were stacks of plates, glasses, bowls and silverware, all seemingly thrown on top of one another and yet stacked to a height of perhaps four feet. Boxes and cans of food had been removed from the cabinets and now ringed the table, forming a foot-high barrier between Bruce, me and the conglomeration of dishes on the table's surface. It looked as though an entire gang of vandals had visited us in the matter of minutes we had been absent from the room!

Eerily, that same strange smell lingered in the air. I didn't mention it to Bruce.

"I don't... I just...," Bruce choked, trying to speak but failing.

Feeling faint, I said nothing, but felt the surface of the wall against my back as I slowly slid to the floor. Suddenly, I collapsed on the tile, with no idea how I had gotten there. I wanted to get up, but I simply couldn't find the strength to stand. I was unable to tear my eyes away from the destruction of the kitchen.

How could something like this have occurred?

"Denice!!" A shrill cry from Crystal shattered my thoughts. She ran into the kitchen, becoming entangled in the dishes, boxes, cans and containers scattered about. Suddenly, her feet flew out from under her and she spilled onto the floor. A harsh, terrified sound came from her throat and she scrambled across the floor to my side. Her hands clutched at my sweater.

"What.... what happened?" she stammered in confusion.

Crystal's terror snapped me back to reality. She stared fixedly around her. Bruce stood rooted in place, his eyes wide and staring.

Somehow, I got to my knees. "Crystal, it's alright," I said. She kept staring. I took hold of her chin and turned her face so that she had to look into my eyes. "Why did you scream?"

"Michael... Michael's room," she finally said.

I got to my feet and nearly collided with Bruce. Taking hold of his arm, I started to speak, but just then another scream sounded in the house. This time the voice was Michael's.

"Hurry," Bruce said, racing up the stairs ahead of me. The door to Michael's room was closed, but we could hear him inside crying. There was another noise too, the sound of something flipping back and forth.

Kenny stood wide-eyed in the hall. "Crystal, Michael and I were playing a game," Kenny said quickly. "Then everything just....just went nuts!"

Bruce twisted the door handle and we went into Michael's room. Stunned, we looked around. The lights in the room were flashing on and off repeatedly, even though no one was near the switch. In fact, Michael was huddled up in a ball on the bed. The "flipping sound" that I heard from the doorway was the sound of the window blinds going up and down, up and down. We watched mesmerized. As if someone had tugged on the cord, they sprung up and then dropped down again with a crash. This happened three or four times and then stopped. At the same time, the lights went out.

In the darkness, Bruce stumbled across something and swore.

I fumbled for a nearby lamp and switched it on. In the dim light we were able to see Michael, still cowering on the bed. When he realized we were there, he uncovered his face.

"What the hell is going on?" Bruce said. He looked around the room as though he expected to see someone else there. He cautiously walked over to the window blinds and raised them. Then he slowly let them down again.

He turned to Michael and Kenny. "Are you okay?" he asked.

Michael nodded and Kenny walked over to the bed. "We were just playing a game," Kenny repeated and gestured to the board, which still lay on the floor. "It was my turn to roll the dice and when I tossed them, they flew clear across the room. I know I didn't throw them that hard, but it was sorta funny."

He and Michael both smiled weakly.

Kenny continued. "Then all of sudden, the cards flew up in the air and all the game pieces went flying over there." He pointed to the far side of the room. I looked over and then had to look again, unsure about what I had seen the first time.

All of the metal game pieces were imbedded in the plaster wall. If the kids had done this, they would have had to fire the pieces from a gun!

Bruce sat down and put his arm around Michael. "What happened?" he asked him.

"It was the people," said Michael. "And a scary ghost was with them."

"What do you mean?"

Michael shrugged. "He was all shadowy and looked mean. He was right there between the windows and he didn't have any legs. Everything started to happen when he came."

"What do you mean, he didn't have legs?" I asked him.

"I could only see him above the waist. He had long hair and he looked mad about something."

"Did he say or do anything?" Bruce questioned.

Michael shook his head again. "No, he just stood there and stared at me, then the dice went flying and the cards…"

"And the lights starting turning off and on," Kenny added.

"Did you see the man that Michael is talking about?" Bruce asked him.

Kenny shook his head this time. "I saw all of the other stuff though."

"Then, what did….?" Bruce started, but was cut off in mid-sentence.

"What's going on in this house?" Crystal interrupted. She had appeared without warning in the doorway and when she spoke, it startled all of us. "Michael has been weird, but this is beyond weird!"

"There is a logical explanation for all of this," Bruce replied, although he sounded more uncertain now than he ever had before.

"No. I'm beginning to believe Michael," Crystal said loudly. "This house isn't normal and you can't ignore it or explain it away."

I walked over to Crystal and tried to put my arm around her. She was obviously shook up by everything that had happened. We were just as frightened, but Crystal had been thrust into our midst with little warning of the strange events here. It was no wonder Crystal had thought Michael was just making stories up. She was totally unprepared for the things she had just witnessed.

Now she shook visibly as she pushed my arms away. She

walked over to her father. "Daddy! Are you going to blame Michael for this?" she yelled at him. "Do you think one of us did it, like you blamed us for the stove? Do you think we turned on all the water faucets earlier, too?"

Bruce sat there silently, just looking at her. Tears streamed down Crystal's face.

"Daddy, this house is haunted...or Michael is on something! But don't you dare blame this on us! And don't you dare say there's a logical explanation!" she shouted and ran past me. I heard her footsteps in the hallway and then the slam of her bedroom door.

Bruce still hadn't said anything. He looked over at Michael. "Are you going to be okay now?" he finally asked.

"Yeah, I'm okay."

"I'm going to sit with Michael for a bit, at least until he falls asleep," I said. "Please take Kenny with you." The two of them walked out into the hallway and their footsteps faded away as they went down the stairs.

I put the game board and cards back in the box and closed the lid. I stared again at the wall, where the game pieces were implanted and promised myself I would try to get them down the next day. Finally, I sat down on the bed next to Michael.

"Are you really okay?" I asked him.

He shrugged. "I guess so, so long as nothing hurts you."

I looked closely at my frightened son and tears came to my eyes. I realized that even without medical tests being finalized I had come to believe that Michael's problem was not physical. "You're pretty brave the way you handle this."

"Most of the people don't scare me. It's just the bad ones who are trying to get me."

Trying to get me? My heart beat frantically. Though he'd

mentioned 'bad people' before, this was the first time he said they were trying to get him. "What do the bad ones look like, Michael?"

"Mostly they look like shadows and they have ugly voices," he replied, then pointed to the corner of the room. "But then there are good ones, too. There's one of the lights!"

I looked quickly, but didn't see anything.

"Grandpa Pierce says they can take different shapes."

"You still see Grandpa Pierce?" I asked incredulously.

"Sure," Michael said brightly, "a lot. He points out the bad people, the ones who say they'll hurt me or one of you if I don't do what they want."

That sent a tremor through me. Until this conversation, I never even considered the idea that Michael or any of the rest of us could be hurt or injured by what was happening. I had wondered if Michael was somehow causing these strange things to happen or if there was a threatening presence in our house. I had wanted to consider every possibility, until now anyway.

After tonight, I agreed with Crystal. I was sure the house or Michael himself was haunted.

"Why do they want to hurt you?" I asked Michael.

"Grandpa says that some of the bad people want me on their side and that I shouldn't talk to them."

"That's probably good advice. Grandpa was a smart man," I told him. I rubbed Michael's back and hugged him. "Why don't you lay down and try to go to sleep?"

"Okay, Mom."

He curled up under the blankets as I watched. Michael was pretty amazing, I thought, and it wasn't just a mother's pride. He had just gone through a terrifying experience and now was able to turn over and go to sleep.

I paused as I started out the door. "Michael?" I said. "The next time you talk to Grandpa Pierce, tell him I miss him."

"He knows, Mom," Michael replied. "He misses you, too."

When I got back downstairs, I found Bruce, Kenny and the dog in the kitchen. Bruce was re-stacking plates in the cabinet and Kenny was sorting boxes and cans on the counter. Katie, whimpering, her tail between her legs, stayed close to Bruce.

Bruce looked at me as I walked in the kitchen. "We have to talk to someone, Denice," he said quietly. "We've got to stop this somehow." His tone of voice was very different than it had been in the past. There was fear in it. A fear we all felt.

"We'll try," I replied.

I went over to him and he slipped his arms around me. "I'm sorry," he said. "I don't know what's happening here, but I know it's not your fault. I'm sorry I doubted you."

"Bruce, I've had my doubts too. It's just that I know Michael better than you and he would never lie about something like this."

Bruce threw his hands in the air. "If you ever told me I would believe in ghosts, I would have told you that was crazy... I just... I really don't know how to explain any of this," he said. He was very confused, scared and probably angry as well.

Suddenly Katie started to howl. I tried to quiet her. "I don't understand it either," I assured Bruce as I stroked the nervous dog. "We just have to try and figure out a way to make all this stop. And, as much as I hate to do it," I said, glancing at Kenny, "we're going to have to find a new home for Katie."

Kenny began to protest, but I interrupted. "Katie used to be a happy, calm, good-natured dog. Now she's a frightened ball of nerves. It's cruel to keep her in this house."

"I guess you're right, Mom," Kenny said sadly.

I looked back into Bruce's eyes. "Maybe one of the letters that I sent out will be answered and someone will be able to help us. We'll just have to keep our fingers crossed."

Three days later, one of my letters was answered.

The telephone rang around 4:00 in the afternoon and I picked it up. The male voice on the other end of the line asked for me. "Yes, I'm Denice Jones," I said. He introduced himself as Tim Sutherland, a psychic and one of the people to whom I'd written. Tim had success helping the police find missing children.

"Perhaps I could help with your predicament, too," he said.

Tim was located some distance away, so he would not be able to help us in person. "However, I hope I can give you some useful advice. I've been involved with supernatural phenomena for many years and have what I believe is good psychic intuition. I've worked with several police departments in the past and with a number of people living in haunted houses."

The initial phone call from Tim eased my mind, but, unfortunately, terrified me as well. He asked me to fill him in about anything that may have happened since I had written my letter and I did. He was very easy to talk to. I had begun the letters I'd sent out by saying, "I know this will sound crazy, but my family is in need of help…"

The thing that Tim said to me on the telephone was "I want you to know, I don't think you're crazy." That made me feel better immediately. He explained, "Situations such as you are going through do happen and more often than most people think." He also said he had helped other families in the past under similar circumstances.

"The first rule of thumb in a situation like this," he explained to me, "is to not show fear, no matter what happens."

"That sounds like good advice," I replied, " but it's a little hard to do."

"I understand that, but you have to realize that if you are dealing with negative entities in your house, they will feed on fear," he said. "Have you noticed that things around Michael seem to be more active whenever the family is stressed out or angry? When you panic, things seem to escalate?"

"Yes, that's exactly what happens."

"There's a good chance at least some of the spirits who are bad are using the energy that you are putting out to manifest themselves and to haunt your home."

"Wait a minute, though…what do you mean by negative entities?" I asked him. I was jotting down notes on a yellow legal pad. I didn't want to miss anything if he could really help us.

"I am talking about spirits whose sole purpose is to create negative situations. In other words, spirits of people who died and who may have been considered bad or even evil in life. They lived bitter, hate-filled lives and their spirit still retains these powerful emotions," he said. "Some people refer to these creatures as 'ghosts.'"

"What?" I gasped. "I don't know a lot about ghosts or the supernatural, but this conversation is scaring the hell out of me! Are you telling me that we have evil ghosts in our house?"

"Yes, Denice," Tim hurriedly replied. "And I am also saying that some feel bad spirits like these don't ever want to leave."

"I still don't understand," I told him. "Michael says that he sees my grandfather. He was a good person."

"Aaahh, there's so much we don't understand," he replied. "And it's impossible for me to say anything definitively over the telephone. I will look into this further and call you back. All of the phenomena seems to be centered around Michael, according to your letter. It is important that he…."

"Why do you think that is?" I interrupted him. "Why do you think that everything happens to him?"

"It's hard to say. It may be that Michael has a gift for seeing these spirits or something they want. They may realize this and center their activity around him. He is the only one who sees them, I understand."

"Yes, he is."

"What I was going to say," Tim continued, "is that it's important that Michael, in no way, should invite the spirits to manifest. I realize that he has had some contact with your grandfather, but what about the other spirits?"

"I don't really know. He often talks of the 'good people' and the 'bad people,' but I don't know what kind of contact he may have had with them. What do you mean by 'inviting them to manifest'?"

"I mean that he should have no contact with them at all. He should not speak to them or allow them to address him in a way that forces him to answer. He has already spoken with your grandfather, but that should cease as well. To continue contact could be very dangerous."

"Dangerous in what way?" I asked him. I had become increasingly frightened the longer we were on the phone. First it had been "ghosts" and now this. Was this man crazy?

"Dangerous in that these spirits are here to enact something.... They are attracted to Michael for a reason. For him to continue to communicate with them invites them to make further contact with him. If these spirits are negative," he finished, "then Michael's very life could be in danger."

Tim promised to call me again and we hung up.

I sank down onto the couch. Was he serious? Or was he in need of heavy medication? To be honest, I wasn't sure. This had all gone so far, so fast for me. I was happy to have talked to someone and relieved to discover that other people had been in the same situation I was in. But what about all of this stuff about "ghosts" and "negative entities"? Was it for real? Could something like that exist?

I was not sure what to think. We had seen some amazing and pretty darn terrifying things take place in our home. I was willing to concede there might be some sort of paranormal activity, although Dr. Holt still held out for an organic cause for these things. I was not sure, however, that I was willing to say they were ghosts.

And what was all this about Michael "inviting the spirits" or having something the ghosts wanted? I looked down at the hastily scribbled lines on my note pad. Was Tim saying that if Michael talked to these ghosts, then something bad could happen to him? Bad? Like what?

As I was rereading the notebook, Michael walked into the family room. He had a book under his arm and was going to turn on the television. He turned around and smiled at me. "Can I have a snack?" he asked me.

"Sure, there are cookies in the cabinet," I answered, "but just take one or you'll ruin your dinner."

"Thanks, Mom."

He did one of those little skips, which turns into a run, the way that only kids can do and started for the kitchen door.

"Hey, Michael," I called after him. He came to a stop near the doorway and looked back at me. "You know whenever you see these shadows...these ghosts? Do any of them give you advice besides Grandpa Pierce?"

He frowned a little and his forehead creased. "Sure, Mom," he replied. "They all do...and Grandpa lets me know which ones are the good ones and the bad ones, but he says he thinks I will be able to tell by what they ask of me."

Great, I thought, *so much for having no contact with them.* "What do they want when they talk to you?" I asked him.

He shrugged. "Just stuff," he said, "but I don't understand most of it, so I just don't say anything to them. Grandpa says I don't have to. The bad people just get mad and go away...or sometimes they do mean things, like all that stuff in my room."

Michael looked down at his feet and then back up at me.

"I'm sorry about that. If you want, I can try to talk to them and then maybe they won't try and scare us," he offered.

I shook my head quickly. "No, no, don't do that. We'll figure something out."

"That's good," he said quietly. "I sure would like it if the bad people went away and left Grandpa and me so we could talk together. Sometimes they really scare me."

It was almost the end of the school holiday. Just as the children had been overexcited at getting out of school, now they began getting restless to return. The new toys had started to blend in with the old ones for Michael and Kenny. Crystal spent most of her time in her room. The only good thing about what had occurred in the kitchen that night was that she seemed to have a new attitude toward Michael.

One of their last free afternoons, I took Kenny and Michael to a movie. Crystal refused to go, saying it was a 'kiddie flick.' We drove to the nearest cineplex. After spending what seemed like a fortune for tickets, popcorn and cold drinks, we sat down to enjoy the show.

The house lights were on and people were still finding their seats when Michael let out a loud shriek. He jumped from his chair. Popcorn flew into the air and his soda spilled onto the floor. Trembling with fear, he literally climbed over Kenny to fall onto my lap.

"Mom, make him get away from me!" Michael whimpered.

"Michael? What is going on?" I questioned. I was so startled that I spilled my own popcorn and was trying not to knock over my soda as I tried to quiet the squirming boy.

He pointed directly over Kenny's head to the empty seat on the other side of where he had been sitting. "That man! Make him go away!" Michael said, frustrated with the fact that I didn't understand what was happening.

"What man, Michael? I don't see anything!"

"Right there!" he cried and pointed again at the empty chair.

"What does he look like?" I begged him to tell me. By now, everyone was staring at us.

"His face is dark, streaked with purple veins and his eyes are yellow," Michael moaned and twisted to bury his face in my shoulder. His eyes were squeezed tightly shut as he whimpered his final words. "He has blood on his teeth!"

Unable to get Michael, who cried louder and louder, to calm down, I whispered to Kenny, "We'd better go," and the three of us left the theater.

As we were walking out, I heard a child who had been sitting behind us say to his mother. "What's the matter with that boy, Momma?" he said, very concerned. "There was nobody there."

What's going to become of us? I asked myself as we walked to the car.

Two weeks later, I talked with Tim Sutherland again. I told him about what had happened in the movie theater. He became very concerned.

"I think that perhaps I was right about the ghosts, Denice," he said to me. "I have been thinking about this a lot and I believe that I should come and visit you."

"That would be wonderful," I told him. My doubts about Tim had been erased with his offer. The idea that anyone would help us was so appealing that I began to make plans in my mind for his visit.

"That's no guarantee that I will be able to help," he told me, "but at least I could get a better understanding of what's going on. That way, if I cannot help you, perhaps we can find someone...."

Click.

Suddenly, the phone went dead in my hands. Tim's voice stopped and a dial tone began to hum in my ear. We must have gotten cut off somehow. I put down the receiver and immediately it rang. I quickly answered it.

"Hi, Denice," came Tim's voice again. "Sorry about that. We must have gotten cut off. Weird, huh? Who knows with the phone company?" He laughed and then continued. "I was saying that I could come out and see the situation first hand. There are people who deal in the cleansing of homes and perhaps...."

Click.

The line went dead once again. *What in the world?* I thought. We must be having problems with our lines or something. Maybe it's the weather? I placed the receiver back on the hook and waited for Tim to call back. Five or ten minutes passed and I began to think that perhaps the problem was on his end. I was just getting ready to call him when the phone rang.

It was Tim. "Denice? Are you okay?" he asked me.

"Yeah, I'm fine. The phone's just acting up, I guess."

"I called back right away, but when it picked up, all I got was an open line. I could hear a man's cackling in the background, but I couldn't understand what he was saying. I wanted to make sure you were alright."

That is strange, I thought. "The phone never rang here, Tim, until just now when I picked it up."

He made a confused sound. "Oh well, maybe I just got a bad connection," he said. "Anyway, I will check into some flights and see what I can arrange. I'll call you back when I've got reservations."

"That sounds great," I replied. "I can't wait to meet you in person."

"Same here. I'll talk to you soon," he said and hung up.

I said goodbye and hung up the phone. I didn't know it then, but it was the last time that I would ever speak to Tim Sutherland. After that, each time I tried to call him, his phone was busy and when I checked, the operator always said there was trouble with the line.

Another incident with Michael took place a few evenings later. We had just finished eating dinner and I was cleaning up and putting away the last of the dishes. Bruce had not come home yet, as usual. His work schedule was brutal, but although he denied it, I was even more convinced that he was also avoiding coming home. He had finally begun to grasp that something evil was going on in our house, or so he said, but it didn't seem like he was ever there anymore.

My musings were interrupted by a pounding noise. *Strange*, I thought, *it sounds like someone beating on the wall.* I tossed the dish towel I was holding onto the counter and began looking around. As I walked into the family room, both Crystal and Kenny turned to look at me.

"What's that noise?" Crystal asked.

"I have no idea. Where's Michael?" I responded.

Kenny shrugged. "He's been playing upstairs since dinner," Crystal said. Something told me that this was not going to be good.

"Michael?" I called, hurrying up the stairs.

The second-floor hallway was weakly lit and filled with shadows, but I made out Michael's form slumped over next to his bedroom door. He was standing, but with his arms folded between his body and the wall. His face was buried in the crook of his arms and one leg was swinging back and forth, knocking against the wall. This was the source of the sound that I had heard downstairs.

I approached him and placed a hand on his shoulder. "Michael?" I said, "What's the matter? What are you doing?"

As my fingers touched him, Michael shrank away from me and slid further along the wall. I had startled him. Apparently, he hadn't heard me come up the stairs, nor call his name. When he realized it was me, he spun around and grabbed for me. I could see by the look on his face just why he had been kicking the wall...he was too terrified to scream!

His body was shaking all over as I held him. He was trying to whisper something to me, but his teeth were chattering so hard I couldn't make it out. Finally, I could understand him. "M-m-my r-r-room," he stuttered over and over. Finally I understood his words.

"Stay right here," I said, my voice sounding much calmer than I felt. A savage churning began in my stomach as I slowly opened the door.

The bedroom was dark. The sun had set early on this winter afternoon, but I knew that Michael would not have played in there with the lights out. I could only assume the lights had gone out by themselves, as they had before. A dim glow from the hallway managed to illuminate the room a little, but it was still darker than I would have liked. Once again, the familiar odor of burning leather or a dead animal permeated the air. *What is it?* I shuddered, but I managed to force my legs to take me further into the bedroom.

Suddenly, only a few feet in front of me, a shadow detached itself from the wall and moved swiftly across the room! A large form passed in front of the window blinds. I could make out a male silhouette highlighted against the streetlights outside. *There's somebody in the house!*

When the shadow moved, a bloodcurdling scream broke from my lips. Backing away from the windows, I stumbled over something on the floor and went down hard. I was squirming backwards toward the door when Crystal and Kenny bounded up the stairs.

"Mom?" Kenny called, his voice sounding frantic.

"Don't come in here! Call 9-1-1!" I screamed at them.

Despite my warning, Kenny came around the corner and into the doorway of the bedroom. I nearly collided with him. He reached his hand into the room and flipped on the light switch. The overhead fixture filled the room with light. Frantically, I looked around, but there was no one there! The room was empty!

"Mom, are you okay?" Kenny asked.

I backed away from the door and pressed up against Crystal. "There was somebody in there," I said. "I saw a man by the window."

Kenny's eyes darted around the room. From the doorway, he even bent down and peered under his brother's bed, but I noticed that he wasn't going inside. "There's nobody in there," he stated. He looked at me curiously. "Are you sure you saw somebody? Maybe it was a car going past outside. Sometimes the headlights hit my window and...."

"A tall man, the color of shadows," Michael interrupted. His voice was very quiet, but so clear it pierced the air around him.

"What, Michael? What did you say?" Crystal asked him.

"He came in my room while I was playing. He held both his arms in front of him like he wanted to pick me up and carry me away. And when I told him to get out, he came at me and I saw his long fingernails."

"I saw something, too," I told the other kids in a shocked voice.

"There's nobody in here now," said Kenny.

Crystal walked over to Michael. "What happened to your neck?" she asked him. She touched him, just above the collar of his shirt.

"The shadow man grabbed me. It was like he was looking for something on me," he said in a puzzled voice. "But I got away."

I pulled back his shirt, from which the top buttons had been torn away, and looked at his throat. Bright red marks spread from his collar to his jaw. It appeared to be the mark of a hand! I could clearly see the hand itself and blotches that looked like fingers. I bent closer to it and touched the mark. It was raw-looking against Michael's pale skin.

"Ow! That hurts," Michael exclaimed.

"It will be alright, Honey," I assured him. "We'll put some salve on it."

I moved a bit away from him. "C'mon, everybody downstairs!" I said and began pushing them toward the staircase. For once, they obeyed. No one wanted to linger behind and they raced down the steps.

My mind was whirling. *What are we going to do?* This was no longer a case of Michael seeing things in his room. Now, I was seeing them too! And what or who had inflicted the marks on his neck? Was I simply imagining that the wound looked like a hand? Or did the "shadow man" really grab Michael? What was he looking for?

Oh God, where is Bruce?

I put some antiseptic on Michael's throat, then put the kids in the family room and grabbed the kitchen phone. First, I dialed Bruce's work number. It rang repeatedly, but there was no answer. Then, I called my mother. I must have been only somewhat coherent because she asked me to repeat everything several times. When I was finished, she told me to try calling Tim Sutherland. Perhaps the psychic would have some idea about what to do next.

I called the number he had given me and a woman who sounded elderly picked up the line. I told her who I was and asked to speak to Tim.

There was a short delay on the other end of the line. "I'm sorry," she finally said. "Tim is unable to come to the phone right now. Who did you say you were?"

I repeated my name. "Tim was helping us with a bad situation that we have here in Connecticut. He was making plans to fly out and visit us," I explained.

"Yes, Tim mentioned that to me. I'm his mother," the lady replied. "Unfortunately though, Tim won't be able to come there. He was in a very bad car accident yesterday and he's in the hospital."

"Oh my gosh, I'm sorry to hear that. What happened?"

"We're not really sure," Tim's mother said. "It was a hit and run accident. He was actually on his way to pick up the tickets for his trip to see you. Tim's car was hit by a black car with tinted windows which took off before anyone could get a license number. Tim has internal injuries... He's lucky to be alive."

I expressed my best wishes for Tim and hung up, even more shaken than I was before. I remembered the way the phone had abruptly cut off the other day when Tim and I were talking, as though someone were trying to interrupt our call. I couldn't believe this new event. It seemed too weird. He planned to come here and coincidentally got in a car accident the day he was getting his tickets? Was there a connection?

You're making too much of this, I told myself, *it was a simple car accident. They happen everyday, all over the country, every single day. There is no way that Tim's accident and our house could be connected!*

Could they?

A vision of the shadowy figure I thought I'd seen in Michael's room came into my mind. I also thought about the weird mark on Michael's neck. Were things starting to happen more often? Were the incidents becoming more serious? Were the ghosts, Michael's "bad people," becoming stronger?

What is next? I wondered. *What will they do to us next? And why? Why?*

❦ 7 ❧

BELOW THE SURFACE

nger seemed to simmer just below the surface whenever we
were all in the house together. Although she was sympathetic
to Michael now, over the next several weeks Crystal took every
opportunity she could to get out of the house, staying with friends,
attending school functions and whatever else she could do. I rarely
stayed in the house alone during the day, preferring to go shopping,
sit in the library or spend hours with a book at a local coffee shop.
The boys now refused to be upstairs in the house alone. They went
everywhere together and called it the "buddy system." And when
Crystal was at home, she too insisted on being accompanied.

Terror was getting to all of us. Once again, I knew I had to
search for some solutions to our problem. I was willing to try anything...but what was there left to try? Where should I go for help
next? Something had to break, I told myself, but I wondered if this
time it would be my family. There was only so much more we
could take.

On a Tuesday in late February, I brought Michael to Dr.
Holt's office for his latest appointment.

"Denice? I wonder if you could come in for a minute?" Dr. Holt asked after seeing Michael.

"Sure," I replied and Michael sat down with some of the toys and books in the waiting room. One of Dr. Holt's staff members sat down with Michael to keep him company.

I went into the office and the doctor closed the door behind me. Nothing had changed here since I had been bringing Michael to see him. The room was still inviting and today was filled with the scent of a vanilla candle. Dr. Holt smiled at me as we sat down in the leather armchairs.

"How are you doing?" he asked me. Dr. Holt had a way of leaning toward you when he spoke, letting you know that his entire attention was focused on you.

"Well, I've been better," I answered. "Things have been pretty bad lately."

He nodded. "So I understand from Michael. I wanted to tell you that both Ms. Ackerman from the school and I have spent a good deal of time with Michael and we've seen no signs of drug abuse, which is always a concern in a case like this. In fact, we have both found that he is a normal little boy in terms of his adjustment."

"Oh, good, I'm relieved to hear that," I said appreciatively.

"Michael has explained to me what has been happening," Dr. Holt told me. "He says that the 'bad people' caused those things to happen, which is what I would expect for him to say."

I felt a jolt of irritation. "Are you still saying that Michael is imagining things? Seeing hallucinations?" I asked him. "Because I can tell you that we all have seen and heard strange things, too! The things that have been happening are bizarre. Even Bruce admits that he can't explain them. And if they are hallucinations, then what did I see in Michael's bedroom?"

Dr. Holt interrupted my breathless speech. "No, wait, Denice!" he exclaimed, "I'm not saying that at all! I think we have moved far past hallucinations…but that doesn't mean that ghosts are at work here!"

"Then, what are you talking about?"

"As I have told you before, the possibility that Michael is manifesting the phenomena is still very strong. These things are not visions being experienced only by a little boy. While no one else sees Michael's ghosts, you have all witnessed some sort of strange phenomena. That still does not mean ghosts caused the phenomena," he said.

"You're saying that it's caused by Michael?" I asked in bewilderment. "I don't know about that...it's just too weird."

"And ghosts aren't?"

I smiled a little. "I guess you've got me there," I admitted, "but I think ghosts are easier to understand than Michael doing these things."

"It's not as strange as you might think," he replied. "Remember the first time you came in and we talked about PK effects and the power of the mind?"

I nodded.

"There is not a single incident that has been related to me that cannot be caused by the power of psychokinesis," he stated. "Not the sounds, the smell, the destruction in the kitchen, the voices...any of it. All of these incidents have been recorded in the past and have been associated with human agents. Any of this phenomena could have been manifested by Michael, even the...."

"What about the shadow of the man I saw in Michael's room and the mark of the hand that was left on his neck?" I cut Dr. Holt off.

He shook his head. "Those can be explained too," he said. "Persons undergoing great distress are often capable of causing physical harm to themselves. As far as the 'shadow' goes, I believe that all of you are in a very susceptible state right now. Your minds are allowing you to see what you believe you are going to see. Michael himself could also influence this. You could be seeing what he imagines is there."

I took a deep breath and let it out. "So, you're saying that all of this is caused by Michael? That the ghosts aren't real?" I questioned him. I had to admit that what he was saying made some sense to me. This man knew much more about this sort of thing than I did. Could he be right? I felt myself whipsawing back and forth between explanations of the rational world and what I was learning of spiritual realms.

"That's my opinion," he answered, "and so far, I haven't heard anything to change that. Tell me, does the phenomena only occur when Michael is in the house?"

I thought about that for a moment. "Yes, I guess it does," I confessed. I considered all of the strange events we had been going through. Most of them revolved around Michael specifically and even the ones that did not, he was still somewhere around, whether it be in another room or asleep.

"That may be our answer then," said Dr. Holt.

"What can we do?"

"Have you made an appointment with the neurologist that I recommended yet?" he asked.

"Yes, I called before the holidays, but the first appointment I could get was in early March. I've got to check my calendar for the exact date, but it should be in about a week or so."

"That's fine. Denice, there is still a very good chance that this could be something organic. Perhaps some brain malfunction that began with his birth trauma. As I've said, I have spent a lot of time with Michael and he does not seem to have any sort of personality disorder. In most cases like this, the human agents for the phenomena usually have a number of serious issues to deal with."

"And that stress causes things to happen?"

"In most cases, but Michael seems to be different. In fact, after talking with you and Crystal and Kenny, I have to say that Michael seems the least fearful of the phenomena. Much less frightened than Kenny is, especially."

"And that's unusual?" I asked him.

He nodded his head. "Yes, outside of the episodes, Michael

is a well-adjusted boy. That's what leads me to believe the cause of all this may be some medical problem which can be corrected."

"I've noticed that things seem to happen more when we are all stressed out in the house," I said and then laughed humorlessly, "and that's been a lot lately. The psychic that I told you about before...he told me that the spirits would feed off that stress and anger and act out."

"That's how the stories of ghosts and spirits get started. Long ago these PK effects were often mistaken for the work of ghosts. The effects were brought on from stress...but how to explain them? Well, the ghosts must be acting up!" said Dr. Holt. "In Michael's case, the stress could be bringing on the episodes as well. It's possible that even though a medical condition is causing the PK release, the stress and anxiety that Michael, and all of you, are experiencing may be triggering the phenomena."

"So, what's our next step?" I asked him.

"Let's get Michael to the neurologist and see what the tests say. If we can find a cause for this, maybe we can get these things to stop."

"But what if the tests don't find anything wrong?" I asked him.

Dr. Holt smiled. "I think they will," he told me with calm assurance. "But if they don't, I'll make you a deal. If the tests don't conclude that anything's amiss, I'll even consider the idea of ghosts!"

I left Dr. Holt's office feeling as though a weight had been lifted from my shoulders. Was it possible that an end might be in sight? I had actually been thinking of canceling the appointment that I had made for Michael at the neurologist, not believing that it would do us any good. When I got home I checked my kitchen calendar and was glad our appointment was scheduled for the next Monday. I called to confirm with mixed feelings. On the one hand, I felt almost hopeful that Michael's medical trauma at

birth could be responsible for some brain glitch which was causing his visions. On the other hand, I was fearful of the same thing.

Keeping Michael home from school, I took him to the
neurologist on Monday, waiting anxiously as head doctor, Maurice
Reagan and his staff put him through a battery of different tests. I
was a bundle of raw nerves and Michael was so frightened that no
one present could help but feel sorry for him. The doctors and
nurses did everything they could to make the tests bearable, but
Michael didn't stop shaking nor did I.

The several days wait for the results of the tests was
excruciating. *What will the tests turn up?* I asked myself over and
over. When the call finally came, they would tell me nothing over
the phone saying simply that I would have to come in. My anxi-
eties heightened. Once there, Dr. Reagan, said "The brain scan
reveals nothing out of the ordinary. There are no signs of damage
due to Michael's birth trauma nor drug or medicine related
impairments. The retina examination also indicated normal functioning." The latter had been conducted with the idea that a visual
imparity might explain Michael seeing ghosts, but the doctors
determined that Michael's eyes were absolutely normal as well.

What are we supposed to do now? As I was leaving the office,
one of the nurses took me aside and advised me to contact a
church. I nodded and left, unable to reply.

We were right back at the beginning.

It was like being on an emotional roller coaster. One day,
we were up and it looked as though an answer could be found to
all of our problems. The next day, the situation looked hopeless
once again and we were down. *What are we going to do now?*

If Michael's condition was not a medical one and his psychological report indicated he was normal, then what was wrong?
If all of the logical explanations had been ruled out, what were we
left with?

Ghosts, I thought, *we are left with ghosts.*

I called and talked to my mother when I got home. I gave her the news about Michael's tests. Like me, she didn't know whether to be happy or sad. She had a suggestion, though. At her favorite charity, she worked with a man who attended the Northern Pentecostal church and she had spoken with him confidentially about the situation in our house. He said that he would be glad to help if he could, perhaps by holding a blessing in the house. "He told me it will change the place and drive out any bad spirits on the premises," my mother explained. "I know it doesn't sound possible, but when you're out of sensible options, maybe a spiritual one is needed."

I figured that it couldn't hurt. This was exactly what I had asked my own church to do and they had refused. I told Mom to find out when it could be done and by whom and to get back to me when she could. She agreed to speak with her co-worker as soon as possible.

The evening wore on and I sent the kids to bed. Bruce was still not home from work. It was a rare occasion now when he was there early enough to see the kids. I was in the family room watching television when Crystal came downstairs. She looked frightened.

"Denice?" she yelled.

I got up from the couch and saw the nervous look on her face. "What's the matter?" I asked, already fearing the worst.

"There's something wrong with my bed. It's shaking," she said, her voice quivering. "It keeps bouncing up and down and when I try to lie down on it, my head keeps going up and down."

"Are you sure?" I answered.

"Yes. I thought it was my music at first, but when I turned off the radio it still happened. Come up and see. The bed keeps doing it. I think it's possessed!"

I followed Crystal back upstairs to her room. The only light came from her desk lamp, which she had turned on when she came to get me. I glanced around, but nothing seemed out of the ordinary. I walked over and placed a hand on her bed. It was not moving.

"It seems to be okay now," I said. It wasn't that I didn't believe her, I was just tired and worn out from all of this. Her face pale, Crystal looked at me as though I thought she was lying.

"I swear it was shaking just a minute ago," she cried.

"Maybe it was a truck going by on the road outside," I said, motioning to the window. "Sometimes I've noticed things vibrate a little when that happens."

"It wasn't a truck."

"Okay, I believe you, but it's not doing it now," I replied. "Why don't you call me if it happens again? Everything will be okay. I'm right downstairs."

I got Crystal back into bed, switched off the lamp and closed her door behind me. I had gotten no further than the top of the stairs before I heard her calling for me again. I went back to her room and opened the door. This time, I flipped on the overhead light.

Crystal was sitting on her bed with a startled look on her face. I could see that she appeared to be trembling, but was she moving or was it the bed? I placed my hands on top of the mattress and sure enough, it was actually vibrating up and down. Were we having an earthquake? I touched the walls and felt the floor, but nothing else was moving.

Crystal jumped off the bed very quickly. "See, I told you it was shaking," she said.

"It certainly is," I mumbled. I bent down on the floor and looked beneath it. I didn't like the only explanation I could think of.

Our visitors had returned and now they were making themselves known to the rest of us.

"Can I sleep in Kenny's room? I'm too scared to stay in here alone." Crystal asked me, already gathering up her pillow and a couple of extra blankets. Michael was already camped out in there. Safety in numbers, I guess.

"Sure, that's probably a good idea," I answered wearily, "We'll worry about this later."

As I walked her down the hall, Crystal turned to me. "You know, Denice, when I first came, I thought Michael was just a weirdo and my father shouldn't have gotten involved with all of you."

"And now?" I asked softly.

"Now I think Michael's telling the truth and we'd all better stick together."

"Well," I said, "at least one good thing has come out of all this."

"What?" she asked.

"We've become a family."

I helped her get settled in the other room, where Michael and Kenny were fast asleep. I stopped in the doorway and looked around, wrapping my arms around myself. Kenny's small green night light had graduated into a larger table lamp, which was left on all night long. I hoped it made the kids feel safe.

At this point, it wasn't doing much for me.

When Bruce finally came home that night and found me waiting for him in the family room, I told him about what had happened. He didn't seem to want to hear what I was saying. Bruce looked disheartened. These days he walked around like he was a beaten animal, no spirit left in him at all. I felt like the chaos in our house had taken everything out of him. He got up each day in a stupor and went to work, then came home when he had to. All that he seemed to have left which was normal was his job and, if he could have been doing it day and night, I believe that during this time he would have.

I also told him about the church group that my mother's co-worker had suggested. Mom called me back earlier in the evening, after speaking to her friend. She told me that a group of them were going to come over in a few days. Mom's friend had even taken a personal day off work to make sure he could come.

"Who is this that's coming?" Bruce asked. He had just taken off his coat and shoes. The coat was tossed over the back of a chair and the shoes were lying nearby.

"Can't you at least put your shoes away?" I asked him. "Are you in such a hurry to leave again that you can't take the time to get them from the closet?"

He ignored me. "What church is this again?" he asked.

I told him and explained that a man from the church worked with my mother.

"Are you talking about the people who speak in tongues? The 'holy rollers?'" he asked sarcastically. "I don't want those people in my house!"

I sighed with exasperation. "Give me a break!" I said. "What can it hurt? These people are nice enough to try and help us. I'm willing to try anything. Aren't you?"

Bruce waved his hands at me and barked a laugh. He rolled his eyes and walked into the kitchen. "Do whatever you want to, Denice," he called, "Just do it while I'm not here."

"Shouldn't be hard to find a time then!" I snapped, but he didn't answer.

Suddenly, the couch in the family room began levitating with me on it. It rose off the floor about two feet and just as I started to scream, the couch crashed to the ground. Trembling with fear, I scurried off it and nearly collided with Bruce who had come running from the kitchen. When I told him what happened he held me tightly and whispered words of apology. "We can't let what's happening in this house come between us anymore. We'll get through this somehow," he promised.

The next morning I explained to the kids that the people from the Northern Pentecostal Church would be coming to our house to cleanse and bless it. The kids were out of school for a holiday and thought the idea was "neat," as Kenny put it. Their mood seemed to brighten the entire afternoon and Bruce even came home early from work that night. His mood seemed brighter than it had been in months and he seemed happy to spend time with the kids. When the three of them got ready for bed, they even agreed to sleep in their own rooms, which was practically a cause for celebration.

Unfortunately, the celebration was not meant to last.

Bruce and I were sitting downstairs in the parlor talking when we began to hear a loud, rolling sound coming from upstairs. It moved continuously like a long peal of thunder. We ran to the steps and just as we started up them, we heard Michael screaming "Mom, help me!" in a terrified-sounding voice.

As we reached his room, the noise abruptly stopped. Bruce pulled open the door and switched on the light. Michael was sitting on his bed, holding onto the foot post with a stricken expression on his face. His chest heaved as he struggled to breathe.

The bed itself was sitting in the middle of the room, a good four feet from where it had been when we had put Michael in it a short time before!

"What happened? What was that noise?" Bruce asked Michael in a strange, muffled voice. I looked at him. His eyes were wide with what looked like terror. Suddenly, it dawned on me. Bruce wasn't acting strangely and avoiding the house because he was angry or because he didn't believe things were going on. He was frightened, just as we were. In fact, at this moment, he seemed terrified.

"I was asleep and I got woken up because my blankets got pulled off the bed," Michael told us slowly. He seemed very happy to see us and was even happier when Bruce sat down and put an arm around his shoulders. His grip on the bedpost gradually eased up. I glanced over and saw that his bedspread and blankets were lying in a pile in the far corner of the room.

"When I looked up," he continued, "I saw this terrible face looking down at me. It looked like it had been burned up. Then it smiled and it went away. When it was gone, my bed started shaking real bad and it slid over here to the middle of the room. It didn't stop until you guys came in. It was shaking so hard I almost fell off."

"C'mon, big guy," Bruce said to him, "let's go downstairs for awhile."

Bruce good-naturedly flung Michael over his shoulder and we headed for the door. Just as we entered the hallway, Crystal and Kenny stuck their heads of out of their rooms. "What's going on?" Kenny asked. "What was all that noise?"

"We're going downstairs to make popcorn," Bruce announced. "C'mon."

The kids were happy to see their dad in a good mood, but this time I saw it for what it really was. Bruce was putting up a brave front, but inside he was scared. Bruce figured that a show of bravado would best serve the kids right now and maybe he was right.

We had just entered the family room when another horrible quaking came from upstairs. It was that same sound as before, which apparently was the noise made by Michael's bed vibrating across the floor!

Bruce put Michael down and I watched as an eerie change came over my husband's face. The blood rushed into it and his cheeks turned a fiery red. I had never seen him in such a state of rage. He yelled something unintelligible and pounded up the stairs! None of us wanted to follow, but we were all afraid to be downstairs alone.

Bruce ran to the door of Michael's room and with a cry shoved the door open. It slammed back at him. He grabbed at it and pushed, but the door would only give a few inches. With a mighty heave, Bruce managed to make it open the rest of the way. We all stared in amazement. Michael's bed had moved all the way across the floor and stood blocking the door. Bruce stumbled into the bedroom, his eyes blazing.

"Leave us alone, you bastards!" he screamed at the top of his lungs. "Leave my family alone! Why don't you attack me? Cowards!"

"Bruce! Stop it! "I cried, but he continued to rant. The kids were all crying now and huddled up next to me, afraid that something terrible was about to happen. Their sobs and cries seemed almost as loud as Bruce's railing.

Finally, it was Crystal who got through to him. "Daddy! Stop or it'll hurt you!" she screamed. Her high-pitched voice somehow managed to cut through Bruce's insane rage. He stopped in his tracks and stared at all of us. His expression changed again and his eyes lost their fire.

"Let's get out of here," he said quietly, pushing us all into the hallway. "Denice, let's put the kids in Crystal's room for tonight." We put the kids to bed and stayed with them until they fell asleep before going to our own room.

There, Bruce sat down on the edge of the bed looking exhausted. I sat down next to him. I knew that he needed to rest. He had told me earlier that he had an important meeting the next day. A short time later, we turned off the lights, got under the covers and collapsed.

Suddenly, there was a crash outside! We jumped up and ran to the kids, but they were all sleeping. We paused in front of Michael's bedroom door. The sounds emanated from behind it. The first crash had been followed by another, then a sound like something being broken into hundreds of pieces.

I saw Bruce's hand reach for the doorknob, but then he pulled it back. He didn't want to be in there any more than I did. Silently holding each other, we walked back to our room.

We went to bed and tried to sleep, but we couldn't. I could feel Bruce's body tense with each sound that came from Michael's room. After a while, he turned to me. "Please call your mother tomorrow and ask her to get those church people to this house as soon as she can," he said to me. "I don't care who they are... Just get someone here."

Bruce looked exhausted when he got out of bed the next morning. "We have to act for the children's sakes like everything's okay," I said and somehow managed to drag myself into the hallway. I had to get the kids up for school and get some breakfast into them before they left.

Michael was in the hall when I opened my bedroom door. "I need some clothes, Mom," he said. He had waited there for me to come out, afraid to go into his room by himself.

We opened his door. The room looked as though a cyclone had torn through it! Everywhere toys were scattered and broken. Michael's bed had been totally stripped and the sheets scattered to the wind. Books lay in piles and opened face down on the floor. His closet door had been thrown open and his clothing covered everything. His dresser drawers had been opened and dumped. His small television set had been thrown down and shattered.

Michael began to wail. "My stuff! My Christmas presents! Who broke my stuff?" His body shook, convulsing with anger and fear. Tears of protest burst from his eyes.

Bruce appeared in the doorway and began to curse. He put an arm around Michael and led him out of the room. "Michael," he said gently, "We'll fix these things and what we can't, we'll replace," he promised. I rooted around and found some clothes for Michael to wear to school. We needed to get him dressed and out of the house for awhile.

Bruce looked at me as we all headed downstairs. "This is my fault, isn't it?" he asked me, nodding towards Michael's room. "Is it because of what I did?"

I shook my head and touched his face. "It's nobody's fault," I answered. "Something did this, but not you."

"You'll call your Mom today, right?"

"I'll call her as soon as I get the kids to school," I assured him.

After telephoning my mother and cleaning up the mess in Michael's room, I spent the next hours the same way I had so many others. I drove to the library and wandered around among the stacks for awhile, pulling and reading books on the paranormal. Then I slept for a couple of hours in the car. I was so exhausted from being up almost every night, but not tired enough to dare sleep at home alone.

Later, I picked Michael up from school and took him to Dr. Holt's office for his weekly appointment. I didn't feel like going in so I took Michael to the desk and then waited for him in the car.

When we returned home, the telephone rang as soon as we entered the house.

It was my mother calling back. She made arrangements with the people from the church to come over the following day. I was relieved, but fearful too. What if they came and things got worse? I thought of the mess that occurred when Bruce had challenged the spirits the night before. In fact, I had spent most of the morning cleaning it up. Or what if they couldn't even get here? What if something happened to them? I felt sorry for poor Tim Sutherland, who had tried to help us, but was now nursing injuries.

Around six o'clock the telephone rang. I picked it up. I had a spoon in my other hand. I was using it to stir spaghetti sauce, which was now heating on the stove. The voice on the other end of the line belonged to Dr. Holt. I had not talked to him since he had called me into his office a few days before Michael's visit to the neurologist. I had asked the neurologist's office to send the results of Michael's tests over to him.

"Denice? Michael told me that a church group is coming over to your house to try and end the problems you are having," he said.

"Yes, they are. I'm sorry, Dr. Holt, but Michael's tests didn't show anything wrong with him. Weird things are still happening here and they are starting to happen to all of us, not just Michael now. Please don't try and talk me out of doing this. I don't...."

Dr. Holt interrupted me. "That's not why I called," he said. "I called because I wanted to know if you would allow me to come over and observe."

I didn't know what to say. A short time before, he had been trying to convince me that Michael was the cause of all of the problems. "That would be fine, I guess" I replied.

"Please understand, I'm still not convinced the supernatural is at work in all of this, but I just don't have any answers for you either. If nothing else, the church group might provide some psychological relief for all of you. I would just like to be there when they come, if that's alright with you."

I assured him that it was and told him what time they were coming. He promised to be there and hung up.

I wonder what the truth was. Was Dr. Holt beginning to believe there was more to our problems than he'd first thought? He was a rational man of science. Was he truly considering the idea that our house was haunted?

I didn't know if that made me feel better...or scared me even more.

❦ 8 ❧

THE BLESSING

They arrived at the house the following day. It was early afternoon when two cars turned into the driveway. I looked out the front window at the clear, calm sky. Spring finally arrived and it seemed a time for new beginnings. I hoped that would be the case for my family as well. I prayed these people would have the power to banish the unwelcome occupants who had taken up residence in our home.

"The people from the church are here," I called to my mother and Dr. Holt who were sitting in the living room quietly talking over cups of coffee. Each had arrived about an hour before, to provide whatever comfort they could. I had kept Michael home from school that morning. He was in the family room, reading a book.

There were eight members from the church altogether, four women and four men. Each was dressed very conservatively in either suits or modest dresses. The women all had very long hair piled up in complicated knots and braids on their heads. I recalled my mother telling me that one of the standards of their faith called for the women to always wear dresses and to never cut their hair. The men were clean-shaven and wore their hair quite short.

Henry, the man with whom my mother worked, introduced us to his church pastor, Brother Frank Hoffman, and his wife, Sister Juanita Hoffman. All of them called each other Brother and Sister, but only the pastor and his wife were addressed by their last names. The other members of the group called my mother's friend Brother Henry and his wife, Sister Ruth. I was puzzled by their customs, having been raised a Catholic, but I was determined to keep an open mind.

We went into the family room and sat down. I offered them coffee, but they politely declined. Next, I introduced them to Michael and Dr. Holt, who I explained as simply a family friend. At Dr. Holt's request, I didn't mention that he was Michael's psychologist.

"Why don't you describe what has been occurring in your house?" Brother Hoffman prodded me. "Brother Henry has told us a little, but we would like to hear about it in your own words."

I spent the next twenty minutes or so explaining all the strange events that had begun with Michael seeing the ghost of his great grandfather and the strange events that continued in our house to that day. They listened intently, although I noticed that Sister Hoffman had closed her eyes while I was speaking. After a while, she began to sway slowly.

Her husband saw me looking intently at her. "My wife is very sensitive to the spirits," he explained to me. "She will be able to sense any disturbance in the house."

We all sat quietly now, watching Sister Hoffman as she continued to rock back and forth. This continued for a few minutes and then she opened her eyes.

"I sense a number of spirits present in this house," she

said quietly. "I have some questions that I must ask before we can proceed."

"I'll answer anything I can," I told her. I glanced over at Dr. Holt. He was watching everything very closely, but I was unable to read his expression. If he was skeptical about any of this, he didn't show it. Of course, he didn't look as though he believed it either.

"Has there been a history of sexual abuse in the family?" she asked me.

"Yes, there has."

"Did any of it involve your son?"

"No, my stepdaughter," I answered.

"Have you and her father both been divorced and remarried?"

"Yes."

I saw her lips draw together in a firm line. Two of the other ladies whispered to each other and then to her. "Did this abuse take place in the house?" she then asked.

"No, in Missouri."

"Has there been any history of black magic, demonic worship or ritual activity in the house?"

"No, of course not."

"Tarot cards, divination, Ouija boards?"

"Well, Michael's father allowed him to use a Ouija board, but that was after Michael saw his great grandfather's ghost and it didn't happen in this house," I replied.

She nodded. "Still, the influence is here," she mentioned. "I believe that someone in the house, possibly your son, has invited evil spirits into your home."

I saw Michael start to open his mouth in protest, but I placed a restraining hand on his arm. "Is it possible that these spirits came on their own?" I asked. "I really don't believe anyone in the house would have invited these things to happen."

"They don't just come on their own," Brother Hoffman interjected.

"What I think Denice means is this," Dr. Holt explained. "Is it possible for this energy to be attracted to the location, perhaps because of a person like Michael? It seems the activity is centered around him."

"It is not merely energy," answered Sister Hoffman in a far off tone of voice. "I have sensed the presence of a number of evil spirits here."

"I'm sorry, I didn't mean to imply that you are wrong," Dr. Holt answered hurriedly. "I just meant that perhaps the spirits have come to Michael, without invitation."

"This is possible. Both God's and the devil's ways are often mysterious," Brother Hoffman replied.

His wife shot him a sharp look and turned back to Dr. Holt. "Whether or not the spirits were intentionally invited or not, they are here. I believe they have come because of sinful practices in this house. Such practices will invite the presence of demonic forces."

"You mean because of the Ouija board and the fact that Bruce and I have been divorced?" I asked, shocked by her words.

Sister Hoffman nodded vigorously. "Yes, these things are not the way of God and if God is not present in your home, you are allowing Satan to take his place," she said. "These practices, along with the introduction of carnal knowledge to the young girl, have invited the evil spirits into your home."

"You're kidding, right?" Dr. Holt blurted out. He was as surprised as I was.

"My wife doesn't joke about such things," Brother Hoffman said sharply.

I really wasn't sure what to think of Sister Hoffman's statements. I didn't believe we had somehow invited the "bad people" into our home. What sins could a little boy as gentle and loving as Michael have possibly committed to deserve this?

Nevertheless, I was so desperate to stop these awful things from happening in our home that I was willing to try anything. Each time a possible solution came about, I clung to it like a person who can't swim holds onto a life preserver. The comparison was eerily similar, too…my family seemed to be drowning in confusion and fear. We needed a way out. I didn't know if those people could provide it or not, but I was willing to wait and see.

"Well, what can we do?" I asked Sister Hoffman.

"We will conduct a blessing in the house and expel the evil spirits who are here. However, before we do that, we need to walk through the house and examine it. This way, we can tell you what you can do to prevent the spirits from returning once they are gone."

"Thank you," I nodded. "Michael, please go with your grandmother and have a snack," I told him. My mother took him into the kitchen for cookies and milk.

After they had gone, the large group of us started meandering through the house. Then two of the men opened doors as we passed by, including bedroom doors, closets, even the front and back doors of the house.

"This will allow the spirits to pass through as they depart," one of them whispered to me.

In every room of the house, Sister Hoffman called out, "I have found a negative influence. This is what has opened you up to ghosts. You need to get rid of all of them to prevent the ghosts from returning." Books, videos, even toys and games, were consigned to the garbage bin. She became especially upset over the rock music posters hanging in Crystal's room. "If this isn't proof of evil influences in the house," she told me, "then nothing is."

Finally, they were ready to start the blessing of the house. We all returned to the family room. My mother and Michael rejoined us and Sister Hoffman announced, "I need to sit down for a few minutes before we can begin." I offered to get her a glass of water and Dr. Holt followed me to the kitchen.

"What do you think?" I asked him.

"What do you imagine my thoughts are?" he asked me with a faint smile.

"Not good ones," I answered. I filled a glass with bottled water from the refrigerator.

"Still, I did promise to try and keep an open mind," he replied. "I just highly doubt that I am going to see anything here today that will change my mind about the source of the activity in the house."

"They are a little odd," I said, understanding his meaning.

Dr. Holt nodded. "I have been willing to suspend my disbelief and at least consider a possible supernatural cause for everything, at least briefly," he smiled again. "But I have to admit that these people tend to set my mind turning in the other direction."

We returned to the living room and I gave the glass of water to Sister Hoffman. After a few sips, she was ready to begin. "Please stand in a circle and hold hands with one another," she said. "Now, pray for deliverance from the dead spirits." Each of the church members began to pray out loud in strong, almost musical voices. The singsong voices continued and even raised in volume after a few minutes. The sound was incredible and almost frightening.

Suddenly, Sister Hoffman let out a loud whoop and began to babble in some weird language I had never heard before. I was worried about her, but none of the others seemed concerned. They simply went on praying and before long, three other members of the church group began to "speak in tongues," as they called it.

Michael stared at me with terror in his eyes, but I smiled at him in what I hoped was a reassuring manner. Dr. Holt, who was standing next to me, let go of his hand and put an arm around Michael's shoulder instead. That seemed to help though Michael still looked panicked. My mother started crying. When I saw this, I began to cry, too. For those who have never witnessed the ardent prayers of this faith, it can be a rather frightening experience. Years before, I had a school friend who had attended an apostolic church and I went with her one Sunday. My feelings on that day must have been a lot like Michael's during the blessing.

The praying went on for several minutes and then I began to notice something strange. The temperature of the room was beginning to drop. It was becoming very cold around us, so cold that I saw goosebumps start to appear on my arms. Looking around, I saw that Dr. Holt had noticed it, too. His eyes were very alert and began to dart around the room. All of the church members were engaged in their prayers. Their eyes were clenched tight, their faces rigid with concentration.

A vibrating noise came from behind us. Dr. Holt and I looked around. The water glass that I had given Sister Hoffman, which had been placed on the coffee table, was shaking very hard. Water splashed and spilled onto the table. Then another tremor came. Suddenly, the glass quickly shot from one end of the table to the other, flying off onto the floor! A few feet away, a framed photograph on an end table clattered over and then skated off in the direction of the water glass.

Dr. Holt, who was on my mother's right, leaned over and whispered something to her. She nodded and grabbed Michael's hand. Together, the two of them left the circle and went out the front door into the yard. None of the church people seemed to notice their departure and continued to pray. Dr. Holt closed the circle by taking my hand. I didn't ask why he had sent Michael outside, but I suspect he believed the strange things would cease to happen with the boy gone from the room, because he believed Michael's fear over the proceedings may have been causing this phenomena.

However, even with Michael gone, it continued!

The air temperature dropped further. Though just that morning I had heralded the arrival of spring, the chill had become almost icy. As the group prayed, clouds of vapor streamed from their mouths.

Suddenly, a loud snapping sound began. I looked over to see the mirror in the hallway shattering. A spider's web of cracks instantly appeared over its surface. Turning to him, I realized Dr. Holt had noticed this, too. His eyes narrowed.

Sister Ruth also saw the mirror shattering. She broke off from her prayers. Her eyes grew very large and round.

On a table next to the wall was a candleholder with several long candles in it. Sister Ruth, Dr. Holt and I stared as the holder began to shake back and forth and then jump up and down, as if it were alive. One by one, the candles began to launch upwards out of their sockets, hitting the ceiling and falling to the floor. One of the candles snapped in half and a piece of it hit Brother Hoffman in the back.

The blood drained from Sister Ruth's face. Suddenly, she grabbed her husband's arm. He stopped praying and she whispered to him. He looked up just as a picture frame, which had been resting next to the candleholder, flipped upwards and slapped flat against the wall. It skittered along the wall from one side of the room to the other and finally flew into the corner.

One by one, the voices of the church group began to falter as they too saw the strange sight. Soon they all stopped praying, except Sister Hoffman, who continued. When she opened her eyes and noticed the others, she looked angry. "Why have you stopped?" she asked them sternly.

Her husband looked at her nervously. He opened his mouth to speak but a loud popping sound cut him off. Everyone jumped and one of the ladies screamed. Tiny pieces of glass showered us as each of the light bulbs in the overhead ceiling light exploded!

Suddenly, all of the church members began to stampede for the door in a panic. As they ran, crying and squealing, Dr. Holt and I were barely able to get out of the way.

Their cries were quickly drowned out by a booming noise from upstairs! It came once, twice, paused, then it sounded again. Over and over the sound repeated. Then I realized what it was. All the doors to the rooms and closets that had been opened earlier by the church members were slamming closed! In the corner of the family room, the closet door swung quickly shut and the loud crack panicked the church people even more. Then I heard the sound of the back door slamming shut.

Just before they reached the front door, it too closed with a resounding bang. Brother Hoffman reached the door first. He pulled and tugged on it, but to no avail. As the rest of the group reached him, they piled into each other. If it had not been for the terrifying events around us, the scene would have been comical. Then, as we all stared, the door popped open on its own. It swung toward them. The group wasted no time in scrambling out.

I began to follow them, having no more desire to be in the room than they did, and motioned to Dr. Holt. He just stood there, as if rooted to the spot in the family room, amazed by what he had seen. He waved me on. After a few minutes, he joined me out on the porch.

Five members of the group were getting into their cars. They and the others looked harried, disheveled and downright scared. Sister Hoffman stood on the front lawn, her arms raised. "Bad spirits are in that house!" she announced in a loud voice. A thick lock of her hair had pulled loose from the bun on her head and was now hanging in her eyes.

"Can't you help us?" I implored her. "This is what we have to live with every day!"

"Only God can help you," she replied. "We are just God's servants. He has tested us today to show us that evil is at work here. This was the deception of the...."

"If you're God's servants, then why can't you help this family?" a voice interrupted her. Dr. Holt stepped down from the porch and walked toward Sister and Brother Hoffman. "You told Denice that you could help, so why did you leave the house?"

"There is evil here I tell you and we feared for our souls," Sister Hoffman said quickly. She looked ashamed for the way they had acted, but was too stubborn to admit it.

"But doesn't the Bible teach that those who trust in God can cast out evil spirits?" Dr. Holt asked Sister Hoffman. His face was flushed and he looked a little angry. He was a man who had just had his whole belief system challenged. I knew he had no explanation for what he had just seen and was confused himself.

"These mischievous spirits used trickery to deceive us and make us vulnerable," she replied. "We could not stay and be deceived by them."

"I can't accept what you're saying," Dr. Holt dismissed her. "You have no idea what was happening in there and now you're using magic to try and explain it away."

"Evil does exist, sir, and it is inside that house," she snapped and then marched toward her car. Dr. Holt's admonishment over her failure to "cast out evils" had apparently touched a sore spot.

That left only my mother's friend, Brother Henry, standing in the front yard. His face was a mask of both fear and embarrassment. "I'm sorry," he said simply. "I really thought we could help you...I'm, well, I'm just sorry." Finally, averting his eyes, he trudged away from us and got into the back seat of one of the cars. No one looked back as they hurriedly drove away.

We stood and watched as their cars disappeared down the road. My mother was holding Michael's hand and she walked over to where Dr. Holt and I were standing.

"I'm sorry about this, Denice," she said. I knew she felt guilty about what had occurred. Henry was a friend of hers and not only had he and his fellow parishioners not been able to help, but the situation with Sister Hoffman had been very disquieting.

"It's not your fault," I answered and embraced her for a moment.

"No, it certainly isn't," Dr. Holt added and placed a hand on her shoulder. "I don't think anyone was prepared for what we saw in this house."

He paused for a moment and looked at me appraisingly.

"I know that I wasn't," he said. "I'll confess, Denice, that I am going to need some time to mull all this over. Frankly, I never expected anything out of the ordinary to occur...at least nothing that I couldn't explain."

He looked at Michael, leaned over and ruffled the boy's hair. Michael smiled up at him and Dr. Holt returned the grin. As my son looked away, I saw the happy expression on the psychologist's face fade away. It was replaced with one of concern.

"It's okay, Michael," I said. "Grandma will take a walk with you so you don't have to go back inside just yet.

Once they were gone, I turned to Dr. Holt. "Do you believe Michael now?" I asked.

"I don't know what to believe," he said, "but God help me, I don't disbelieve."

"God help us all," I murmured and with that I bid Dr. Holt goodbye and went back into the house.

As I walked in, I thought about the people from the church. I didn't think they were charlatans. They truly, I believed, had wanted to help us. They just found themselves more than a little over their heads. I had hoped blessing the house might rid us of its terror. Instead, the strange church group's prayers had brought more.

I took a deep breath. *There has to be a solution out there.* I just wondered if we would find it before something really terrible occurred.

❧ 9 ❧

ENDLESS NIGHTS

I took Michael with me to pick up Kenny and Crystal from school after Dr. Holt and my mother left. The children both asked how things went and I told them the unsettling story. We were all filled with dread as we walked into our home late that afternoon.

When Bruce arrived from work and I told him what had occurred, he took a deep breath. "Somehow, we have to conquer our fear of this house," he said.

"Maybe we should move somewhere else," I said slowly.

"Don't be silly, Denice," Bruce responded. "I struggled to afford this for us all. We have to live here."

Of course, that is easier said than done, I thought as I walked into the kitchen and turned on the light. I expected the room to be in shambles, as it had been at times before, but all was quiet. In fact, the entire house felt still and empty. It was as if whatever had been there departed. I knew better though. I knew they were simply hiding, waiting for our family to return.

And I was right.

Around 2:00 A.M., Michael awoke screaming, as he often did. Bruce and I ran into his bedroom.

"There are bad people in here pinching me," he wept.

His pajamas were torn off. The buttons were gone. We looked closer. There were angry marks on him. Red and blue welts and blemishes appeared on his forehead, his back and his shoulders.

We sat down on the edge of the bed and somehow got him back to sleep.

"It's like they are looking for something on Michael," I said to Bruce as we walked back to our room.

"Looking for something?" He said, puzzled. "Like what?"

"I don't know. I wish I did."

Later that same night, Michael called out again. I hurried down the hall, almost colliding with Crystal who had also come running when she heard Michael scream. Together, we entered his room to find Michael standing on top of his bed. In his hands he gripped the edge of his blankets, which he was pulling towards him. The opposite side of the bedspread was curling around beneath the end of his bed. It looked like someone was pulling it under.

Crystal and I grabbed hold of Michael's end of the blanket and pulled along with him. I could feel the tension in the fabric. Something or someone seemed to be on the other end pulling in the opposite direction! Suddenly, the covers jerked from our hands. They vanished beneath the bed. It took me a few moments to get up the courage to look under it. When I did, I saw the blanket folded neatly as if by human hands.

We were all exhausted the next morning. Between the bizarre episodes with Michael and the time it had taken to calm him down afterward, none of us had gotten much sleep.

Regardless, Bruce had to go to work and he departed early. I allowed the kids to stay home from school for the day. The four of us went back to sleep and didn't get up until lunchtime.

I was fixing sandwiches in the kitchen when Kenny called to me. Walking into the family room I asked, "What is it, honey? I'm trying to fix lunch." He and Michael had been playing a video game on the television while Crystal lounged on the couch with a book. She was wearing a set of headphones, listening to music, and hadn't heard Kenny call for me. She took off the headset when I walked over to them.

"What is it, Kenny?" I asked him.

"Watch this," he walked towards the opposite wall and pointed to a framed picture that hung a few feet from him. We all looked at it.

"What?" I asked.

"Shush." Kenny continued pointing to the picture.

A few moments later, it began to rock back and forth on its hook. It swayed in one direction and then another, apparently under its own power. Then it slowed down and came to a stop, suspended in the air as if held by an invisible finger. Afterward, it swung back again.

Crystal jumped up off the couch and placed her hand flat on the wall above the picture. "I bet there is some vibration in the wall that's causing the frame to move." I don't think any of us believed this to be the reason, but we watched her anyway.

"Is it the wall?" I asked and she shook her head.

"It's the shadow man who's doing it," Michael announced quietly. We all turned to stare at him. He was standing now, his arm outstretched and pointing at something none of the rest of us could see.

"Stop it, Michael," Crystal said, her voice trembling. "I hate it when you do that."

Kenny had quickly scrambled away from the wall and moved very close to me. He was usually more afraid of Michael's "people" than anyone else. "Make it stop," he told Michael. "Make it stop."

Michael turned and looked at him curiously. "I can't make him stop. He won't listen to me."

"Try it, Michael," I urged him.

He shrugged and turned back towards the wall. "The bad people never listen to me, but I'll try," he said simply, then raised his voice in the direction of the swaying picture. "Stop moving that!" he said loudly.

Incredibly, the picture stopped moving! The pause lasted for a few seconds. Then the glass over the picture shattered, splintering from the middle as though a fist had been pounded against it. Pieces of glass fell to the floor and then the frame launched itself from the wall! I ducked quickly, taking Kenny with me as the frame flew over our heads. It landed with a crash on the far side of the room.

"Wha...what happened?" asked Crystal, her voice shaking.

Michael turned back to us. "He left," he said, "the man got mad and left."

But whatever it was, it was far from finished.

Later that evening, as I walked into the family room something grabbed hold of the back of my hair giving it such a hard tug I gasped in pain. Tears sprang to my eyes. It felt like some of my hair had been pulled out by the roots. I spun around to confront the prankster, but there was no one there.

I wondered for a moment if I had somehow caught my long hair on the doorframe or something. Sure, it was improbable, but I wanted to believe anything rational that explained the irrational. I shook my head and walked on. Then, suddenly, my hair was pulled again, this time even harder. It was yanked so hard that I literally took two steps backward from the force. I whirled around. Still, there was no one there, at least that I could see.

There was little doubt that someone, or something, was present however. The hair pulling was followed by the sense that someone was standing very close behind me, so close that I could feel warm breath on the back of my neck. A hot rush of air crawled across my skin. Someone was there!

I was unable to move, frozen by fear. My hand clenched the doorframe. My knuckles began to turn white. Then, the presence behind me growled. It was no louder than the low rumble in the back of a man's throat, but it was enough to break the paralysis that gripped me. I screamed and whipped around, but the presence was gone!

Running wildly, I stumbled out of the room and ran into the downstairs bathroom. For some reason, it was the only place where I felt I would be safe. Perhaps it was because of the size of the tiny room, I don't know. Regardless, I crashed inside, slammed the door behind me and locked it. Just as the latch clicked, the overhead light winked out! I stood there in the blackness, screaming for Bruce, when a loud pounding came at the door.

"Denice! What's the matter? Are you okay?" came a voice. It was Bruce. He had been on his way downstairs when he heard me cry out. I fumbled with the lock and the door swung open. Bruce stood there in the doorway and reached for the light switch. It immediately came on, which meant either I had accidentally bumped if off when I ran into the bathroom or it had been switched off by something else. I didn't take time to think about it and instead fell into Bruce's arms crying.

"What happened?" he asked me. I was shaking uncontrollably and it took me a minute or so to calm down. When I could speak again, I explained to him what had happened.

"Are you sure you heard a growl?" Bruce asked.

"Yes, it growled," I replied. "I know someone was there."

Bruce leaned back on the edge of the sink. "It's like whatever this is, it gets stronger all the time," he said. "First it was just Michael, then we all started hearing and seeing things and now it's attacking us, too. My God, what's next?"

"That's a good question," I sighed. I leaned back against the wall and looked at him. "The other question is, what are we going to do about it?"

"We've got to get some help."

"We tried that yesterday, remember? It didn't do much good."

"Let's not give up now," Bruce replied. He stood up and hugged me again. "There has to be someone who can help us."

The next night was no better than the previous one. This time, it was Kenny who was assaulted first. I heard him screaming. Bruce and I were still downstairs watching television, although the kids had gone to bed an hour or so before.

I ran upstairs to find Kenny standing outside of his bedroom door. His face was pale and he actually looked blue around the mouth. He was having difficulty breathing, I realized. I hugged him and asked what had happened. "I was asleep and dreamed that something was smothering me. I couldn't breathe."

This was not uncommon. All of us, including Bruce, had been plagued with terrible nightmares. In fact, Kenny had experienced the same dream before.

"The difference this time," he explained tearfully, "was when I tried to get up, it felt like two big hands were holding me down! Somehow I wiggled out from beneath it. No one was there. Please," he pleaded, "go in and see if anything is in my room."

Just as I walked into the bedroom, I smelled that same

terrible odor I had experienced so many times before. It made me nauseous for a moment and then was gone. I searched everywhere in Kenny's room, though I already knew that whatever it had been was no longer there.

Later on that same night, it was Crystal's turn. The clock read 3:00 A.M. Unable to sleep, I had gotten out of bed to check on the children. I put on my bathrobe and left the bedroom. When I entered the hallway, I saw Crystal's light on. I went into her room to see what was wrong and found her sitting up in bed. "I had a bad dream," she wept. In her nightmare, a loud voice had been calling to her over and over again. It had been so deafening that eventually she had actually awakened from the sound. As she became aware of her surroundings, she realized the voice had not been in her dream, but had been real! It was coming from inside of her room! "I quickly turned on my bedside lamp and the sound stopped," she said, her voice quavering.

I was comforting Crystal and getting her back to sleep when I heard a loud thumping sound. It seemed to come from my own room and I hurried back there. The sound had been Bruce, falling out of bed and onto the floor. He seemed to be struggling with something in the darkness. I could hear him grunting with exertion and swearing under his breath.

"Bruce?" I hissed out a whisper. I didn't want to alarm the kids, but at first I only made out his darkened form and heard him tumble over and over again on the floor. Then he laughed with triumph. I could see him, in the street light from the windows, stand up.

"Bruce, what are you doing?" I asked him quietly. I walked over to him, wondering if he had lost his mind. I could see a white shape bunched in his hands. It was his pillow and he was holding it like it was a trophy won in some hard-fought contest. As it turned out, it was.

"I was sleeping," Bruce explained to me. "All of a sudden I woke up when my head hit the mattress. I thought that I had somehow knocked my pillow off the bed. I looked and it was on the floor. I picked it up and then tried to go back to sleep."

He tossed the pillow back onto the bed and lay back down. I climbed into bed beside him. "I was just lying here," he continued, "when the pillow was jerked out from under my head...again. It fell on the floor and once again I picked it up. This happened three or four times before I finally got tired of the game and hung onto the pillow next time."

Bruce went on to tell me that no matter how hard the pillow was pulled away, he clung to it and yanked back in the other direction. I was reminded of Michael and his bed covers. Eventually, the battle for the pillow became a tug-of-war that had pulled Bruce onto the floor, which is where he had been when I walked in the room.

"I managed to end up with it though," he said and tried to smile. It wasn't much, I know, but Bruce kept that victorious feeling all through the night. He had beaten the spirits this time! His triumph would last until the next occasion, when the chaos started all over again.

It was almost as if our bringing the church people to the house had angered whatever was there, because Michael's "bad people" began to intensify their visits. He said they appeared now not only at night, but in the daytime, too. "They want things," he said, although he couldn't seem to explain to us just what they wanted. I wasn't sure he was old enough to understand yet, but these spirits didn't seem to care. They continued to harass him and nothing he did to ignore them seemed to work. Other spirits continued to appear as well, although Michael described them as "the good people." They would appear to him, but distantly, as though they were having trouble making themselves known.

He wasn't so lucky when it came to the "bad people". They became stronger. I believe they decided that if they couldn't get to Michael directly, they would use the rest of the family to do it. And now all of us began to suffer the effects of the spirits as they began what can only be described as a campaign of terror.

Frightening episodes went on night after night. They began to run together and to blur into one terrifying experience. All of us were afraid, but as always, Michael bore the brunt of the spirits' abuse.

Unseen hands tugged and pulled at his clothing. Though he said his great grandfather tried to control them, Michael seemed especially scared by something even he was unable to see. Our entire family witnessed the invisible fingers plucking and pulling at his clothing and hair, searching for something we still couldn't divine. Red marks appeared everywhere on his skin, but especially on his face and on his scalp, where they appeared to be searching for something.

I tried to move the children from bedroom to bedroom and usually stayed with Michael until he fell asleep. I was hoping to stay one step ahead of the frightening events that continued to take place at night. One night after I put Michael into Kenny's room, I checked on Crystal only to find her bed shaking and jumping just as it had before.

The spirits plagued us night and day. We had the constant feeling of being watched. Crystal, unable to shake the feeling that leering eyes were upon her, refused to take a shower or undress unless I stood nearby on guard. I shared the same uncomfortable sensation and stopped taking baths in the house. We began taking quick showers with one of us on patrol outside the bathroom.

On the occasions when I was in the house alone, I felt my hair pulled and heard whispering voices which had no visible source. I continued my daytime escape trips, mostly staying at the library reading everything on psychic phenomena I could find. I had two reasons. One, I still kept hoping to find answers in the books and two, so that I wouldn't have to be home alone.

We were falling apart, I realized frantically. *What will it take to finally push us over the edge?*

One night, I was awakened just moments after I had closed my eyes. Unfortunately, it had taken until around 2:30 in the morning for us to settle down. We had moved the boys, who we had sleeping together tonight, back and forth between Michael's and Kenny's rooms three times and each time had been driven out by flying objects, weird sounds and the constant whispers.

Loud, angry voices awakened me. They seemed to come from the hallway. It sounded as though several people were out there shouting at one another. In my half-awake state I wondered at first if the voices belonged to the kids, but then realized they sounded like those of two men and a woman. I couldn't understand what they were saying. The voices were distant and speaking very fast. They also had a hollow sound, as if they were in a tunnel. I lifted my head to try and hear them better and they stopped.

Thinking that in my exhausted state I must have imagined the sounds, I wearily put my head back down and closed my eyes trying to get back to sleep. As soon as I did, the voices came again. This time, I realized why I couldn't quite understand them... one of the voices was speaking in what sounded like a foreign language! I knew that couldn't be the kids! I jumped out of bed and ran to the door. I flung it open. The voices stopped again.

"What's going on?" Bruce asked groggily. I felt so sorry for him. He had to be up for work in just a couple of hours.

I shook my head. "Nothing. Just the usual weirdness, I guess."

"Come back to bed," he mumbled and turned over. In moments, he was asleep again.

I had just pulled the blankets over myself when the door to our room burst open. Crystal rushed in, crying and upset. "Denice! Daddy!" she wailed. I sat up wide awake again. Bruce stirred, rubbing the sleep from his eyes. "What's wrong?" I asked.

"Something woke me up and I heard voices outside of my room," she told us.

"I thought I heard something, too," I said, wondering if she heard the same voices I did, but she hadn't. She went on to explain, "I heard the voices of little children, crying and calling Michael's name, saying that they were lost and needed him to come with them. I tiptoed to my door and opened it just a crack to take a look, but the hallway was empty," she wept.

Crystal sat down on the edge of the bed. I held onto her until she stopped crying. "It really scared me," she said. "Do you think they were some of the spirits that Michael sees?"

"Probably so, honey," Bruce said and turned over.

"But they sounded like scared little kids, Denice," she said. I felt her body shudder. "And there was something even scarier about them wanting Michael to come with them."

I agreed with her and she sat there quiet for a minute.

"Denice?" she said and looked into my eyes. I couldn't see her very well in the darkness, but could just make out the paleness of her skin and the glistening reflection of the tears that were still wet on her face. "Is there some reason they want Michael?"

I wasn't sure how to answer that. "I don't know," I answered. "He just seems to be tuned into something the rest of us aren't. Maybe it's because he almost died so many times as a baby or maybe there's something special about him or maybe it's physical. I just don't know," I said wearily.

"My friend Jenny has a sister who goes to Michael's school and she says that a lot of the other kids make fun of him."

"Kids can be cruel sometimes," I said. "You know that." I resolved to have another conference with Kathy Ackerman, Michael's school counselor, so that I could apprise her once again of Michael's problems.

Crystal nodded. "I know. It just bothers me. I never tell anyone what goes on here. I don't think they would believe me. I know that some of my friends wonder why I never ask them to come over here, but can you imagine?"

She gave a nervous laugh and I laughed along with her. It was good sometimes to be able to find a little humor in the situation in which we found ourselves. Unfortunately, we didn't find it often.

Bruce rolled over at the sound of our laughter. He had drifted to sleep again. "Everything okay?" he asked.

"It's fine, Daddy, go back to sleep," Crystal told him. She stood up and I climbed out of bed and walked her back to her room. Crystal got into her bed. I tucked her in. "Denice, can you leave the light on next to my bed?" she asked sleepily.

"Of course I can," I said, patting her shoulder.

Believe me, I understood.

When I returned to my own bedroom, I found that Bruce had not gone back to sleep. In fact, he now seemed wide-awake. He looked at me as I walked in, softly closing the door behind me.

"Is she okay?" he asked me.

"She's fine, just a scare, that's all," I said and then laughed humorlessly. "Who would have ever thought I would say 'just a scare' about anything that happens in our home?"

I lay down next to Bruce and he put an arm around me and drew me close. He spoke very quietly. "I don't know how much more of this the kids can handle," he said. "What am I saying? I'm not sure how much more of this any of us can handle. We're all nervous wrecks around here; we're up half the night with these strange happenings. No wonder the kids are scared to be alone. I spend all day worrying about what's happening when I'm not here...."

"I know, I know," I soothed him. "We'll figure something out."

Bruce's voice rose, although he wasn't angry, just agitated. "We keep saying that...not just you, me too," he said. "We keep thinking we'll figure something out, but we don't. Everything we try turns into a worse disaster. There's no one we can turn to here...not your church, not the people from the Pentecostal church that you had here, not Dr. Holt, nobody."

"Maybe we should move," I said, once more advancing the idea of escape, but Bruce shook his head.

"Well, what do you want to do?" I asked him.

He smiled at me sadly and held me even closer. "I don't know. I wish that I did," he replied. "Anytime I think of telling someone about this, I stop myself. They would think we were crazy. Jeez, maybe we are crazy."

"If this goes on much longer we're going to end up that way."

"Well," Bruce said cryptically, "that's really something to look forward to."

We both began to laugh despite ourselves. It was nice to be able to laugh. It was the second time that evening. It had been so long since I had done it and really meant it. Suddenly, Bruce sobered a little.

"Have you noticed though that things seem to be getting worse?" he asked me.

I nodded. "I have a bad feeling, as if this is just the beginning and things are going to get much worse until something awful happens."

"Like what?" He asked slowly.

I didn't reply. I just lay there in the darkness worrying.

❧ 10 ❧

SOMETHING BAD IS GOING TO HAPPEN

Several days passed with no further incidents. I began to think we would be safe for a while.

One morning after I dropped the kids at school, I went in to update the school therapist, Kathy Ackerman. I told her what had been happening and that Michael was continuing to see Dr. Holt, though not on a regular basis. She was pleased to hear that Michael was doing well and that things were calmer at home. Her positive outlook inspired even more hope in me that perhaps this period of peace was just the beginning. The whole family seemed more upbeat. Bruce had been home more than usual and we had spent several quiet evenings playing games in the family room and watching television together.

Maybe they are going to leave us alone, I thought. I had been watching the calendar and with each new day that passed without an incident, I thanked God and hoped for another one. We had been through a lot already; there was no doubt about that. *Could it really be over?*

I hoped and prayed, but, unfortunately, it wasn't meant to be.

That Tuesday night, Bruce and I had settled on the couch to watch the news and spend some much-needed time together. The children had gone to bed and the hands of the clock were creeping toward midnight.

It had been a long evening. After dinner, Michael had started crying. Apparently he had told one of his friends at school about the ghosts he had seen and the boy started making fun of him. The boy told some other kids and soon, most of the kids in Michael's class were teasing him and calling him "Spooky." The only one who stuck up for him was a boy named Justin, Michael's best friend. He finally got the other kids to stop and leave Michael alone. By then, however, the damage to Michael's feelings had been done.

Bruce and I talked to Michael about how to handle the teasing. I told him I would talk to his teacher. All of us tried to lift Michael's spirits, but nothing we did seemed to work. I reminded him his tenth birthday was just a few days away and suggested he invite some friends over for cake, but Michael didn't want anyone coming over.

"I just want it to be us this year," Michael said sadly.

We all knew why Michael felt the way he did. Truthfully, I am not sure any of us really wanted to talk about ghosts. Things were so quiet around the house now that I think all of us felt the mere mention of them could invite trouble.

Finally the boys and Crystal had gone upstairs to bed. Bruce and I had just started to relax. The lights were turned down low and Bruce leaned over to kiss me when suddenly we heard Kenny's voice.

"Mom! Michael is trying to call you!" he yelled. "I think he's crying again!"

Bruce and I ran up the stairs, our tender moment together abruptly coming to an end. As we reached the second floor, I could hear Michael sobbing in his room. Crystal and

Kenny were both huddled together in the hall. They were both too afraid, after the incident with the "shadow man," to see what might be in store for us in Michael's bedroom.

Bruce and I went inside and found Michael crying too hard to even speak. Bruce didn't bother to try and talk with him. He simply picked Michael up and rocked him back and forth and spoke softly to the boy, as though Michael were a baby again. Michael just kept crying and mumbling "another man, another man."

After a few minutes, Michael's crying jag began to subside. He sat there curled up on Bruce's lap, looking small and pitiful. "What happened, Michael?" we asked. He tried to explain.

"It was another man," he said, still breathless and hoarse. "One I had never seen before."

"One of the bad people?" I asked him.

"No, he was nice and had that light around him like Grandpa Pierce, but I was scared of what he told me," Michael replied.

"What did he say?" Bruce asked.

"He kept talking to me," Michael explained. "I tried not to hear, but he kept asking me to listen to him. He said he was a friend of Grandpa Pierce's and Grandpa couldn't come tonight, but that he wanted us to know that bad things were going to happen and that we should not sleep, but keep watch or something like that."

"Are you sure that's what he said?" asked Bruce. He looked as confused as I felt.

"Yes," Michael grumbled. "So I just started yelling for Mom and he went away."

"You can yell for me anytime you want to, Michael," I told him and patted him on the leg. I tried to smile at him. I wanted him to feel better, but I didn't feel much like smiling. I had hoped all of this was over. And now, after a brief respite, it was beginning again.

We put Michael to bed in Kenny's room for the night and turned on a light for them. Kenny and Crystal were pretty shook up about this latest incident, too. I think they had shared my hope that it was over. Now, to find out that it wasn't finished shook all of us.

"What do you think?" I asked Bruce after we went back downstairs.

He shook his head. "I don't know. I still don't know what to make of all this," he replied. "Things have been so quiet lately. What do you think Michael was talking about when he said they told him something bad was going to happen?"

"Some kind of warning maybe?" I suggested.

"I have to admit, to me, it really sounded like a bad dream," Bruce said. I started to protest, but he held up his hand. "I'm not saying that it was, just that it sounded like it. Even so, it wouldn't hurt to be especially careful...just in case."

"Just in case," I agreed, thinking for a moment about Tim Sutherland. Had he not been extra careful on his way to pick up those airline tickets?

The weekend arrived and found us in preparation for both Michael's birthday and a visit from Bruce's mother, Mary. We all loved her dearly and missed seeing her. She had a bad heart and didn't get to visit as often as she wanted to. Because of this and with my parents out of town, we were especially glad to have her spend a couple of days with us and to have another person on hand to celebrate Michael's birthday.

We spent Saturday morning cleaning the house and preparing food. I planned a big dinner that evening, turkey and all the trimmings, followed by a chocolate cake—Michael's favorite. I had a lot to do, so I asked the kids to clean their rooms so they would keep busy and out of the way. This was not an easy job, but somehow I managed it.

As I was basting the turkey, a terrible thought ran through my mind. What if something happened while Mary was at the house? When we invited her I had not considered this. Not only had things been quieter lately, until the incident a few nights before, but also it seemed as though nothing out of the ordinary ever occurred while guests were at the house. In all honesty, I would have loved for someone outside the immediate family to witness something, but not Mary. Her health was bad enough already and if something happened like the episode in the kitchen... well, I just didn't want to think about it.

Putting the potholders on the counter closest to the oven, I left the kitchen and went to check on the kids. They were still cleaning up their rooms. Everything seemed happily normal. I stayed upstairs for a little while and then went back to the kitchen to check on the turkey. Opening the oven door, I reached up for the potholders I'd left on the counter. They were gone.

Thinking I'd misplaced them, I looked all over the kitchen, but they were nowhere in sight. I told myself not to get nervous. After all, it was a minor matter. And though things had disappeared before, like cereal bowls and the kids' toys, they always turned up again, though often in mysterious places. I looked everywhere, however I still couldn't find the potholders. Then I smelled smoke coming from the oven. Whipping open the oven door, I found the potholders sitting next to the roasting pan. I pulled them out with a pair of tongs and tossed them into the sink. Was it me? Was I losing my mind? With Mary due shortly, I didn't even want to consider the alternative explanation.

Mary arrived in the early afternoon and the entire family spent the rest of the day together. She planned to stay until Monday morning. We didn't want her to have to climb the stairs, so I had made a day bed up for her in the family room. She was a little unsteady on her feet, but a joy to be around. Mary's spirits were always good. She prided herself on being able to make the kids laugh over just about anything.

It was because of the absence of her usual sense of humor that I began to notice something was bothering Mary as the day went on. Around four o'clock we were sitting at the kitchen table playing Monopoly when I saw Mary acting rather peculiar. Several times, she turned quickly and looked back over her shoulder as though she thought someone might be standing behind her. "This house gives me the shudders," she finally said.

Bruce had just rolled the dice to take his turn when his mother suddenly jerked upright and shuddered. "My goodness, it's freezing in here!" she exclaimed. "I just felt a terrible draft. Does anyone else feel that?" Mary hugged her arms around herself.

Bruce looked over and his eyes met mine. He looked almost scared, but when he turned to Mary, he smiled at her. "Yeah, Mom, it is a little chilly," he said, getting up from the table. "Let me turn up the thermostat a little bit."

Mary shivered. "There's something strange about this house. I think you should sell it and leave."

I looked around the table at each of the children and found them all staring back at me. A silent question seemed to hover in the air between us.

Now what?

Somehow we got through dinner. Our spirits were lifted for a short while as we sang "Happy Birthday" and Michael blew out his candles. But after having our cake and watching Michael open his presents, the tension returned. Mary continued to seem uncomfortable throughout the evening. I saw her looking around corners and toward the staircase. I had experienced this same feeling myself and recognized it. She was seeing movement out of the corner of her eye, but when she looked to see what it was, nothing was there.

Finally, around 10:30 that evening, Mary said, "I'm really tired. I'd like to go to bed." I breathed a heavy sigh of relief. We had made it through the evening hours with nothing going wrong. We got Mary settled and I suggested all of us turn in. "We could all use a little extra sleep," I said.

The night passed in silence...at least on the second floor of the house.

Early the next morning I decided to come downstairs to start some coffee. We planned this Sunday as a relaxing day for all of us. Bruce wasn't working and we hoped to do something as a family. The kids would be up soon, too. We were all excited about spending another day with Bruce's mother.

Quietly, I eased downstairs, not wanting to wake Mary quite yet. I assumed she was still sleeping in the family room. A light was already on in the kitchen though and I smelled coffee. As I came into the room, I saw Mary sitting at the kitchen table. She was still in her robe. She looked tired.

"Hi Mary, good morning," I greeted her cheerfully.

She looked up at me with a sour look on her face, frowned and just shook her head.

"What's wrong?" I asked, "Are you feeling okay?" I reached for an empty cup from the cabinet but stopped and looked at her. I peered a little closer and saw dark circles under her eyes. Mary looked as though she hadn't slept at all.

"No, I'm not feeling okay and I'm ready to go home," she snapped.

"Mary, what's wrong?"

She slapped her hand down on the table and raised her voice at me. "I have had enough of this awful house and of your awful children!" she said.

I was stunned. I had never seen her act like this before or heard her say such things. She loved the kids and they adored her. What was she talking about? "What happened?" I asked her.

"Well, for one thing, I didn't sleep all night! Someone was walking around upstairs all evening. I could hear everything through the ceiling and then there was the dog!" she explained.

I knew that no one had been walking around the evening before. The kids had been asleep before we were. None of us heard a sound all night. "I have no idea what you mean! And what dog?" I asked.

"It kept scratching at the door," Mary said, "and whining. I could hear it whimpering all night and scratching to be let out. I kept getting up and opening the door for it, but it always ran away before I could let it out."

"Mary, we don't have a dog anymore! We had to give Katie away!" I didn't tell her why.

"Yes, you do," she insisted. "I heard it. Furthermore, Michael doesn't like me and I have no intention of staying in a house where I am not welcome!"

"How can you say that?" I questioned her. "Michael loves you. Why would you say such a thing?"

Mary was obviously very upset. Her face was flushed and she looked up in surprise to see Michael, Kenny and Crystal standing in the doorway. How long they had been standing there, I didn't know, but all of their faces were marked with expressions of dismay.

"Last night, when I was in bed and half asleep," Mary explained, "He whispered in my ear, 'I hate you, you bitch, get out of my house.' I have never heard such a thing in my life!"

I gasped in amazement. "Michael would never say something like that! Did you see him?" I asked quietly.

"I didn't see him, but I heard his voice. I know it was him."

"Mom, I never said that to Grandma, I didn't," Michael spoke up.

Mary sniffed. "Well, it must have been Kenny then, because I heard it."

"I'm going to get Daddy," Crystal announced and ran upstairs.

I sat down next to Mary at the table and put my hand on her arm. "I promise that neither Michael nor Kenny would have said such an awful thing to you. Both boys love you, Mary. They are thrilled you are here."

At that, she burst into tears. "I know that I heard someone cursing at me, Denice. I didn't want to think it was the boys," she said. She held her arms out and the boys came up on either side of her. She embraced them.

"We're sorry," Kenny spoke up, "but I promise that Michael and me didn't say anything bad to you."

Just then, Bruce walked into the room. "Mom?" he asked "You okay?"

"I'm fine now," she said and wiped the tears from her face. I handed her a tissue and she blew her nose. "I was just upset. I didn't sleep well. I must have had a terrible dream."

"Crystal said that you thought one of the boys said something awful to you."

Mary looked up at Bruce and smiled. "I must have imagined it," she told him. "It's this house. It's scary and makes all kinds of sounds. Look at these two angels. Do either of them look like they would say something mean to me?" She hugged both of the boys again and let them help her out of her chair.

Mary and the boys, accompanied by Crystal, went out into the family room. I was left alone in the kitchen with Bruce. He looked tired and worn out. He ran a hand through his already tousled hair.

"Well, that's one bullet we've dodged," he said.

"What do you think happened?"

"This house is what happened, or whatever it is that's living here with us," Bruce said grimly.

"What do we do about your mom?" I asked him.

"Let's keep her out of this, Denice," he stated firmly. "I don't want her to know what's really going on here."

"That's fine," I said, "but right now, she thinks she's going crazy, hearing voices and thinking we have a dog in the house. Is that really fair to her?"

As soon as I asked, I realized Bruce was right. Mary was simply too fragile for us to try and explain to her what had been going on. She treasured the kids and literally wept with joy every time she had an opportunity to see them. We had no idea how long she would be around and we didn't want to burden her with what we saw as our problem.

"You know it has to be," Bruce answered. "She's only going to be here one more day. Let's just keep our fingers crossed and pray that nothing bad happens."

It seemed like our prayers were answered. We spent the rest of Sunday out in the backyard. The boys played, Crystal read and we had a barbecue.

The next morning, I was up early again. Mary wanted to get started for home when the kids left for school. I had promised to get her up so she could have breakfast with them. The previous day had gone better than we could have hoped. Mary's outburst in the morning had been forgotten and the rest of the day and evening we enjoyed each other's company. We had gone to bed around midnight and Mary had been fast asleep when I went upstairs.

I decided to wake Mary up before I started fixing something to eat since I knew that it would take her a little while to get ready. As I walked in to the family room, I noticed that the day bed was empty. *Maybe she's already up*, I thought, *I'll check the kitchen.*

Unfortunately, what greeted me in the kitchen was all too familiar! The cabinets and drawers all leaned and tilted open, their contents strewn about. This time however, the plates, bowls and cups were scattered on the floor. On the table was a tower of boxes and canned food that leaned precariously to one side.

How did we not hear a commotion last night? But then I remembered the last time it had happened. On that occasion, Bruce and I had only been out of the room for a few moments; we never heard a thing and yet the room looked like a war zone.

Suddenly these thoughts vanished from my mind and a more ominous one surfaced... *Where is Mary?* I looked around in a panic. *Did she get frightened and leave?* I looked out the back door window. No, her car was still parked in the driveway. So, where was she?

"Mary?" I called her name. No answer.

I continued to call and walked around the house, listening closely for a response.

"Den..."

What was that? Suddenly, I heard it again and realized it was the very feeble sound of my name being called. It had to be Mary, but where was she? Going toward the sound, I walked around a stack of plates on the floor and eased close to the basement door. We rarely used the cellar, except for storage, and I couldn't remember the last time I had been down there.

"Mary?" I called again. I heard her answer once more and realized where her voice was coming from. She was in the basement! What was she doing down there?

Hurrying to the door, I jerked on the handle to pull it open. It jolted my arm, refusing to budge. I knew the door didn't lock, so what was holding it closed? I looked carefully at the door jamb and saw a twist of bent metal that had somehow been hammered into the edge of the door and the doorframe. The metal piece had effectively sealed the door shut. *What is that?* I looked closer. It had a vaguely familiar shape, I thought, and then

I realized it was a metal bottle opener. It had been stretched and pulled beyond recognition and then pounded into the wood to make a lock for the door!

How in the world?

I yanked on the door again, but it still wouldn't move. I could feel the panic rising in my chest. What if Mary was hurt? I ran over to the doorway and screamed up the stairs for Bruce.

"Denice," a faint cry sounded. Mary was calling to me again. I needed to get to her, but how? As I went back towards the door, I noticed our tool drawer standing open. A heavy metal screwdriver was on top. I grabbed it, rammed the point of the screwdriver into the wood of the door and tried to pry the metal loose. My hands were shaking and the blade slipped down the door.

Get a grip on yourself! I screamed inwardly and stabbed at it again. The tip slipped between the wood and the metal. I pulled back on the handle. It began to pry loose and in moments, the remains of the bottle opener crashed to the floor. Suddenly, the basement door opened!

"Where are you?" I called out loudly. Descending the steps into the dark basement, I looked around for Mary. I still couldn't understand what she was doing down there.

"Denice?" she groaned.

Looking down, I saw her stretched out on the cold concrete, wearing only her robe and a thin nightgown. Her pale legs poked out from beneath the hem of the robe. She turned to look at me and tried without success to get up.

"Mary! My God, what happened? What are you doing down here?" I rushed to her side and tried to support the older woman. Her face was deathly white and she was having trouble breathing. Something was seriously wrong.

Bruce appeared at the top of the stairs. "Denice?" he yelled down, his voice filled with panic. He had undoubtedly come upon the mess in the kitchen and seeing the basement door ajar, feared something had happened.

"It's your mom. She's been badly hurt," I hollered up the steps. "Call an ambulance!"

I turned back to Mary, who was still laboring to breathe. The grayish tinge of her skin scared me. She clutched at my sleeve and tried again to sit up.

"Please, just lie still," I said soothingly. "We're getting you some help."

"I was in the kitchen getting a glass from the cabinet so I could get a drink of water. I thought I heard…heard Michael call to me," she said. "He seemed to be in the basement. I opened the door to the basement so I could get down to Michael. That was when I felt someone behind me saying 'Mary.' I turned towards him…"

"Him?" I said, a cold chill passing through me.

Mary coughed. She was gasping for breath.

"It's okay, just be still, " I tried to tell her, but feebly she waved me away.

"No, no, I have to tell you," she said breathlessly. "When I turned all I could see was a shadowy form like a very tall, skeleton-thin man. But before I could cry out, he put some kind of kerchief with foul smelling stuff on my face. He said, 'You bitch, you told them to leave.' Then I felt myself being pushed down the stairs. I passed out while I was falling. I think I woke up here."

I looked down at her legs again. They were covered with welts that I hadn't seen a few moments ago. Some formed a pattern like the very same red marks I'd seen on Michael. I also noticed the way that Mary's body pitched to one side. I guessed that her hip was broken. I began to cry and I could hardly hear the last thing she said.

"Something…," she managed to utter, "something bad here."

Her eyes rolled back. I could still feel her chest heaving for air, but she was unconscious and did not speak again. She was still unconscious when the paramedics arrived.

Bruce rode in the ambulance with his mother while I stayed home with the kids. He called me from the hospital to say Mary had been placed in Intensive Care. The doctors told him that she had suffered a heart attack and a broken hip and wrist from her fall down the stairs.

The paramedics told the doctors that Mary had apparently had a heart attack while rearranging the cabinets in the kitchen. Confused, she had opened the basement door instead of going through the one to the family room. This had resulted in her fall down the steps.

No one questioned why she was in the kitchen fixing cabinets in the middle of the night. Bruce didn't volunteer any information to dispute this theory.

"She's in really bad shape. Her heart has stopped twice," Bruce explained when he called later that night.

I shed tears of grief and fear. What had happened to Mary? Had the "bad people" done this to her? I couldn't get her last words out of my mind. She had seen the shadow of a man. Was it Michael's "shadow man?" Had he pushed her? But why?

I spoke with Bruce for another few moments and then hung up the receiver. He was coming home, but my mind was in turmoil. What had really happened to Mary?

Mary remained in critical condition that week. Just as Michael had when he was born, she seemed several times to be close to death and then be pulled back. One night when we came to visit and she was feeling a bit better she told us about a man who came to her several times in the hospital when she was at her worst. She explained, "I kept seeing this kindly old man with white hair. Once he bent to kiss my cheek and his face was so clean shaven and smelled of a heavenly, minty scent."

Mint. I bolted upright. That was the scent of Grandpa's favorite shaving lotion! I pulled from my wallet the photo of Grandma and Grandpa Pierce my dad had given me.

"Is this the man you saw?" I asked Mary, showing her the picture.

"I don't believe it. My goodness," she said, "It is him." Bruce and I just stared at each other.

When she was finally ready to be released from the hospital, we wanted Mary to come home with us so we could take care of her, but she refused. "I'll never set foot in that house again," she said firmly. And she was as good as her word. From then on, whenever we wanted to see her, we had to go visit her at her home or take her out.

❦ 11 ❧

THE GHOST HUNTERS

For a short while after Mary's recovery, things were almost peaceful. On this day, two of the kids were away: Kenny at a friend's house and Crystal playing volleyball with her class. Michael was upstairs playing with his friend Justin, who had come home with him from school. The sound of their laughter filtered down the stairs. It made me feel good. With all of the problems my son had experienced, he needed a friend he could count on and Justin was certainly that.

The two boys had taken to each other right away when Michael had started the school year. That first week, I came to pick him up one afternoon and was introduced to a grinning, redheaded boy. Michael announced, "This is Justin." Soon Justin became Michael's best and really only friend. There was something very special about him. He was always helpful and very polite. When he came to our house, he always sat down and talked with Bruce and me, which at first surprised us since most boys his age shy away from grown-up conversation.

Justin was the only child from school who ever came to our home. Kenny and Crystal did not invite friends over because of a combination of fear and embarrassment about what might happen. Justin, however, just wanted to be with Michael, whatever was going on. He accepted the fact that strange things were going on at our house. He had seen some of them and had no doubt they were real. The sweet thing about Justin was that even if he had not seen them, he still would have believed what Michael told him. That's just the kind of friend he was.

Up until this point, the incidents Justin had experienced in the house were minor ones compared to some of the violence our family had seen. I was afraid that something terrible might happen when he was there and Justin would be frightened away. This would mean that Michael would lose his only friend and I would lose a boy to whom I had grown really attached. We all had.

A short time before, Justin had been getting ready to go on vacation with his parents. His family planned to be gone for eight days and my birthday fell during the time he would be away. I teased him as he was leaving our house. "You'll be gone over my birthday. I expect at least a postcard from you." He laughed and promised to send one. The next morning, the phone rang quite early. It was Justin. "We're just about to walk out the door to go on vacation, but I wanted to wish you a happy birthday before we leave." He had called just in case the card wouldn't arrive in time. I explained, "I was only kidding about that." He laughed and told me to have a great day anyway!

It was an isolated incident, but it spoke volumes about Justin's true character. I knew that he would grow up to be a person that others would always be able to count on.

My reverie about Justin and Michael suddenly came to an end as a loud crash reverberated. It came from upstairs. I jumped in surprise. It sounded as though a huge piece of furniture had just fallen.

"Denice!" came a shout from upstairs. It was Justin's voice. He sounded frantic. I raced up the steps and into Michael's room. Michael lay on the floor and Justin was kneeling beside him. Michael's closet door was flung open and a trail of clothing poured out of it, leading straight to where my son was lying.

"What happened?" I questioned them, squatting down next to Michael. He seemed to be okay, but his breath had been knocked out of him. He strained to pull air back into his lungs, breathing hard.

"We heard something in the closet," Justin explained. "It sounded like a dog was howling in there or something. Michael went to look and the door just flew open!" He pointed to it, then went on. "The door swung open so fast that Michael didn't even see it coming! Luckily, it missed hitting him."

They said the bureau in the closet fell forward and the clothes rushed out of the closet so fast it was like someone had shot them out of cannon! The tangle of shirts and jackets had hit Michael in the chest and knocked him onto the floor. Justin helped Michael to his feet while I walked over to look in the closet.

I approached the door slowly, as I had learned to expect anything in this house. Sticking my head around the corner, I peered in. The bar hanging across the middle held empty hangers, which tinkled softly together. In front of the bureau, shoes, dirty socks and a few bits of clothing littered the floor. This wasn't the work of ghosts though. This was how Michael's closet always looked.

I started to leave and took in a breath. As I did so, the terrible odor that had come before accosted me.

Justin cried out, "It stinks in here like something died!"

I placed my hand on the closet door, sensing the smell grow stronger. What was it?

"Go away!" came a shout from beside me and I jumped. My head banged into the clothing bar and the hangers jingled wildly. Michael pushed past me and into the edge of the closet. He repeated his stern words. "Go away!" he said again.

I felt the bad air slither around me, permeating my hair and clothing. Then suddenly it was gone. Until I tried to speak, I didn't realize that it had taken my breath with me when it had gone. "What was that?" I managed to ask Michael. My hand had found its way to his shoulder and I pulled him with me as I exited the narrow closet.

"One of the bad people," he replied. "Didn't you see him?"

I shook my head.

He frowned at me. "Mom, you were touching him. I thought you must have seen him too," he said and I felt a shiver go down my spine. I had been touching one of those things? Was that the source of the odor I smelled?

"What did it want?" Justin asked him.

"I don't know, I never asked him." Michael gave his friend a cock-eyed grin. It was the kind of joke that only ten-year-olds can appreciate. But I knew having Justin around kept Michael from being too scared and for that I was grateful. It helped me as well, though in truth, I was still frightened, but I always tried to keep from showing too much fear in front of the kids.

I was trying to put on a brave face for both of them, but I could only be so heroic. "Let's go downstairs and watch television for awhile," I said, trying to smile. It came as no surprise when they readily agreed.

Luckily, as it so often is with children, they quickly moved to another subject as soon as we flipped on the television. Soon, the three of us were arguing over from where we wanted to order pizza for dinner when the front doorbell rang. Michael ran to answer it and I heard him greet Dr. Holt. Surprised, I walked out to see him standing in the foyer.

I could see he wanted to talk to me alone. "Michael, why don't you and Justin go tell Kenny it's time to come home," I

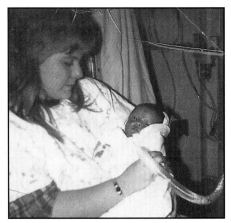

In the hospital fighting an infection, Denice holds her newborn son Michael who is critically ill.

Denice's grandfather, who Denice asked to watch over Michael, is the first ghost Michael sees.

Denice's parents hold the photo of her grandparents in which Michael recognized his great-grandfather as the first ghost who came to him.

Bruce and Denice's new home where Michael first begins seeing ghosts.

On Christmas day, Michael receives a new bike and excitedly anticipates riding around the neighborhood with his best friend Justin.

Katie, the Jones's pet, becom‹ so skittish and agitated becau‹ of the strange occurrences in the Jones's home that Denice has to give the family dog aw;

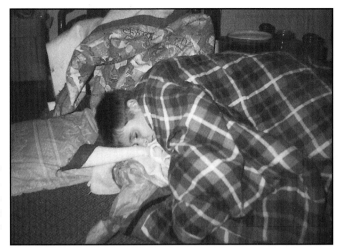

Plagued through the night by spirits and demons, Michael is too afraid to sleep in his bedroom, choosing the family room instead.

Fear of ghosts begins to bother both Michael and Kenny who, terrified of sleeping alone in their rooms, pass many nights together in the hallway.

Denice watches for several minutes as this picture sways back and forth on the family room wall.

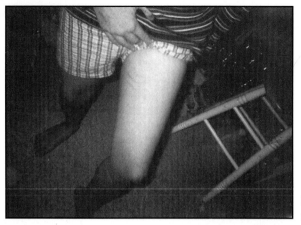

Michael bears scratch marks after an attack by a demon.

The entire Jones family, terrified of nighttime ghostly assaults, spends the night together sleeping in the living room.

Michael near the front door of the family home—one of many places where he saw th shadow man. Note the black cloud in the upper left-hand corner and the face in the small windows of the front door.

Michael visits the gravesite of his best friend Justin.

Devastated by Justin's tragic death, Michael wraps in plastic trucks, toys and other items his best friend had given him.

The cemetery where Justin is buried. Note the large spectral orb above the tombstones.

The Jones family comes to this church for Michael's exorcism.

After his exorcism, Michael spends much time praying and holding religious articles that have been blessed.

Several religious articles blessed by the bishop who performed Michael's exorcism are placed on this table.

Upon seeing a ghost in his bedroom one night, Michael grabs a camera and takes this photo.

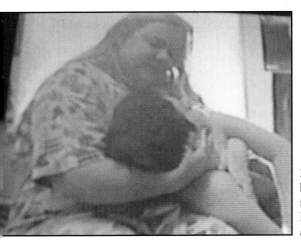

Denice spends almost two hours trying to rouse Michael from the semi-conscious sleep-like state in which the demons attack him.

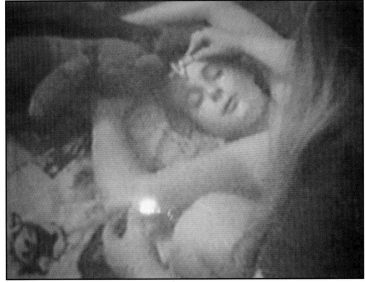

ce Michael tells Denice that the ons are keeping m from waking, e places crosses other religious ifacts on him to lp him fight the evil spirits.

The Jones family, brought together by this ordeal, remains a strong and supportive unit as Michael continues to see ghosts.

suggested. Kenny was over at his friend Jim's house. Jim lived a couple of blocks away and the time it would take for them to go there and get back would give me fifteen minutes or so to talk to Dr. Holt.

"I have some information that might help you," he said quietly. I was anxious to hear what he had to say.

The boys ran out the door and I led Dr. Holt into the family room. I offered him something to drink, but he declined, explaining that he had dinner plans. "I've been thinking of that scene with the church group," he said, shaking his head. We sat down and he withdrew a business card from his pocket, placing it on the coffee table.

"I decided to give you this," he told me. "I can't vouch for these people personally. My receptionist passed along their names to me. You remember Janice, don't you?"

I nodded and picked up the small, white card. On it was printed *Betterman Paranormal Investigations* and beneath that were two names, *Steve Betterman* and *Paul White*. In the corners were an address in Hartford and a telephone number. Across the bottom were the words *Confidential Investigations*.

"What are these guys, ghost busters?" I asked, not really sure what to think.

Dr. Holt chuckled. "That's exactly what I asked Janice, but she assures me they aren't. Actually, she has been dating Steve on and off for several months. I met him at the office Christmas party. He seemed like a nice guy," he said and then shrugged. "Although that's pretty much been the extent of my contact with him."

"So, what do you think?" I asked him and at the same time was asking myself how I felt about this. Paranormal Investigators? That was something out of the movies. Did people do this for real? "I mean, are they going to charge me to come and get rid of the ghosts or something? I've seen some pretty strange things, but I'm not sure what to make of paranormal detectives. I can tell you one thing for sure, Bruce is never going to buy it!"

"I asked Janice about that aspect, too," Dr. Holt assured me. "She said that they have a non-profit group. She said they don't rid of ghosts, but if they can determine a place is really haunted, they can help you find someone who will."

"But what do you think?" I asked again.

Dr. Holt took the card from me and looked at it. He shrugged again. "Honestly, Denice," he said, "I just don't know. If you had asked me three months ago if I believed in ghosts, I would have said absolutely not and that you all needed professional therapy. If you had asked me a month ago, I still would have said that I wasn't sure. But after what happened at your house during the blessing by that Pentecostal group, well, I don't know anymore. I have no reasonable explanation for what I saw." He looked away from me and then back again.

I nodded. "It's okay. Say what you're thinking. I've heard a lot of crazy ideas lately."

Dr. Holt looked at me, his eyes serious, and gestured toward the white card. "My psychology can't seem to solve your problem," he said frowning. "I don't know if these people can help you or not, but I figured you might want to try them," he added.

"Well, we certainly haven't found relief anywhere else," I conceded, nodding slowly. "I don't imagine that it can hurt, but I would appreciate it if I could call you. You said that your psychology can't solve our problem and that may be the case, but we do need a friend."

"Please call if you need me." He smiled warmly. "I care what happens to Michael and to all of you. Besides that, I'm looking for some answers here myself.

He inclined his head toward the card. "So, do you want me to get in touch with them for you?" he asked. "I thought since Steve and I had met before, he might be more inclined to follow up on the case than he would be if all this came from someone he didn't know."

"Yeah, I can imagine what kinds of calls he must get," I replied. "Thanks, that would be great."

Dr. Holt stood up and I started walking with him towards the front door. "I'll give them a call from the car," he said, "and if possible, have Steve Betterman get in touch with you this evening. There's no sense in wasting any time on this."

"I'm not sure yet how I'm going to convince Bruce to allow these investigators into the house," I told him. "I'll worry about that after I talk to them."

"Well, if there is anything I can do, let me know."

"Thanks so much for trying to help us," I answered. "It really means a lot to me."

"That's why I got into the psychology business, to try and help people. So many of the children I work with seem to come from impossible environments. So often I feel like I'm not really curing the problem, but just putting a band-aid on it."

He took my hand and held onto it for a moment. "But yours seems like a fine family and Michael's a great kid. I admit that I have felt pretty helpless when it comes to him. If I can even do a little bit to bring this thing to an end," he went on, "I will feel as though I have served a purpose."

Dr. Holt squeezed my hand and smiled at me. He let go and placed his hand on the doorknob. "It'll be okay, Denice. All isn't lost." He waved and stepped outside.

I watched him as he walked to his car. "No, it's not lost...not yet anyway," I said quietly to myself. Suddenly, I saw Michael, Kenny and Justin running down the block toward our house. I looked down at the white business card, slightly rumpled in my hand. I couldn't afford for all to be lost...nor did I dare give up either.

Steve Betterman called later that evening. He sounded like a serious person, though I still wasn't sure whether to trust him or not. He asked me to explain to him what was going on in our home. He had spoken with Dr. Holt, but wanted to hear it all first-hand from me. Our first conversation lasted about an hour and when I was finished, Steve asked if it would be possible for him and his colleague, Paul, to come over to the house for a preliminary interview which they would record. We set up a time for the following evening and said goodbye.

As I hung up the receiver, I felt a tightness uncoil in my stomach. I had not realized how tense I was, nor how nervous, until the conversation had ended. Though I wasn't sure I could believe in Steve, I wanted desperately for him to believe me and not think we were crazy. I had spent the entire hour on the phone trying so hard to sound sane. How could the incredible events that had been taking place in our home not appear to be lunacy to someone hearing it for the first time? I prayed that Steve Betterman would believe me and that he would be able to help.

I felt anxious about how to tell the family, but decided to do it right away. The kids were in the family room watching television. They seemed delighted when I told them Steve and his colleague would be coming here. "Spook Detectives" was what the kids labeled them. Bruce was less enthusiastic, as I thought he might be.

"They do what?" he asked me, frowning. I explained what Dr. Holt had told me.

"I don't see how it could hurt, Bruce," I told him. "Someone has to help us. I know it sounds crazy, but maybe they can."

Bruce sighed. "Okay, do what you want," he said. "What can it hurt? I don't like the idea of a couple of kooks wandering around the house though, so keep an eye on them while they're here."

"You won't be here?" I asked him, surprised.

"I'll be home as soon as I can. I have an afternoon meeting, but I'll try to get back before dinner," he replied. He paused for a moment and took my chin in his hand. His eyes looked into mine. "Sorry, Denice," he said. "I don't mean to sound like I don't care. I do. I just don't want to get my hopes up over something even weirder than what's already happening in this house—two possible flakes."

"I know," I told him, "I don't either."

His hand left my face and began running through my hair. "You say that, but we both know you're already counting on this to work...to get rid of these...these things, right?"

I didn't answer, but I could feel my face get hot. A tear squeezed out of the corner of my eye and ran down my cheek. Bruce wiped it away.

"Believe me, I understand," he went on. "I just don't want you to get hurt by this. You put all of your hopes into every possible solution that comes along and you keep getting disappointed. Look what happened with the people from the church that your mom brought here."

"I know, but I have to have faith that something will work," I told him. "I can't just go along thinking that everything we try is going to fail. If I give up, what will become of us?"

"I'm not saying there's anything wrong with a little faith. I just don't want you to get crushed by these people."

"Don't you want this to end, Bruce?"

"More than you know," he answered solemnly. "It is tearing us all apart, but don't get your hopes up too high about these two so-called detectives, Denice, that's all I'm saying."

"I'll try not to, okay?" I told him, "but that's all I can promise. I want so badly for all of this to be over that I will do just about anything at this point."

Late the next afternoon, my mother came to stay overnight with the children and hopefully provide a little of her usual TLC for me. "I am concerned about these investigators," I told her. "While Steve seemed quite credible on the phone, I'm still not sure what to think of someone who goes looking for the sort of things that are going on in our home. Whatever it is has targeted our family, but these two detectives are seeking it out on purpose. Who in their right mind would do something like that?"

My mother nodded and patted my arm. "But you have to try to stop what's happening here, Denice, so I think you've done the right thing. Let's be optimistic." Hoping to alleviate my worry, I decided to call Janice, Dr. Holt's receptionist, who had recommended Steve and his friend in the first place. After I explained my concerns, Janice assured me that her boyfriend was not crazy. "He has been interested in paranormal phenomena for many years, starting with a strange experience he had when he was a boy."

Apparently, he had been staying at his grandparent's house in the Midwest and had seen a ghost, or what he believed to be a ghost. It had appeared at the end of his bed one night and had spoken to him. When he described the figure to his grandmother, she informed him that his description matched that of an aunt who had passed away many years ago. The bedroom Steve had been staying in had once been hers.

After that, Steve had collected all of the books and data that he could find on ghosts and hauntings. After college he decided to get into investigations. Paul was a high school friend who also shared the same interests. Together, they and several other members of their team had investigated alleged haunted houses. They were not "ghost busters," Janice told me again, "They collect evidence about ghosts to ascertain if they are real. If they can determine that a house is haunted, they can recommend someone who might be able to assist the owners."

"How will they be able to decide if our place is haunted or not?" I asked.

Janice explained that they use a variety of equipment to do so. "In addition to cameras and recording devices," she said, "they also have an array of high-tech pieces of electrical equipment that can sort out phenomena." Janice said that she really wasn't sure how it all worked, but she had seen them in action before and it was impressive. She also said that Steve was very careful about taking on new cases. Many of the cases he had dealt with in the past had been ruled out as nothing more than old houses settling and overactive imaginations.

"Not that I'm saying this is the case with your house," Janice added quickly. "I just wanted you to know they are pretty careful."

I thanked her, hung up and conveyed to my mom what Janice had said. "I feel better after talking to Janice, but I'll wait and see what I think of Steve and Paul after meeting them. Bruce thought they sounded like flakes and although I won't go that far, I still think it best to remain cautious."

The two men arrived just before 5:00 in the evening. They were both young, very polite and very serious about what they were doing. We had agreed that this would be a preliminary interview, so they hadn't brought any of the equipment that Janice had told me about. Paul carried with him a small, black case that I soon learned contained two video cameras, a laptop computer and a 35mm camera. Steve carried a thick notebook and a folder under his arm. The tab on the folder was printed with our name.

Neither of them looked like what you might expect. I'm not sure what image I had in my head, although perhaps it was of elderly English men with tweed jackets and pipes. In fact, they looked more like athletes than scientists.

Steve was the larger of the two men. He was heavy, but not overweight, and he wore a navy blue blazer over a white shirt and striped tie. The collar looked very tight around his thick neck and I felt a twinge of sympathy for him. He had blond hair, clipped very short, and a deep voice that was strangely comforting when he spoke. He was one of those people who made you feel at ease and, as I soon discovered, was easy to talk to.

Paul was the polar opposite of his friend. Thin and wiry like a runner, he was very quiet and introverted. Although he smiled a lot, he said little. He had thick black hair and his dark eyes were framed by wire-rimmed glasses. "I handle the technical aspects of our investigations," he explained, "while Steve deals primarily with the witnesses and homeowners."

I introduced them to my mother and to each of the kids. Steve made it a point to talk to each one of the children individually. He seemed to know that to learn what was going on at our house, he would need to gain the confidence of everyone who lived there. He asked each of the kids about school and even engaged Kenny in a discussion about his favorite sports team.

After a while, he turned back to me. "Well, let's get started, if that's okay with you, Denice," he said. "Everyone take a seat," he added and placed himself in a chair directly across from me. "As I explained on the phone, we would like to record this interview if we can. That will give us a record of the events that have taken place. I would like to have you do most of the talking, Denice, but please, if anyone has anything they would like to add, feel free to speak up."

I took a deep breath. "It's okay with me to record it," I told him, settling into my seat and looking around nervously. I didn't really like being on camera, although the kids didn't seem to mind. They smiled, enjoying the novelty of the situation.

"Also, while we are doing this," Steve said, "I was hoping to get your permission to have Paul take a look around the house. He won't bother anything. He just needs to take some photographs and run a little video. This will give us a better idea of the layout of the place when we put together a report."

I told him this was fine as well and Paul unloaded the black case he had brought with him. He handed one of the video cameras to Steve and draped the 35mm camera around his neck. He also placed the tape recorder on a nearby table. It had an external microphone leading away from it and he placed that on a small stand. He pushed the "record" button, then left the room to look around the house.

Steve placed the other video camera on a tripod and pointed it in my direction. He turned it on and spoke aloud, stating the date, time and our home address. "This is Steve Betterman," he added, "conducting an interview with Denice Jones about the events reported at her home. Also present are her children, Michael, Kenny and Crystal." Steve also mentioned my mother was there and then he asked me to begin.

I spoke for the next hour, trying to recall everything that had happened in the house. The kids chimed in often, adding memories and incidents that had slipped my mind and details about Mary's 'accident.' Steve asked a number of questions, too, and we answered them as best we could.

At one point, while Michael was talking to him, I looked at Steve closely. I was trying to read his expression, to get an idea of whether this man believed us or not. He smiled often, but his face remained inscrutable. His remarks were never harsh, but were always questioning. I didn't know what to make of him. Were we guilty until proven innocent? Did Steve automatically disbelieve us until he saw something that would convince him otherwise? I remembered Janice's warning that Steve was always "careful" about taking on new cases and that many of his old cases had turned out to be the result of "overactive imaginations." I wondered what he was thinking while he was conducting the interview with us? Did he think we all were simply confused, crazy or even outright liars?

As we sat there all was placid. For the first time, I really wanted something terrible to happen in the house. I wanted one of Michael's "bad people" to appear...for something to go flying across the room, as things had so many times before. Where were the strange thumpings and the unexplained noises that had awakened us all on so many nights? I wanted these things to occur during the interview. I wanted Steve and Paul to be as scared as we had been, as we always were!

Yet nothing like that occurred. The house remained quiet, so quiet that it was almost frightening in itself.

Paul returned to the family room about the time Steve was concluding our interview. He had videotaped the entire house. "I used two rolls of film documenting each room." He turned to us. "Would you mind giving me a tour of the place so that I know which rooms belong to which family member?"

We gladly agreed and I let the kids lead him around. I wanted to have a word with Steve.

"Well, what do you think?" I asked him.

He smiled and began wrapping up the cord to the video camera. Paul had left the case open and when Steve was finished he carefully placed it inside. "There's really no way for me to say just yet," he answered. "I am going to need to review the tapes and take a look at what Paul has recorded."

He stood up. "I can say that I certainly found your story convincing," he said. "You stated that you had no knowledge of unexplained phenomena; yet your encounters seem to be pretty consistent with cases in my files."

"Cases that you've investigated before?" I asked him.

He shook his head. "No, not that we have done, but in my records."

Steve unhooked the cord and microphone of the tape recorder and began packing it away. I felt he had avoided really giving me an opinion about our house and about the story I had just finished telling him. He didn't seem very talkative now and I wondered again if he believed any of the events we had related to him.

"Steve, can you stop for a second?" I placed a hand on his elbow.

"Sure, I can," he replied. "I'm sorry about that. When I get working on something, my mind goes somewhere else." Steve grinned and shot his hand out like an airplane.

"I want an honest opinion from you. Are you going to be able to help...?"

Steve started shaking his head before I could even finish what I was saying. "Denice, there's no way for me to answer that right now," he stopped me. "I have to look over the material we've collected. It would be really irresponsible of me to try and even give you a guess at this point. I wish that I could, but I'm not a psychic or anything. I don't claim to be able to come in here and magically say that you've got ghosts. Do you under-stand what I mean?"

"Yeah, I do understand," I said. I realized what I had been doing to him and immediately felt guilty. "Sorry about that. It's just that this has been going on for so long..."

"It's been going on so long that you really need an answer, right?" Steve asked me.

"Right," came a voice from behind us. Bruce was stand-ing in the doorway from the kitchen. He had his briefcase in his hand and his coat draped over his arm. I didn't know how long he had been standing there, but he looked pleased with what he had heard. He stepped forward and held out his hand. "Bruce Jones," he introduced himself.

Steve placed the recording microphone on the table and shook his hand. "Steve Betterman," he replied. "I was just telling Denice that..."

Bruce waved him away. "No, that's okay, I heard you. I respect the fact that you aren't claiming to wave a magic wand and make it all better. We have just been living with this stuff for a long time and obviously would like to know that an end is in sight."

"I understand that completely and I'd love to tell you that. It's just that...," Steve shrugged and left the sentence hanging.

"We know, you have to do your job," Bruce finished for him.

"Exactly. We're going to need a few days on this and I promise to get back to you as soon as I can. We'll let you know what we find out, then we'll go from there."

"Thanks," I told him. Bruce put his coat and briefcase on the couch and came over to stand next to me. His arm went across my shoulders. "I apologize again if I seemed too pushy with you," I told Steve.

"No need," he replied. Steve looked up as Paul and the kids, with my mother trailing behind, came back into the room. They both finished packing up their things and got ready to leave.

"Thanks again for allowing us in," Steve said. "I'll call you as soon as I can. In the meantime, just try to sit tight and don't worry too much."

"That's easier said than done," I replied.

"I know it is," he said and smiled at me again. He helped Paul pack up the rest of the equipment and they both shook our hands and left the house.

"I promise to get in touch with you as soon as I can," Steve repeated, calling back over his shoulder. All of us watched as they climbed in their car and drove away. As the car vanished out of sight, I had a sinking feeling in the pit of my stomach. It was as if our last, best hope had just disappeared.

"I hope they come back," I said and followed my family inside.

The next morning, after Mom left, Paul telephoned. "Would it be okay if I come by the house and do some recording in Michael's room?" I told him that it would be all right and he offered to explain further when he got to our place.

Paul arrived around 2:00 P.M. and brought with him another black case. This one contained a very large tape recorder and a microphone like the one he had used the evening before.

"I want to record for a little while in Michael's room," he told me. "I was getting some distortions in the tapes in there last night and wanted to see if there may have been something wrong with my equipment."

"What kind of distortions?" I asked him.

"Really kind of hard to explain," Paul replied quickly. "I just wanted to check on the equipment so that we can evaluate the material that we got last night."

Trying to get straight answers from these guys is like pulling teeth, I thought, but I told him that it was fine. "You know where it is, right?" I asked.

"Yes, thanks."

Gathering up his recording device and cords, he started for the staircase to the second floor. "Oh, and one other thing," he said, turning back around. "I will be here for a little while, but I was wondering if you could make sure that no one comes upstairs while I'm recording? And also, that no one turns on a television or any music in the house either? Is that okay?"

"Sure, I guess," I shrugged. I wanted to catch up on a book that I had been reading anyway.

"Sorry about that. I just need a very controlled environment," he explained. Paul seemed very shy and hesitant about asking, but I assured him once again that it was fine. Then he disappeared upstairs.

Sitting down on the couch in the family room, I opened my book. I could hear Paul moving around upstairs. His footfalls crossed and recrossed the floor in Michael's room and I heard several small thumps, which I guessed were the sounds of him setting up the recording equipment. After a few more scrapes and screeches, things grew very quiet for the next hour or so. What were once unnoticeable noises, like the hum of the refrigerator, suddenly seemed very loud. In fact, the ticking of a clock on the other side of the room became so distracting that I almost couldn't concentrate on my book.

Suddenly, a loud, sliding noise, like something moving across the floor of Michael's room, came from upstairs. *What is Paul doing up there?* I heard the tap of Paul's feet cross the floor in the direction of the noise, cross back and then more silence. A few minutes later, I heard the sliding sound again, although it was much longer this time. Once more, I heard Paul walking, then more silence. I confess that I was becoming a little irritated. We had very nice hardwood floors in Michael's room, and whatever Paul was doing sounded like it could cause some damage. I listened for a repeat of the sound, but heard nothing. I went back to my book.

Twenty minutes or so passed in silence. Then I heard the sound again. This time, it began as a low scraping noise that grew louder as it swiftly went along the ceiling above me. *That is it!* I knew that Paul had asked me to stay downstairs and stay as quiet as possible, but this was ridiculous! *What in the world is he doing up there to make this kind of noise?*

I jumped up off the couch and started for the staircase. Just as I reached it though, I heard someone racing down the top steps. It was Paul with his tape recorder jammed up under his arm. A confusion of cords dangled down from the device. They twitched back and forth as he hurriedly descended the stairs and we almost collided. Paul's face was flushed and his eyes looked anxious.

"Paul? Is everything okay?" I asked. "I heard a strange noise up there and... What's the matter?"

He pushed past me into the family room. "Yeah, uh, I was trying to set up some more microphones," he answered nervously.

What had happened to him up there to make him so skittish, I wondered.

"S...s...sorry about the noise," he stuttered.

"That's okay," I replied, watching him. He had gone over to the table where he left his case and started packing up the recorder. I followed him and stood by his side. "Are you all done up there?"

He nodded. "Yeah, I'm all set for today." He smiled weakly at me, but clutched his stomach, looking as if he was going to throw up.

"Are you okay? You look like you're not feeling well."

"I'm fine," Paul answered and snapped shut the latches on his equipment case. "I'm just feeling a little under the weather. Ate something that didn't agree with me last night, that's all."

I shrugged. *This guy is a little strange,* I thought. "So, when can we expect to hear something from you and Steve?" I asked him.

Paul was now marching toward the front door and I had to stride quickly along with him to keep up the conversation. He seemed to be in a big hurry to get somewhere. I wondered if he was late for a meeting or something. At least that was how he was acting.

"Uh, I'll have Steve give you a call as soon as we finish things up," Paul promised. He opened the door and I followed him out onto the porch. He looked down at his watch for several moments and shook his head as if he was late for an important appointment. "Sorry," he said distractedly, " I just have to get back to work. I didn't realize it was after five."

"No problem. I have to start dinner soon anyway."

He waved and walked quickly toward his car.

I called after him. "I hope you got what you needed," I said.

Paul stopped in his tracks. His back was toward me, so I have no idea what he looked like at that moment, but I saw his shoulders hunch up. He turned back around. That same nauseous expression was on his face again, and once more I thought he might vomit. "Thanks," he called, so quietly that I could barely hear him. "I got a lot more than I planned on."

With that, he waved weakly and climbed into his car. A few moments later, he drove away.

That night was one of the worst yet.

Around 11:00 P.M., after the kids had gone to bed, Bruce, who had come home from work late, was eating a warmed-up dinner in front of the television in the family room. The lights were turned down and I was having a glass of wine while we tried to unwind from our day. Suddenly, Michael's screams shattered the calm of the house!

They were blood curdling, frightening me so badly I spilled the drink I had been holding. A single thought flashed through my mind. Whatever was happening must be really bad as I had not heard Michael scream like that for some time. He had seemed to me to be coping with things so much better lately. Whatever had frightened him now, I thought, must be truly terrifying!

I jumped up out of my chair. Bruce was right behind me

and we pounded up the stairs together. Michael was still screaming and, if anything, his cries had gotten louder. We ran into
Crystal as we reached the top of the steps. She was knocking on
Michael's door. Kenny peered out his own door, afraid to come
into the hallway.

"Something is really wrong!" Crystal shouted, "I can't
get the door open!"

We've been through this before, I thought, watching her twist-
ing the knob back and forth. Her small fists beat on the door.
"Michael! Michael!" We could still hear Michael crying inside the
room.

"Step back out of the way!" Bruce ordered as he grabbed
hold of the doorknob himself. Crystal and I pressed against the
wall on the opposite side of the corridor, while Bruce tried in
vain to get the door to open. He banged against it with his shoulder, but it still refused to budge.

"There has to be a way in there," he muttered and
slammed against the door again. The door shuddered, but would
not open.

At that same moment, a knocking sound began. It
mounted, doubling and tripling as though a hundred tiny hammers had become trapped inside of our walls. They all began
tapping at once. Knocking and rapping sounds came from both
sides of the hallway, climbing up and down and back and forth.

"Stop it," Crystal yelled, and the sounds immediately
ceased. The moment of silence was followed by two thundering
raps, like a sledgehammer pounding against the outside wall of
the house.

"Leave my family alone!" Bruce shouted. His words were
followed by two more knocks. He threw his body against the
door again and this time it swung open. I pushed up behind him
and we smelled that horrible odor. It was there for only a few
moments and then it was gone.

Entering the room, we saw Michael standing on top of

his bed, moaning and weeping with fear. As we came closer, he looked up and saw us. His hand shot out and he screamed at us. "No!" he cried, "stay back! He's under the bed!"

Involuntarily, we all froze. Bruce was the only one brave enough to step forward. "Who's under the bed, Michael? Who's under the bed?" he demanded of the boy.

"The shadow man."

As these words left Michael's lips, the bed suddenly began to violently shake! It vibrated up and down, only an inch or so, but so fast and so hard that it began to move out away from the wall. Michael slipped from where he was standing and fell down. His head cracked against the wall and he was flung onto the mattress.

Bruce jumped back, colliding with Crystal and me. We all huddled together for a few seconds, then Bruce ran toward the bed and jumped on it. He scooped up Michael, leaped from the bed and brought Michael over to me. Then he warily approached the bed again, trying not to get too close to it. The frame continued to shake and jump.

"Be careful!" Michael warned through his tears. "He grabbed my leg while I was sleeping and wouldn't let me go!"

Bruce reflexively stepped back, not relishing the idea of being grabbed by anyone, but then, as if his decision was made, he rushed forward to the bed and grasped the mattress and box springs. He grunted and flipped them both upward into the air. All of a sudden, they were standing on end against the wall. The bed stopped shaking.

My heart pounding, I knelt down to see what was under it. There was nothing beneath the bed but two toy cars and a sock. Silently, I shook my head at Bruce.

He swore under his breath and sat down heavily on the bed frame. "Why won't they leave us alone?" he asked and while his question was asked out loud, he was muttering to himself.

Then Bruce spoke much louder. "Leave us alone, damn you!" he shouted.

From the hallway came two hard thumps. The vibration they caused made some of the toys on the shelves rattle together.

Bruce looked slowly upward. "Will you leave us alone?" he spoke loudly.

The two knocks sounded once more.

"Do you want something from us?" he asked now.

I was growing more frightened by the minute. I didn't doubt the fact that our house was haunted by ghosts or some sort of spirits. The idea that they could somehow communicate with us was frightening me. Michael already had a connection to them that I would never understand, but I wasn't sure that I wanted the rest of us to share it.

"Bruce, please stop," I urged him.

The foul odor was returning to the room. I had experienced this too many times already. I knew what it meant. Something was close to us...very close.

The knocking sound came again, but this time only once.

"Is there something we can do to make you leave?" Bruce asked.

"Bruce, stop," I whispered to him. Crystal and Michael were clinging to me now. As much from fear as from the odor, which now pervaded the room.

One knock sounded in the wall.

"Are you here because of the house?"

Two knocks.

"Is it because of one of us?"

One knock.

"It's because of me," Michael whispered.

One knock sounded on the wall, this time very loud.

Bruce looked over at Michael. "Why do they want you?" he asked him.

"They want me to do things, I told you."

The single knock sounded once more.

"What do you want from him?" asked Bruce.

Only silence greeted his question. Then, a few minutes later the rapid knocking began again. The hundred hammers were back, beating from inside our walls. The sound grew louder and louder until it was almost deafening.

Bruce cursed them and got up from the bed, herding us toward the door. We found Kenny standing in the hallway. He had been too scared to come in and yet too scared to want to be there by himself with chaos in the house all around him.

A clamorous noise made us all jump! The door to Crystal's room had slammed closed. Now a heavy, shifting noise, followed by a series of solid thumps and then breaking glass sounded.

"My room!" Crystal groaned in dismay. She pulled away from me and started down the hall. The rapping sounds finally began to dwindle and then faded away.

"Wait a minute!" Bruce called after her. He brushed past me and hurried to catch up with Crystal. "I don't want anyone going into a room by themselves, especially after the sounds we just heard coming from inside."

Crystal turned and waited for Bruce to reach her. He grabbed the doorknob and turned it. The door started to open, but collided with something on the other side. It stopped moving. Bruce pushed against it and the door slowly opened. As it did, the sound of something dragging across the floor came from inside the room. Bruce eased the door open about a foot and a half and squeezed through. Crystal followed him in and flipped on the overhead light. I heard him yell, "Don't come any further!" and then Crystal groaned loudly.

"Denice?" I heard Bruce call to me. "Come take a look at this and watch where you walk."

Taking Michael and Kenny with me, we eased through the opening to Crystal's room. I looked around. The room was a disaster. The bed was the only thing in the room that did not appear to have been moved, although all of the sheets and blankets had been pulled off it. The door had been blocked by a chair and by Crystal's dresser, both of which had somehow been moved from the far side of the bedroom. Clothing had been pulled from the dresser and scattered all over the place, and books were tossed about, but the most ominous thing was the broken glass from Crystal's treasured perfume bottles. They had been smashed and littered the floor. Had anyone rushed in here barefoot, they would have been badly cut.

Bruce had cleared a space to walk and Crystal was sitting on the end of the bed crying, when we came in following the path. Michael walked over to her. "Crystal, I'm sorry," he said to her. "This is all my fault."

She shook her head. "No, it's not...it's nobody's fault," she answered. Her eyes were blurry with tears and her face was red and blotchy. Somehow she managed to smile at him anyway. "You have to help me clean up this mess though," she said.

Michael grinned a little. "Okay," he replied.

"First let Bruce and me clean up the glass," I said quietly.

Kenny was still standing at the door by himself. He was crying. "I'm afraid to go back to my room," he said.

Easing his way over to him, Bruce wrapped one arm around Kenny and hugged him tight. "Nobody's going back to their room," he stated. "Let's worry about this stuff tomorrow. Let's everybody go downstairs. We'll all sleep together in the living room."

We edged out of the bedroom and into the hallway. My

family continually amazed me. I didn't know how they managed to make it through all of this without cracking up. I looked at each of the children. Their faces were masks of weariness and fear. Yet there was also love and a bonding between them generated, perhaps, by uniting against the things which were attacking us.

Was it that we were so used to the strange things going on in our home that they didn't bother us quite as much as they used to? I'm sure that was part of it, but I also saw there was an inner strength in our family. We were now determined to stick together and to outlast this nightmare. Our growing love for each other was the only thing that gave me hope each day. Yes, I admit that I was often too afraid to stay in the house by myself, but on the other hand, no matter how scared I got, I knew that if we met this threat together, I could keep my grip on sanity.

I can keep my grip as long as we don't have too many nights like this one, I corrected myself. *What had caused the destruction to escalate as it did?* Could it have been the visits by Paul and Steve? Was there a reason the spirits didn't want them to come here? *Perhaps my imagination is getting the better of me,* I thought, *but that's how it seems to me.*

Could the night's horrible events been meant as a warning from the spirits to keep Paul and Steve out of the house? Did they sense some sort of danger from them or perhaps from where their investigations might lead? I prayed that was the case. There was no doubt that we needed a weapon with which to fight back. Maybe these ghost hunters would turn out to be what we had been looking for!

The ghost hunters called us the following day, or rather Steve did. "Would it be possible to meet with you this evening after work?" he asked. I told him that it would and prodded him for some hints as to what their initial findings had told them about our problem. He dodged the question until I told him about the things that had occurred after they had left the night before. There was silence on the line.

"Let's just say that I'm not surprised by what you're telling me," he finally said.

That was all I could get out of him, but he promised to explain that night.

The doorbell rang that evening at the agreed upon time of 7:00 P.M. I opened the door to find Steve, Paul and a young, dark-haired woman. They introduced her to me as Kirsten. She was Paul's girlfriend and worked at the computer business with him. She was also a frequent assistant on their paranormal cases. Steve further explained, "Kirsten is skilled in photography and develops all of our photographs in a darkroom in her basement."

Kirsten seemed very nice and outgoing, like Steve was. She doted on Paul though, and they appeared to be very close. She took one of the cases he carried and placed it on the dining room table.

"Denice? Would it be okay to hook this camera up to your television? That way we can play back the tapes that we want to show you," Kirsten explained. I told her it was fine and she went to work in the far corner of the room attaching the camera to the set.

"I'm assuming you got something on your tapes?" I questioned Steve.

He nodded. "Yes, we did," he told me, "and we wanted to show what we think is important to you this evening." He nodded at Paul. "We first thought that we would just talk to you and Bruce alone, but Paul felt the kids should hear what we have to say, too. This definitely involves everyone."

"I became convinced of that," Paul cut in, "after what happened in Michael's room."

"Exactly what did happen?" I asked him. I knew that something was wrong with him when he left and I suspected it had to do with the weird phenomena in the house. Apparently, I was right.

"We'll explain in a minute," said Steve. He was handing tapes to Kirsten and setting up a cassette player as well.

"I'm sorry about rushing out of here like that yesterday," Paul added. "I had just never seen anything like that before."

As soon as he said this, he walked away from me. I wanted so badly to ask him what he was talking about, but obviously I would have to wait. Steve and Kirsten finished getting everything set up, then we sat down to hear what they had to tell us.

"With only our preliminary investigation to work with," Steve began. "We have come to the possible conclusion that your house may be haunted by ghosts. I am hesitant to say this, only because we have a limited amount of data to work with."

"To say what?" I asked. "It doesn't sound like you're saying anything at all. We can tell you that this house is haunted. What we need to know is what can you do to help us."

"I understand what you want," Steve answered. "It's just that we don't work that way. You have to understand that we have not experienced the things that you have in the house. As I told you on our first visit, it would be irresponsible of me to say automatically that a haunting is occurring here. There are a number of further steps that we have to take to confirm our initial findings. At that point, if we can rule out all other explanations for the reported activity, then we can conclude it's paranormal."

"What sort of steps?" Bruce asked.

"We will need to do a full-scale investigation of the house," Kirsten spoke up. She was sitting on the end of the couch next to Crystal. She turned to face Bruce and me. "This may take more than one visit."

"Unfortunately, a thorough investigation can be pretty

invasive," Steve added. "So we have to make sure that you will agree to the whole process."

"We agree!" I blurted out, but Bruce frowned a little.

"How invasive are we talking about?" he asked Steve. "I mean, I want to get to the bottom of this, but we don't really know you very well to let you have complete access to our home."

I elbowed Bruce in the ribs. Sometimes he was about as subtle with his comments as a baseball bat upside the head. He had basically insinuated that Steve and his group might be "casing" our house in order to burglarize it. I knew what was running through his mind and I think Kirsten did, too.

Kirsten answered, "We have no problem with all of you being here while we work," she said. "I know that would make you feel better about the situation."

"Basically," said Steve, "an investigative team would consist of the three of us, plus a few other members of our group, coming in and setting up a variety of recording and monitoring equipment. We would remain behind to observe anything that might occur."

"Which means what?" asked Bruce.

"Well, if we can determine through our investigations that the house is haunted, then we can present the evidence to someone who specializes in 'cleansing' residences," Steve answered. "There are people who deal in just that end of the paranormal. We have worked with some very good people in the past and we would approach them about your situation."

"What are the possibilities that you're going to find something?" I asked them.

Steve, Paul and Kirsten all exchanged looks.

"I'd say pretty good," Paul finally spoke up.

"But, we have to keep that off the record for now," Steve

smiled. "I don't want to jump the gun on this, but we do have some rather interesting things to show you from the other night when we were here."

"I'd also love to hear what happened when Paul came over yesterday afternoon," I said. I was as curious about Paul's activities as anything else.

"We'll get to that," Paul smiled uneasily.

"First, let me show you some of the photographs that Paul took while he was looking around the house during our interview," Steve said. He opened an envelope and took out some photographs. He carefully laid five of them out on the coffee table in front of us.

"Were these taken the other night?" Bruce asked him.

"Yes," Steve answered. "The film was all developed by Kirsten and each of the anomalies you see here also appeared on the negatives. We tested and enlarged the negatives, but weren't able to find any natural explanations for what you're seeing here."

"Notice the odd images in each one of the photographs," Steve said, pointing to each one. In four of them, strange streaks of light appeared in various rooms of the house. Each of the streaks began with what appeared to be a ball of white light, just like those Michael had described. A smoky-looking tail protruded behind each of them, as if the lights had been in motion while the shutter of the camera was open. I asked about that and Steve agreed that this was exactly what he believed to have occurred.

"This photo is probably the strangest though," he said and pointed to the final one.

The last photograph showed my mother, the kids and I talking to Steve at the end of the interview. Michael stood a few feet off by himself in the frame. All around him was a white and gun metal gray smoke-like substance. It appeared just over his left shoulder and wrapped behind his head, then emerged again on his right side.

"What is this?" I questioned Steve.

"It appears to be some sort of ectoplasm-like material…a spirit energy," he replied. "We looked at the negatives many times and enlarged the prints and have ruled out any natural explanations, like reflections or lens flare, for the phenomena." He pulled out a larger version of the photograph and then another one, which had been enlarged to show a close-up of Michael's right arm.

He pointed at this shot. "You can see here how the energy wraps around Michael's arm," he said to us. "This tells me that we aren't talking about some effect caused by the camera flash."

"Well, what are we talking about?" Bruce asked. He had passed the photos over to the kids to look at and had turned back to Steve. I noticed that Michael looked particularly disconcerted by what he saw in the photographs.

"It could be earthbound ghosts," Steve shrugged. "Again, that's off the record, but that's what it appears to be to me."

"What in the world are earthbound ghosts?"

"Earthbound ghosts are those that have lived and not passed over. They are trapped between worlds."

"That sounds awful," I said slowly, not knowing for sure if I believed him or not, but feeling that what he said might explain the horrible things we were going through. "How can you take pictures of them?" I asked.

Kirsten shook her head. "I have no real explanation for how it works. The best that I can figure is that spirit energy occurs at a different light spectrum than what we can normally see. This may explain why the camera can pick up the energy…plus, it may also explain why Michael sees things the rest of us don't."

"What do you mean?" I interrupted.

Steve continued. "Some people seem to be able to see things that others can't, that's the best that I can explain it."

"But we had Michael's eyes tested," I protested. "The doctors said they were perfectly normal."

"I wouldn't say that it's a physical condition," said Kirsten. "It may have more to do with a part of the brain that few can use. Science tells us that we use very little of our actual brain capacity. I believe that some people may use more of it than others. In Michael's case, this may mean that he is capable of tapping into that portion."

"Does that mean I'm smarter than everyone else?" Michael asked.

"No!" Kenny and Crystal both answered at once, then laughed.

Kirsten laughed along with them. "It just means that you see in a different way," she assured him with a smile but her eyes catching mine were more serious as if she wanted to say more but not then.

Bruce spoke up. "Let's get back to these investigations," he said. "Would this be the kind of stuff you would be doing?" He gestured to the photographs.

Steve nodded. "Along with other things," he replied. "We would also want to measure any electrical or magnetic disturbances in the house, seismic activity and other things like that. We would also have cameras and video going most of the time. Additionally, I would like to test Michael for psychic abilities. Dr. Holt explained to me that he first believed that Michael might be manifesting some of the activity through PK abilities."

"I don't think that Dr. Holt feels that way now," I said.

"Yes, and most likely this is not the case," Steve said. "However, I want to completely rule it out so that we can proceed."

Bruce nodded and gestured to the photos on the table. "So are these what convinced you to go ahead and do the investigations?" he asked.

"They are part of the reason," Steve told him. "We also want to show you some of the video that Paul recorded..."

"Or have you at least listen to it," Paul cut in. He went over to the camera they had set up through our television. It had been temporarily wired into our VCR and when he turned the set on, the television picture displayed what was recorded on the tape.

An image flickered to life. It showed a view of the upstairs hallway. The picture was very murky and tinted a weird green color.

"What you are seeing is shot through an infrared lens," Kirsten explained. "That's why it's colored green. Often, anomalies will show up through this lens that may not show up any other way. Also, we can use it to film under low-light conditions. That way, we don't disturb any kind of activity that only occurs in the dark."

As we watched, the camera panned down the hallway as its operator moved and then entered the master bedroom. It scanned the entire room for a minute or two and then went into the hallway again. There was no sound on the tape other than that of Paul's footsteps as he walked. The camera entered Crystal's room, Kenny's room and then went into Michael's bedroom.

"Here's where it gets interesting," Paul spoke up.

All of us leaned closer toward the television, our eyes and ears straining to catch any little nuance that seemed out of ordinary. The door to Michael's room swung open and Paul's camera entered it, slowly moving from left to right. Paul moved further into the darkened room and the camera showed different views, then we watched as the scene changed to the hallway again.

Bruce and I looked at each other and shrugged. "I didn't see anything," I said. The kids and Bruce agreed they hadn't either.

"Actually, there isn't anything to see," Paul explained. He had been standing near the wall. Now he walked over to the machine and backed up the tape to the spot where he had entered Michael's bedroom. Then he turned the volume on the television up quite loud. "You have to listen very closely," he instructed us.

The tape began to roll again. The speakers on the television set hissed loudly and we could hear what sounded like jarring thumps on the audio portion of the tape. These sounds were Paul's footsteps as he had entered the room that night. As the lens swung to the right, a heavy and slightly garbled voice came from the television. The sound repeated once, twice, then again. I wasn't quite sure what I had heard, but a chill went down my spine. Someone seemed to be talking.

"What was that?" Bruce questioned the investigators.

"We believe it was a voice," Paul replied. "It's what we call EVP, or Electronic Voice Phenomena. It's thought to be, well, basically the voices of ghosts. These sounds aren't normally heard by the human ear, but can sometimes be picked up by recording devices."

"Like the photos you showed us?" Bruce asked.

"Just like that."

"What did the voice say?" I asked them. I had a feeling that I already knew. It sounded pretty clear to me, but I wanted someone else to tell me they had heard the same thing.

Paul and Steve looked at each other. Paul finally spoke up. "Well, what I did was isolate the track from the tape," he explained. "I had to be sure that the voice was not mine to be able to use it as evidence...I had to be able to prove it to someone else."

He withdrew a cassette tape from his shirt pocket and placed it inside of our stereo. He turned it on and stood there, poised with his finger on the "play" button as he continued. "I got rid of all of the background noise and placed just the track of the voice on this tape that I'm going to play for you. It got much clearer once I got all of the garbage out of it."

Paul pressed the button on the stereo and I heard the click of the gears as they went into motion. He turned up the volume and the hiss of stereo silence filled the room. A few seconds passed and then the voice of a man echoed all around us. The voice was menacing in its volume although it actually had the throaty sound of a whisper.

"Michael," it railed. "Michael, Michael...."

Then the voice trailed off.

I looked over and saw my son visibly tremble at the sound of his name being called on the tape. Everyone in the room looked very uneasy, including the investigators. *Great*, I thought, *they're the professionals and they are already scared.*

Bruce swore under his breath. Then he asked another question. "So how do you explain something like this?"

"Although I haven't made my final judgement, I believe it's a troubled spirit who wants to cause havoc for anyone who lives here," Steve answered. "That's what got us interested in continuing the investigation into your case."

"And that's what made you want to come back and do some recording in Michael's room yesterday?" I asked Paul.

He nodded. "Yeah, I wanted to make sure that it wasn't a fluke or something. You know, some sort of natural effect or anything else at all."

"So, what happened? Did you record more?"

"No," he said and again he looked very uneasy. "I didn't record anything unusual, but," he paused and then went on, "I saw something...well, unusual instead."

"What?"

Paul glanced over at Steve. The other man nodded at him, so Paul continued. "I had placed the recording equipment on the floor in Michael's room," he told us. "I had been recording for a few minutes, when all of the sudden the recorder moved."

Suddenly, it dawned on me. That had been the sound I had heard. "It slid all the way across the room, didn't it?" I asked. "I heard the sound from down here and couldn't figure out what it was!"

He nodded quickly. "It just took off!" he said. "I have never seen anything like that before. It happened two more times and each time, the recorder slid a little bit farther. That's when I decided to call it a day." He looked a little sheepish at this and I recalled the frightened expression that had been on his face when he left.

I looked over at Bruce, who was frowning. "Here's the thing," he said, leaning forward in Steve's direction. "We see that kind of stuff around here all the time. Don't get me wrong. I'm not happy about it, but I am wondering if you guys are up to this? I mean, if you're scared by a moving tape recorder, then I have to wonder what you'll think of some of the more terrorizing stuff?"

Steve looked a little put out by Bruce's words, but quickly recovered. "Look, we consider ourselves professionals in this field. We have conducted...."

Bruce interrupted him. "I'm not trying to accuse you of anything and I'm not trying to imply that you don't know what you're doing," he said. "I think we just need to know if you've ever handled a case like ours before?"

"Well, no, not exactly," Paul, looking uncomfortable, answered before Steve could.

Steve didn't appear pleased about Paul speaking up and cut his partner off. "What Paul means is that we haven't seen so much activity occur in the early stages of a case before," he said. "We can handle your case. We've investigated dozens of cases very much like yours in the past. We just need you to give us a chance."

I noticed that Paul and Kirsten exchanged a strange look between them. I didn't even want to wonder what that look meant, because if I did, I was sure that I wasn't going to like it. Were they really as competent as they tried to come across? I didn't know.

All I could think about though was that at least this group was willing to try and help us. Perhaps more than willing, I realized, looking at Paul more closely. Still, like Bruce, I wondered what might happen if they witnessed some of the destructive acts that we had experienced in our house. What would they think?

It doesn't matter, I thought, *they are going to try and help us.* That was more than anyone else had been able to do, with the exception of Dr. Holt. Even my own church had refused to try and assist us. How could I turn down an offer from these investigators? At that point, I didn't care if they had the right experience or not.

"You can do your investigations," I said, breaking the silence that had followed Steve's statement. "All that we ask is that you don't abandon us." I tried to meet his eyes, but he was looking down.

"We won't," Steve replied in a firm voice. "I promise."

I clung to that vow.

❧ 12 ❧

The First Investigation

We were filled with anticipation about the impending detective work. Surprisingly, everything was quiet, or so we thought. On Monday morning I was busy getting the kids ready for school. They were upstairs finishing some last minute homework and putting their clothes on while I was in the kitchen making breakfast. Michael's friend Justin had slept over the night before, but I was startled when I looked up and saw him standing in the doorway. I had no idea how long he had been standing there, but he looked upset, his face pinched and nervous.

"What's the matter?" I asked. I knew immediately that something was wrong, either with him or Michael.

"It's Michael," he replied. He shifted his feet back and forth. "He's upstairs crying."

I started toward the door, but Justin didn't move. I stopped in front of him. "What is it?" I asked gently.

He sort of shook his head a little. Several expressions crossed his face, from confusion to nervousness to outright fear. "Denice, I know that weird things are going on with Michael. I just...I really care about him." His voice cracked and he looked as if he were going to burst into tears.

I reached for him and hugged him briefly. "I know," I assured him. His face was buried in my shoulder and he trembled a little. I think that he was embarrassed for me to see him cry. "Sometimes, it's just so hard to understand. It's pretty scary sometimes too, isn't it?"

Justin leaned back and looked up at me. He nodded his head. "I'm just worried about Michael," he said. "I'm afraid that something is going to happen to him, that's all."

I smiled at him, as warmly as I could. Once again, I was simply amazed at what a good kid Justin was! He wasn't worried about something happening to him; he was worried about Michael. "How about we make a deal?" I asked him. "We agree that we won't let anything bad happen to Michael. How about that?"

He grinned. "Okay, that sounds like a great deal."

"I figure between his mom and his best friend, we ought to be able to keep him safe," I told him. *Let's hope so anyway,* I mentally added. However, I wasn't going to say that to Justin.

"C'mon," Justin urged me. "He told me not to say anything to you, but I think he's pretty scared."

That was enough to get me moving. He led me upstairs to Michael's room, where I found my son sitting on the edge of his bed. His face was red and streaked with tears. When I walked in, he quickly wiped his cheeks and gave Justin a quick glare. "I told you I was fine," he said to his friend.

Justin just shrugged. I sat down on the bed next to Michael. "What happened? Why are you upset?" I questioned him.

"Some of them have been hurting me the last couple of days, ever since Steve and those guys were here."

"I thought the house had been quiet all this time! Why didn't you say something?" I asked.

"I didn't want to scare you," he replied with an uneasy shrug. He sniffed loudly and wiped his nose. "It's not that big a deal."

"Yes, it is," Justin spoke up from the doorway. "Show her that place."

I looked back and forth between the two boys in confusion. "What place?" I asked Michael. "Show me what?"

Michael looked even more uncomfortable. "Remember the shadow man that you saw in my room that one night?" he wondered. "Remember how he searched my room and touched my neck as if he were looking for something?"

I remembered it vividly. It had been the first time that I had felt one of the "bad people" who had been bothering him. It had been so real that I actually thought someone had broken into the house. I also recalled the strange handprint that had appeared on Michael's neck, when the spirit had forcibly grabbed my son.

"I remember," I told him.

"Well, it keeps happening, only it's been a lot worse the past few days."

Michael lifted his shirt and turned away from me. I looked down at his shoulder and upper back and saw a large, round welt. A painful red color suffused the edges. The center of it was a purple and blue bruise.

"What happened to you?" I asked him.

"They keep poking me, especially around my head and whispering 'We have to find it,'" he replied. "I don't know what, but they hurt me. It's like pointy fingers and they poke me so hard that it's like it goes all the way through me. It doesn't leave a hole, but it feels like it should."

"Heck, it looks like it should too," Justin added.

I gingerly touched the mark and Michael winced in pain. "It hurts," he hissed at me. "Don't touch it!"

"Sorry," I apologized. I pulled his shirt down. I didn't want to look at that horrible mark anymore. "Why didn't you tell me about this? Do you have more of them?"

He nodded. "Yeah, they've been poking and pinching me, but they don't always leave a mark."

"Some of them do though," said Justin. "Show her the ones on your chest."

Michael frowned and lifted his shirt again. I looked down and saw a small collection of round welts and small bruises on his skin. Some of them were round and a few were elongated, much like the mysterious finger marks I had seen on him before. Most of the marks were faded, although a couple of them were the same vivid colors of the bruise on his shoulder and upper back.

"Some of these are old," said Justin, then he pointed to one of the darker ones. "But not this one, that happened last night. We were watching a movie and Michael jumped up and started crying. He showed me this place and made me promise not to tell you." Justin looked a little sheepish. "Sorry about that."

"That's okay," I touched his arm. "Michael, when did you get this one on your shoulder?"

He pulled his shirt back down and turned his back to me. "It just happened this morning. It was a little while ago."

"But why didn't you come tell me?"

"Because Mom, I'm not a little baby," he answered stubbornly. "I knew that you'd just get all upset and I didn't want to worry you."

"Michael," I said, but he refused to turn and look at me. I repeated his name, then reached over and turned his head in my direction. "Look at me," I directed him.

"What?" he questioned. I saw that new tears had appeared in his eyes.

"It's my job to worry," I reminded him. "I'm your Mom. I want to know when things like this happen. I'm not going to think you're a baby because you cry and neither is Justin."

Michael looked up at his friend and Justin grinned reassuringly at him.

"It's okay to cry," I told him. "It really is. We're not going to think any less of you if you do."

I hugged him tightly. Silently, I prayed that Steve, Paul and Kirsten were truly going to be able to help us. It was one thing for my hair to be pulled or for Bruce and me to be awakened at all hours of the night, but it was another thing for Michael to be tortured. No one can really understand the despair and the fear that I felt unless their own children are placed in danger. And what were the demons looking for? Kirsten had said Michael might see things others didn't. What?

I was a walking bundle of nerves, but I knew I had to try to act calm for the sake of the children. It was okay for me to tell Michael that he could cry whenever he wanted to, but it was quite another for me to weep all the time, even though I felt like it. No matter how justified my crying jags might be, I had to stay strong for Michael. He could cry all that he wanted to, but I couldn't. At least, I couldn't when he was right in front of me. Later on would be another story altogether. I had lost count of the times that I had spent curled under a blanket on the family room couch, weeping.

I prayed again these detectives could help us. My sanity, indeed, our very lives, depended on it.

For now, the best that I could do was to hold onto my hope and try to instill a little into my family. I smoothed Michael's hair back from his forehead and smiled at him once more. I pulled Justin over to us and hugged and tickled them both. Their laughter was like soothing music to my troubled mind.

One more crisis somehow passed. I certainly had not found a solution for what was plaguing us, but we had managed to get past it, at least for the moment. For now, that seemed to be the key to coping with our situation, just drawing together and holding onto the love we all felt for one another. Our affection for Justin, and in this case, his for us, had helped us through another terrifying experience.

In the back of my mind though, that very familiar question returned...*What next?*

It happened soon enough.

In the late morning, after taking the kids to school, talking to Michael's counselor and running some errands, I cleaned up the kitchen from breakfast and then took some laundry I had put in earlier out of the dryer. I folded the clothes, placed them into a basket, then went upstairs to put them away. As I reached the top of the stairs, I saw it. I'm not sure if the light in the corridor was just right or what actually occurred to make it visible, but suddenly I got a glimpse of a series of vivid marks on the wall overhead. They ran in a long, straight line about three inches below the edge of the ceiling.

My first thought, as I drew closer and put down the laundry basket, was that the words had been scribbled there by one of the kids. The writing in the hallway had a primitive, looping quality to it that looked like something a child would do. The question was, however, exactly how could Kenny or one of the other kids have managed to write so high up on the wall? And even if they could manage to do it, why would they?

I squinted my eyes, but couldn't make anything out. I would have to get closer. I knew that Bruce stored a wooden stepladder in the garage and went outside to get it. Somehow, I managed to carry the ladder back inside and up to the second floor. From this teetering perch, I was able to get a closer look at the strange writing.

I didn't like what I saw.

The marks appeared to have been scrawled with a crayon or perhaps a stick of charcoal and some sort of red substance. They stretched about five feet down the hallway, never wavering any farther than a few inches from the top of the wall. As I began to read them, I experienced a sinking feeling in my stomach. The first word filled me with dread. There, in that poorly written script was my son's name....

MICHAEL

As I looked closer, I was sure these were not crayon marks, placed on the wall by a mischievous child. There was something sinister about them, something that filled me with dread. At that moment, I became convinced that the writing was in some way connected to the ghosts who were haunting our house.

Michael's name was repeated again in a string of words that ran together, which roughly read: *MICHAEL WE'RE COMING TO GET YOU YOU KNOW WHY* and then the number 3 and a roughly drawn eye with red drops dripping from it. My dread turned to terror, but somehow I managed to maintain my grip on the ladder as I stared at the words. They were glowing like neon now. I wondered how long they had been there and what their meaning and purpose might be. It was a message, a threat, but from whom? And why Michael? Who had made these marks? What did they want with my son?

Running to my bedroom, I grabbed the Polaroid camera and took several photographs of the writing. Things had a habit of disappearing around our house and I wanted to have some evidence that these words had really been here, should they vanish later on. Afterward, I decided to call Steve and the other investigators. They ought to know about this, I reasoned, so they'd be prepared to deal with it during their investigations tomorrow. I got Steve's answering machine. I left a message detailing not only the writing on the wall, but the strange marks which had appeared on Michael's body as well.

Hanging up the phone, I went back upstairs. I wanted another look at the weird writing. I climbed back up on the ladder and looked at the wall...but the writing was gone! It had disappeared as mysteriously as it had come! *How long had it actually been there? Could it have appeared only this morning?* I didn't know, but I guessed that it was possible. Regardless, I thought I had been wise to take the photos when I did. But when I went to get the pictures to show Bruce later, they had faded to nothing.

The following evening the children and I waited for the investigators. Steve arrived first, bringing with him a number of cases of equipment, coolers packed with food, drinks and enough film as well as blank recording tapes to outfit a movie set.

I pulled him aside where the kids couldn't hear us and told him more about the frightening writing on the wall. To my surprise, Steve didn't seem interested. He murmured, "Sorry you were exposed to that," and got right back to his own agenda. He seemed almost obsessed about not being diverted, but since he was our only hope and my fears for Michael had escalated after seeing the crude threat on our walls, I let him get on with his work. I didn't want to risk antagonizing the only man who might be able to help us.

Paul arrived about a half-hour later, around 4:30, bringing more equipment. He had several cases of video cameras and monitors that would be set up throughout the house. Kirsten followed a few minutes later with more equipment and three additional volunteers, John, Lisa and Amanda. By the time they arrived, I felt as if we were preparing for a war.

In a way, I guess we were!

The children were remarkably subdued, despite all the activity that was going on. Steve put them to work handling small tasks and they gladly helped out where they could. I imagine that he felt it was better to keep the kids busy than to have them underfoot. Feeling rather helpless, I spent my time mostly watching what was going on. Bruce had not yet come home from work, although I hoped he would arrive before the actual investigation began.

One of the first things Steve's group did was to designate the family room as their headquarters, a "safe area" as Steve referred to it. Here, they unpacked and unloaded their equipment and supplies and placed their coolers. I offered to make food for the researchers while they were in our home, but Steve declined. He explained the investigation will be invasive enough. "I don't want you to go to any more trouble than you already have."

Paul began setting up the video equipment. He had brought along two portable tables and now placed them in one corner of the room. With Lisa's and Amanda's help, he began unspooling cable and getting the monitors up and operational. Four cameras were hooked up to a central monitoring system in the family room and the cameras themselves were placed in various parts of the house, including Michael's bedroom, Crystal's bedroom, the upstairs hallway and the kitchen. Each of them would send their images to the main monitors, which were hooked up to four separate video recorders. Any activity could be observed and recorded in the downstairs room. In addition, all of the cameras had been fitted with the same type of night vision lenses the investigators had used during their first trip to the house. "Hopefully," Steve explained to me, "this will record anything beyond the range of normal human vision."

After Paul placed the monitors on one of the portable tables, Lisa began the complicated task of wiring things up correctly. Seeming funny and outgoing when she first arrived, with long dark hair pulled back into a glossy ponytail, Lisa set about her tasks silently, with the solemnity of a scientist.

Amanda, on the other hand, was Lisa's opposite. She was constantly laughing and cutting up. She was short, stocky and had blond, curly hair that looked so tousled that it probably hadn't seen a brush in awhile. She was also engaged to be married to John, who was across the room helping Steve with the rest of the equipment.

Amanda started to draw a diagram of the entire house, putting in a few cartoon figures for fun, and began marking on it the various areas being monitored by the equipment. As the evening went on, she would keep track of the areas where activity took place.

John was tall and stocky with the same build and short haircut as Steve. The difference was that John's cropped hair was black. He also had an olive complexion with a narrow face and sharp features that would have been menacing if he didn't smile so much. He began running some cables away from a laptop computer that Steve had placed on the dining room table. Once that was done, he carried several large cases upstairs to Michael's room.

The computer Steve was carefully adjusting had been loaded with a software program Paul had designed to monitor paranormal activity in a location—in this case, Michael's bedroom. Here, they placed various monitoring devices that would send signals, via the cables, back to the computer. The program would then monitor and provide a record of any strange activity that occurred. The sensors included two meters to measure disruptions in the electro-magnetic field; a device that would monitor changes in visible and ultraviolet light; a negative ion counter and a small base with a glass dome over it to track any seismic activity which might occur.

They also set up recording devices in Michael's room, equipped with sensitive pressure zone microphones that could pick up low level activity coming from any direction. In addition to all that, the investigators also brought 35mm cameras, video cameras and black, gun-like devices that could take instant temperatures readings from the atmosphere.

I stood off to one side as Steve placed the last of the stationary monitors, a digital thermometer that he wanted in Michael's room. It was calibrated to measure any sort of sudden temperature drops. He placed it near the camera that was monitoring the room. "This way," he explained to me, "we'll be able to see if any cold spots are present without having to be in the room." I remembered some of the terrible chills we had all experienced in the house before and I hoped his equipment was prepared for the sudden way they could come and go.

Steve led me out of Michael's room and closed the door behind us, being careful to make sure the numerous snakes of cables running into the room fit into the space beneath the door itself. After closing the door, he pulled out a wide roll of clear, heavy tape and attached it to the door and the surrounding frame, effectively sealing the room. He inserted a piece of paper behind the tape and signed his name on it.

"Why are you doing that?" I asked.

"Well, this way, we have evidence that we sealed the room," he answered and nodded to the video camera at the end of the hall. "If anything happens inside, there is no way that a person could have gotten inside. On the other hand, thanks to the monitoring system, if the tape is broken, we have to assume that it was done by other than human hands."

"I wondered if you were securing the room in some way."

"It's more of a formality than anything else, but it's something that I like to do."

I gestured to the same video camera he had just pointed out to me. "If somebody were in this hallway," I asked, "wouldn't the camera see them?"

"If they could be seen," Steve smiled a little, showing a small glimpse of his rarely seen sense of humor. He bent down over a black case that he had brought upstairs and popped it open. Inside were several plastic squares, about six inches tall. Each of them had a circle of glass on the front side. Steve took one out and handed it to me. He carried another one over and placed it on a small table near the video camera.

"These are motion detectors," he told me. "They send out an infrared beam and if that beam is broken, it causes the alarm on them to sound. If a person walks up here, the detectors will pick that up...."

"How does it work for ghosts?" I interrupted him. "I'm assuming that's what you will be using it for."

He nodded. "They can protect your area from the living and also pick up anything else that crosses its path. The beauty of it is that the infrared beam can pick up things that are not visible to the naked eye—that fall outside the light spectrum we can see. It won't activate because of the wind or something, but only if something solid breaks the beam."

"Have you had much luck with them in the past?" I asked him.

"Actually, we have," Steve replied. He took another of

the motion detectors out of the case. "A year or so ago, we were called to investigate an allegedly haunted church. According to a maintenance worker, who only worked at night, and a few other people, ghostly figures in robes were seen walking up and down the main aisle of the church very late at night. The story had it that these people had been killed in a fire at the church back in the 1920s. They were choir members—which explains the robes—who were practicing one evening when the fire broke out. It did some pretty heavy damage to portions of the church."

Steve paused in his story long enough to go over and place another of the motion detectors outside the door to Crystal's room. One of the video cameras had been set up there, as evidenced by the cord running beneath her door.

"The interesting thing was that, after I got this call and heard a little of the story, I looked into the history of the church," Steve told me. "It turned out that the fire and the deaths actually happened. Based on that, and some pretty convincing anecdotal evidence, we decided to go ahead with the investigation.

"We got there late in the evening and set up some cameras, although we didn't have the kind of equipment we have now. Then we placed motion detectors along the aisle of the church."

"Where the ghosts were supposed to walk?" I broke in.

Steve nodded and set about putting a motion detector in front of Michael's door as he continued with the story. "We had been sitting there about an hour when the alarms starting going off, on one sensor after another, right up the church aisle. It was just like someone was walking from the back of the church...up to the choir loft."

Steve shook his head and took the last motion detector from my hand. "I never was able to find a logical explanation for it," he said. "We took all sorts of photos and video that night, but we never captured anything else, although one of the audiotapes Paul recorded had something that sounded like organ music on it."

"Was it?"

"I don't know," he answered. "The weird thing was, there was no organ in that church. There hadn't been one in years. The last one had burned up in the fire."

"That's a creepy story," I said, suppressing a little shudder. Not much could affect me, after experiencing all of the things that I had in my own home, but Steve's story was more than a little unnerving.

"It was a creepy place," Steve admitted, placing the final motion detector at the top of the staircase. He hurried back down the hallway and quickly activated all of the sensors in the corridor.

"Well, that's it," he stated. We went swiftly down the stairs, not wanting to activate any of the motion detectors. "I think we're ready to get started."

"I'll keep my fingers crossed," I promised. "I really hope you'll be able to pick something up with all of this equipment, some real evidence which proves that we aren't all crazy."

"Denice, listen to me," Steve said. He turned to face me. "What little evidence we already have tells me that you aren't crazy. If I didn't believe that something was going on here, I wouldn't be here. What I need to do is to document the activity so that we can get you some real help."

"That's what I want," I said quietly. "We need whatever help you can send us."

"I know that, and you can depend on us, I promise you. We just need for something to happen that we can record and authenticate. Then, you can leave the rest up to us. We'll steer you in the right direction," Steve assured me.

"Thank you, you don't know how much that means to me, to all of us."

"That's okay," Steve replied, then he smiled warmly. "C'mon, let's get to work."

Unlike all the activity that had taken place in order to prepare for it, the investigation began quietly. The house was almost silent, except for the sounds of the groups' whispers and the tapping of Lisa's fingers on a computer keyboard. She had an additional laptop, other than the one monitoring the system in Michael's room, and would be preparing a complete report of the evening.

I sat behind the researchers with Michael and Kenny, trying to stay out of the way. Crystal had left to spend the night at a friend's house. Bruce still had not returned home from work.

Most of the lights in the house had been turned off, including those in the family room, enhancing the glow from the computer screens and the greenish tint of the video monitors. The faces of the investigators were washed with stark light, causing the area around them to fall into the shadows.

After an hour, Lisa, Kirsten and Amanda, who walked backwards part of the time, lightening the atmosphere and amusing the boys, made a trip through the house with the portable instruments and cameras, checking for disruptions in the electro-magnetic field, searching for any out of the ordinary temperature drops and taking photographs. As they went up the stairs, we all watched on the monitors and heard the high-pitched squealing of the motion detector alarms as they crossed the infrared beams.

"At least we know they're working," Paul said with a slight grin.

Kirsten turned off the sensors while they checked out the upper floor, entering all of the rooms except for Michael's. They appeared and disappeared from the monitors that were hooked to the cameras in the hallway and in Crystal's room. Then we heard a loud voice from the audio on the hallway camera.

"There's a severe temperature drop here," Amanda said, her usually joking voice had a breathless, distorted tone through the monitor speaker. We could see her back on the screen. She was turned and facing down the hallway toward Michael's room. Next to her stood Kirsten, camera slung around her neck and holding one of the black temperature guns in her hand. I could see the small screen on the temperature gun glowing brightly in the green light of the monitor that we all watched in the family room. She pulled the trigger and activated the temperature sensor again.

"I have a reading of twenty-eight degrees around Michael's doorway," she announced, then added. "I hope you can hear me on the monitor." She then grabbed for her camera and took several quick photos in the direction of the door. She had explained to me earlier that her camera had been loaded with very sensitive infrared film. This would provide her with the best chance of actually picking anything up with the camera.

Kirsten continued to activate the sensor. Lisa and Amanda now joined her on camera. Both of them carried electro-magnetic field detectors. As Kirsten took temperature readings, Lisa walked toward the doorway. We could hear both Lisa and Kirsten talking at the same time.

"Readings have dropped to twenty-six degrees."

"I'm picking up some high-level disruptions here. They're getting stronger as I approach the door."

"Now dropping to twenty-five degrees, no, twenty-four degrees."

"The disturbances are reaching the maximum point for this meter."

"Down to twenty-three degrees."

"The needle on the scale is now buried."

The monitor showed Lisa standing just to the left of Michael's door. The small, box-like instrument in her hand could be heard making an annoying whine as it reached the highest levels of electro-magnetic activity. Kirsten moved closer and continued to call out her temperature readings. I also saw Amanda quickly writing everything down on a clipboard she was carrying.

The next voice came from within the family room. "Steve, we have some activity now, inside of the room," John called out. He had been monitoring the elaborate system that had been placed in Michael's bedroom. I followed Steve over to the table and saw that the computer screen had a thick yellow line across the bottom of it. The line had several numbers on it and above each number was a red or blue colored bar. Each of the bars rose to various heights from the yellow bar at the bottom.

"Both of the EMF sensors are showing activity," John pointed out. His finger tapped the screen and highlighted two red bars, both of which were much higher than the others.

"What are you getting for a temperature reading in the room, Paul?" Steve called back to his assistant, who was still manning the camera monitors.

"It looks like twenty-six degrees," he answered. "Remember though, you have to allow that the digital will be about two degrees or so behind the infrared scanners on the guns."

"Is Kirsten still calling out her readings?"

"Yeah, she's at twenty-three degrees still, no change. She's about six feet or so from the door."

"The EMF readings are still strong," said John. "Do you think we should have them go inside? That's obviously where the source of the activity is."

"You may be right. I'll want to unseal the door though and record that on the...what the...?" Steve started to reply but then faltered and went silent.

"What's going on?" John demanded. He tapped on the computer screen and then punched at several buttons on the keyboard.

I looked over and saw that the red bars that had marked the strength of the electro-magnetic energy in the room had vanished! The readings had dropped off to zero, as if something had been there and then had abruptly left.

"All readings returning to normal," John stated.

"How in the...what in the world happened here?" Steve asked, speaking more to himself than to the rest of us. He was still staring at the computer screen and wondering what had gone wrong.

"Kirsten says they are getting no readings in the hallway now," Paul called out from the other side of the room. "No thermal changes and no EMF activity. Plus, the temperature in the room has risen about forty-two degrees in the last minute or so. It's now reading a steady sixty-eight degrees."

"I don't get it. What happened?" Steve mumbled to himself.

From over at the side of the room came a soft voice. "The bad people," Michael whispered, so faintly that he could hardly be heard. He was sitting on the couch, his arms wrapped around a pillow. Both his and Kenny's eyes had been wide just moments before, amazed at the equipment which flashed and whirred around them. Now, Michael sat with his head down and his eyes turned towards the floor. Steve walked over to where the boy was sitting and hunkered down in front of the couch.

"What did you say, Michael?" he asked.

"It was the bad people," the boy replied. "They don't like all your stuff. They don't want you here."

The next four hours were spent in almost utter silence. The investigators were both confused and discouraged by what had occurred. Unable to explain, they simply sat and stared at the monitors, wondering if something would occur. About every thirty minutes or so, Kirsten, Lisa and Amanda made a circuit of the house, checking everywhere with their portable equipment and cameras. They found that nothing out of the ordinary was occurring.

When Bruce arrived home, I told him what had happened. He stayed with us for several hours, but eventually he and Kenny dozed off on the nearby sofa. Michael stayed awake with me, watchful of what was going on, his eyes like small round beams reflecting the dim light.

Just a little before midnight, Steve came up to me. "Could we talk for a minute," he asked. I nodded and he led me into the kitchen. We stood next to the back door, out of range of the camera and its intrusive microphone.

"I have an idea that I would like to run past you," he said.

"What is it?"

"Well, as you can see, after that initial excitement, we've had no other readings on the equipment," Steve replied. "What I would like to do is to try and stir up the activity a little bit using some sort of catalyst."

I shrugged. I had no idea what he was talking about. Why was he asking me about this? Wasn't this all part of his job? "Okay," I finally said, a little hesitantly. "What did you have in mind?"

"Michael."

"Michael?" I echoed.

He nodded. "I want him to go into his bedroom and see what will happen." I had told Steve not only about yesterday's weird event, but also about the repeated attacks on Michael since the investigators had first come to the house. Now, the person who was supposedly here to try and help my son, wanted to intentionally expose him to more danger by using him as bait to stir up paranormal activity! It was like sending Daniel into the lion's den…and I wasn't having any of it!

"Absolutely not!" I answered firmly. "You can't expect him to go in and do your work for you. He's just a little kid. Some of these things attack him. Haven't I made that clear to you? He isn't…"

"Wait, Denice," Steve cut me off. "I'm not asking him to do anything. I just wanted to send him into his own bedroom and then observe if anything occurs that we can record on the equipment. Believe me, I don't want anything to happen to him. If it looks like things are going to get nasty, we'll pull him out of there right away."

"Well, if he's going to be there, I'm going to be there, too."

"No, Denice, you can't. You're not there every night."

I started to protest, "But I usually stay until he's asleep or one of the others sleeps with him."

"We would be watching him the whole time," he insisted. "He sleeps in there every night. I know these things harass him, but this time it will be safer than usual, because he will have all of us watching and ready to help him if he needs it."

It was true. They only wanted to see what we observed when Michael went to sleep, but I had an uncomfortable feeling about the whole thing. Steve's motives did not seem to be as clear as he made them out to be. Yet we had to save Michael and the rest of us somehow. I was so desperate for help after our months of torment I would have tried anything.

Steve shook his head. "You know, Denice," he said, "if we can't document that you have ongoing activity here, there's no guarantee that we can get anyone in here to help you get rid of it." Despite the way it sounded, Steve said these words in a very friendly and concerned tone. He truly wanted to help us, his voice assured me, but the message hidden beneath his words should have rung warning bells in my mind.

What was he saying? Did he mean that if they couldn't provide evidence of the activity, evidence only they could collect, then we wouldn't be able to get anyone here to help us get rid of these things? Yes, that was exactly what he meant, I realized, which in turn meant that Michael might be in more danger from these things later on. He would be more threatened than he would be tonight, under the controlled setting which Steve had described.

What choice did I have?

"Okay," I finally answered. "Let me talk to Michael. If it's okay with him, we'll go ahead and do it, but I have to be able to see everything going on in his room."

I talked to Michael, who agreed. We gathered outside of his bedroom. Bruce, who I had awakened, was against the idea of sending Michael into the room alone. I probably should have listened to him, although at the time I just thought he was being difficult.

Michael said, "Don't worry, guys. I'm not afraid." He was afraid though; I could see it in his eyes. For a moment, I thought of calling the whole thing off, but then the threat of the day before—*MICHAEL WE'RE COMING*—rose in my consciousness and I didn't, telling myself this was my only way to save my son.

A few minutes later, we all went upstairs. Steve explained to Michael, "I'm going to open the door for you, but I don't want you to go inside until I go back downstairs and monitor the equipment. Can you do that?"

Michael nodded and we all watched as Steve removed the seal from the bedroom door. Kirsten took two photos of him while he was doing this. I looked over at her and was startled by how nervous she looked. Paul had an expression on his face that I couldn't really read, but I wasn't sure he liked what was going on either. Before we had come upstairs, he and Steve had gone into the corner of the family room and had held a strong, but whispered, discussion about something. Paul looked unhappy with the outcome of it then. He appeared to be even less pleased now.

I watched Michael. He looked so small, standing there next to Steve's powerful frame. There was no question that he was scared, but I don't think we could have talked him out of going through with it if we had tried. Unfortunately, none of us did try.

The door to the bedroom swung open and only darkness came rushing out. The room was cool and silent. Only the flicker of lights on the equipment and sensors could be seen in the blackness. I know that I would not have wanted to go in there alone. Looking around at the investigators, I realized that none of them would have wanted to either.

"Okay, Michael," Steve leaned down and smiled at him. "Are you ready?"

Michael nodded, but he didn't say anything.

Bruce elbowed gently between Steve and Michael. "Buddy, you don't have to do this," he told the boy. "Nobody's going to make you. I'm sure not going to think badly of you if you decide you don't want to."

"It will be okay. We'll be keeping an eye on you," Steve interrupted.

At that, Bruce stood up and turned toward him. Steve may have been a strong, burly man, but Paul cut him off. "Just shut up for a minute," he said. Steve's face flushed. Bruce crouched back down beside Michael.

"You just make sure that you're doing this because you want to," he said. Bruce inclined his head toward the ghost hunters. "I don't want you thinking that you have to."

"I know," Michael said in a quiet voice. "I want to do it." He looked up at me and smiled. I had a feeling, for just a split second, that Michael was doing this more for me than for anyone else. Could he feel my fear? He smiled again, then turned back to the open doorway.

"Uh, ready?" Steve asked him, careful not to anger Bruce.

Michael nodded again.

"Okay, give us just a few minutes and then we'll be all set. I'll have Kirsten call to you when we're ready to have you go in."

Michael said this was fine and we moved away from the door. The investigators re-activated the sensors on all of the motion detectors, except for the one at the bedroom door. Nothing was going to be able to get to Michael's room without one of the sensors or cameras picking it up. Paul and Steve returned to the family room. Paul still didn't look very happy. I was more concerned about my son and searched for him on one of the television screens. In moments, I located him standing in the hallway, just outside his room.

"Okay, we're ready," Steve said, looking over to Kirsten, who was standing at the bottom of the stairs. Kirsten called up to Michael that it was okay for him to go into the room.

I looked back at the screen which showed the interior of Michael's bedroom. He was entering the room and closing the door behind him. I breathed a small sigh of relief. Through the camera lens, we could see everything. Michael, careful to avoid the equipment that had been set up on the floor, walked over to sit down on the bed. He perched on the edge of the mattress, glancing back and forth, obviously waiting for his eyes to adjust to the dim light.

"Now what?" I asked Steve nervously. Michael looked so small sitting there. I felt a pang of dismay, wondering again if I had done the right thing.

"We wait," the investigator answered. He poured himself a cup of coffee and sat down near Paul, his eyes fixed to the monitor. He had left John and Amanda watching over the computer system while Kirsten and Lisa talked quietly in the corner. Bruce and Kenny were sitting on the couch behind us, looking tense and anxious.

Minutes went by. The only sound I heard was my own heart pounding.

About one half hour after Michael had gone into the bedroom, one of the motion detector alarms in the hallway began to ring! The noise startled all of us. I jumped up from my chair. Paul immediately turned to the hallway monitor.

"We have movement in the hallway," he called out. "I don't see anything on the monitor though!"

Steve peered over his shoulder. As they watched, another of the motion detectors sounded. Steve called to Paul, "Can you tell which sensors were triggered from the camera?" Apparently, small red lights flashed on top of the sensors when the alarm was going off.

"It looks like the one nearest to the camera went first, followed by the one outside Crystal's bedroom," Paul answered quickly.

Kirsten stood near the staircase, trying to see if anything was happening at the top of the steps. She turned back to the rest of us. "The movement is coming from down the hall toward Michael's room and moving closer to it," she announced.

We looked back at the bedroom monitor. Michael looked as startled as we had been by the sound of the alarms in the corridor. Other than that, everything appeared to be calm inside of the room.

"We have activity here!" John called from the computer system.

Steve hurried over. I was right behind him. He leaned

past John and looked at the computer screen. I could see the same charting system as before with the red bar marked as EMF starting to rise from the yellow base at the bottom. Another bar, this one orange, was rising up and down.

"We have both EMF disruptions," he explained, first tapping the red bar and then the new orange one. "We also have seismic activity above the parameters I set when Michael went into the room."

"What does that mean?" I questioned him, my voice rising despite my efforts to keep calm.

"It means there is movement in the room that is not being caused by Michael," John replied.

Moments later, a loud, rattling noise coursed through the audio speakers from Michael's room. The noise radiated down the stairs from the second floor. It was a metallic sound, as if something was shaking very hard. On the television screen, Michael looked fearfully toward the door.

"Where's that sound coming from?" Steve demanded.

"It's the doorknob," Paul stated. "The doorknob is rattling and shaking the entire doorframe."

Bruce spoke quietly. "What is at the door?"

"I don't know," Paul replied. "Nothing that can be seen."

My heart beating furiously, I looked back at the monitor. Michael was now staring at the shaking door and sliding back on the bed, slowly working his way into the corner. Bruce had come over and was standing to my left. Kirsten came over to my other side and put a hand on my shoulder. When I turned to look at her, she smiled comfortingly at me. I touched her hand once, then turned my attention back to the screen.

"EMF activity is climbing!" John called out.

"We have a major temperature drop here!" Paul said. He pointed to the image of the digital thermometer on the screen. The backlit screen read twenty-four degrees.

Suddenly, the rattling sound of the door ceased and was replaced by a banging and tapping sound that I recognized. It sounded like hammers inside the walls. We had experienced it once before on the night that Bruce had tried to communicate with the spirits. The same night they told us they wanted Michael!

The investigators jumped up. The sound was coming not only through the speakers from Michael's room, but from the audio track of the camera as well. The rapping grew louder and stronger until it was no longer coming from just Michael's room, but reverberating from the hallway, the stairs and even the walls around us.

"What's going on?" Amanda cried out. Her voice was strained and fearful, but I couldn't worry about that. I could only focus on Michael. He still seemed calm as I watched the screen.

"Okay, we have EMF activity off the scale!" John said loudly. He and Amanda were bent over the machine while the rest of us were crowded around the table where the monitors were. He spoke up again. "We also have more seismic activity. I can't keep track of it so I am going to shut it down."

"No!" Steve shouted at him. "Don't shut anything down! Just let it run and we'll sort through it all later."

"We're going have false readings here!" John argued.

"Just leave it I said! I'll deal with that later."

On screen, we saw something blur past the camera! The camera itself shook for a moment, teetering and then righted itself again. It was still focused on Michael, but now seemed a little askew. Another blur passed by and this time was followed by a cracking sound, like wood splintering into small pieces.

"What was that?" Lisa asked.

"It looked like...," Paul began, then paused as another blur whizzed past the camera. "Something just flew past the camera! Things are flying around in the room!"

The next image left little doubt about the fact that Paul was correct. A book narrowly missed the camera tripod, passed in front of the lens and smacked against the wall above the bed. Michael ducked down out of the way. Another object passed close by the camera and connected solidly with several pieces of equipment the investigators had placed in the room. A resounding crash and tinkle of glass crackled through the speakers.

A yell went up from John. "We just lost everything but the number one EMF detector!" he cried. "Everything else just went down!" He tapped frantically at the keyboard in front of him.

"Just keep monitoring the last sensor," Steve directed him. His eyes were glued to the screen in front of him.

"Take a look at the thermometer," Paul told him. He pointed to the image on the screen and we saw that it now read nineteen degrees. Was that even possible?

I stared back at the screen. Michael was now cowering in the corner of the room. As loud as the knocking sounds were in the family room, they must have been deafening in the boy's bedroom. The temperature on the gauge had now dropped down to fourteen degrees and as Michael breathed, I could see puffs of warm air emerging from his mouth. He had wrapped his thin arms around his body and he appeared to be shaking, from cold, fear or both. I wasn't sure how much longer I could stand for this to continue!

The pounding noise continued to get louder. I watched Michael cover his ears. I saw Kirsten looking at me closely. I turned to her and I could see she was frightened. She knew that I could stop this whole thing, but I was as terrified as I was every day and night for Michael. I was more terrified that if I ended this, Steve would desert us and we would never get the help we needed to make these things stop. I felt torn apart inside.

I started to speak to her, but before I could, another

crashing sound blasted from the camera speakers. We all stared and saw that the camera itself had toppled over on the floor, apparently hit by one of the flying objects inside of the room. It was still transmitting. The image now was cantered at a wild angle and peered up at Michael.

As we watched, a bright, white smear of light appeared from the edge of the camera lens. It was a dozen shades lighter than the greenish tint provided by the night vision lens. The light slowly arced upwards in a painstaking loop and then moved sideways, almost filling the screen. As it turned and moved past the camera, Michael began to scream!

That scream erased any fear that I might have felt about stopping the investigation. My son was in danger and that immediate threat was more powerful than anything else was. I stumbled into Bruce and pushed past him toward the stairs. "I'm putting a stop to this right now!" I called out.

"What's happening?" Paul said, not even realizing that Michael was screaming. He was utterly transfixed by the white, blurry image on the screen.

At the same time, Steve put out his arm as if to stop me but I pushed past him. "Denice! Wait a minute!" he yelled after me. "You can't go up there yet!"

"Shut up, Steve!" Kirsten snapped at him. She followed me as I ran up the staircase with Bruce at my heels. As we reached the top of the stairs, the last motion detector alarm began to squeal.

I reached the bedroom door first. It was jammed. Bruce pushed me aside and yanked the door open. Suddenly, a black object hurtled out at him and struck him in the chest. His legs went out from under him and he fell to the floor. He painfully turned to the side and as he did so, the video camera rolled onto the hallway carpet. It had been snapped apart, but was solid enough to leave a good-sized welt on Bruce's chest for over a week.

He climbed to his feet as Kirsten and I ran into the room. I shivered. The room was ice cold, and for a split second, the image of a meat locker flickered through my mind. Over to the right, a toy truck was shaking and trembling on Michael's dresser. Without warning, it vaulted into the air, narrowly missing Kirsten's head. She ducked and ran over to the bed. I was already there, scooping Michael up into my arms.

At the same moment I picked him up, the pounding sounds suddenly stopped. The room was plunged into silence. Only the beeping of the motion detectors alarms in the hallway could still be heard. Slowly, the temperature of the room begin to return to normal.

Michael was trembling against my body. His voice murmured something at first garbled and indistinguishable. When I listened closer, I realized that it was "I'm sorry, I'm sorry...," he kept repeating.

"Sorry for what?" I asked him.

"I messed everything up," he replied. "I got scared...I wasn't supposed to be afraid, but the people were so mad at all of the stuff. They scared me and then they broke everything."

"Michael, you are the bravest boy in the world," I soothed him. Kirsten stood close to us and gently said, "It can all be fixed. It's not your fault."

Bruce hobbled over to us, in pain from the jolt of the camera striking him and his fall. "She's right, pal," he told Michael, taking him from me. He held the boy tightly in his arms, despite his bruised chest. "This isn't your fault," he assured him.

The motion detector alarms in the hallway stopped sounding. I saw Paul, Steve and the others appeared in the doorway. One of them reached over and flipped on the light to survey the damage. I heard a groan emerge from John when he saw the wreckage of their equipment, the shattered video camera and the now scattered cables. The only thing that did not look destroyed was the audio recorder and the microphone. Somehow, it had escaped the wreckage. Steve bent down. He righted the camera tripod and looked over the sensors that had been hooked to the computer downstairs.

"It's not as bad as it looks," he announced. "We can get this all fixed before the next time."

"There won't be a next time," Bruce said. He put Michael down on the floor and I slipped an arm around the boy's shoulders. He still looked upset, but whether it was because he was afraid of the spirits or because he felt that he had failed the investigators, I didn't know.

Steve looked up quickly at Bruce. "I thought we had agreed that we needed to get to the bottom of this to get you guys some help," he said.

"I think you've got plenty," Bruce answered him curtly.

Steve shook his head. "Unfortunately, what we have is a half-finished investigation, faulty readings and a lot of broken equipment," he replied, looking around the room. "I certainly can't put together any valid findings with that."

Paul and Kirsten exchanged a look between them. "Why can't we use what we already have?" Paul asked him.

Steve spun around. "Because this is all incomplete, Paul, you know that." I think he hoped for some stronger support from his partner, but Paul just looked uncomfortable and turned away in silence.

Bruce's voice had a razor edge. "No way are we doing this again," he said. "Our house is in shambles, Michael is petrified and now you're telling us that this wasn't enough for you."

"All that I'm saying is that I can't recommend a cleansing

with the evidence that we have collected here. We lost most of our sensors and...," Steve started to explain.

I interrupted him. "How much more do you need?" I asked him.

Bruce looked at me in surprise. "You're kidding me, right?"

"What else do you need, Steve?" I repeated. I ignored Bruce and turned to the investigator. I was beyond rational thought at this point. I simply couldn't see why Steve was balking at trying to help us. I was determined to see that all of the terror in our house stopped. I was willing to do anything I could. Had he asked for money, I probably would have emptied my savings account if I thought that it would help.

"Well, I would still like to test Michael for psychic abilities," he answered, taking two casual steps away from Bruce. "It's obvious that he is attracting the activity in some way, but I would like to have evidence of that. Secondly, I would like to try another investigation to record more of the activity in the house."

"The one thing I'm not going to do is to put my son in greater danger than he already is," I said, gesturing around the room. "This is not going to happen again, at least not with Michael in the room. If you want to record activity in here, then you guys can sit in here yourselves. I don't want Michael placed in this situation again."

Bruce walked over and poked a finger into Steve's chest. "This is your deal," he snapped at him. "I don't want my family directly involved in your investigation. We'll be here if you need us, but from now on, you are the ones who sit in the room and get stuff thrown at you!"

"Fair enough," Steve answered, his eyes locked on Bruce.

Bruce reached over and took Michael by the hand. The

two of them left the room, leaving me and the investigators standing there looking at one another. I watched as they began picking up the pieces of their broken equipment.

I turned and walked out of the room. God help me, at that moment, I felt our family was as beaten and battered as that equipment.

I was once again gripped with a terrible, paralyzing fear. My mind flashed back to the different people I had been in contact with about the disturbances around Michael. I thought of Tim Sutherland and his warnings and how Michael should "refrain from inviting the ghosts to manifest." I also thought of Sister Juanita, who had said that evil was at work in our home. What if these people were right? Would the ghosts do more harm to my son and destroy my family?

❧ 13 ❧

BETRAYED

Two evenings later, Steve and Paul returned to the house to see Michael. They planned to administer some tests they felt would determine whether Michael had psychic ability. Originally, I had dreaded the notion that Michael had any sort of strange powers at all. In fact, when Dr. Holt said he believed that Michael, through psychokinesis, was possibly causing the events to happen in the house, I shrank from the idea. When the doctor eventually abandoned this theory, I was glad. Now, Steve seemed to be advancing another variation of PK and I didn't like it any better. He disagreed.

"It's not that we think Michael is responsible for the activity," he explained. "We don't feel these are random acts of PK. We think that Michael is somehow attracting the spirits to him. That's why everything seems to be centered around him and why he seems to be the only one who can see these things. If we can determine that he has some psychic ability, this will show that our theories are correct."

I pretended to understand it all and gave them permission

to test my son. They arrived at the house about seven-thirty one evening with some video equipment to document the tests and a case containing some pasteboard cards and a screen. Placing the screen in the center of the dining room table, Steve sat on one side of it and Michael on the other. Paul placed a video camera on each side of the table and then moved out of the way to watch the tests on two separate monitors. I stood next to Michael while Crystal sat beside him on the floor. We weren't about to leave Michael alone again.

On his side of the screen, Steve opened the pack of printed white cards with a variety of symbols on them. There were five basic designs: a cross, three wavy lines, a circle, a star and a square. With the solid screen between them, Steve made sure that Michael was unable to see the cards. Steve held each one up in front of him and asked, "Michael, what is the design imprinted on this card?"

I watched in amazement as Michael guessed card after card correctly. Paul looked over at me, his eyes widening. Steve ran through the cycle of cards several times, shuffling them and presenting them, hidden, to Michael. Occasionally, Michael gave an incorrect answer, but most of the time his identification was right. Even someone as ignorant of the process as I was could see that Michael had psychic powers.

After about an hour, Michael was starting to get tired. Before he finished with the test, Steve did one more thing. He handed Michael a small wooden box that Steve had sealed shut with thick, clear tape.

"I want you to tell me what's inside this box," he directed Michael.

Michael took the box from Steve and turned it over and over in his hands.

"Clear your mind," Steve instructed, "and just try to concentrate on it. Try to tell me what you think is in there."

Michael nodded and held the box in both hands. He closed his eyes. It was several moments before he spoke. "I don't know for sure...," he said haltingly. "I think it has something to do with a door...but not really a door. I see the color red and I see the number five a lot."

Steve glanced over at Paul and the two of them shook their heads at each other.

Michael opened his eyes and handed the box back to the investigator. "That's all I can see," he said.

"That's fine," Steve said and took the box back. He placed it on the table and scribbled something down in his notebook. He looked over at Michael and smiled. "That's it, you're done," he told him.

"Good," Michael replied and added, "So, what's in the box?"

Steve took out a pocketknife and sliced the tape from the box. He popped it open and took out a key. "You couldn't have been much closer," he said. "You said that you saw a door, but not a door. This is, however, a key, which might go to a door, but in this case, it goes to a motorcycle...a red, Five-Fifty motorcycle."

I gasped in surprise. Crystal stared at Michael and shook her head. She was as stunned as I was. "So, what does it all mean?" I asked the two investigators.

"Well, as we suspected, Michael has above average psychic ability," Steve said. "Maybe that explains why the ghosts seem to be especially attracted to him."

"The best way to describe it," Paul cut in, "is to say that Michael is like a campfire burning in the woods. If you were walking along in the darkness, you would be able to see the fire from a distance and would be attracted to it. The same thing is happening with the ghosts. They are seeing the light given off by Michael and are attracted to it."

"That's perhaps a bit more poetic than I would have put it," Steve smirked, "but you get the idea."

I turned to Paul. "So, what you're saying is that the ghosts are lost spirits and they see Michael as someone they can communicate with, as opposed to people like us, who aren't psychic at all?"

"Exactly," Paul agreed, nodding his head. "I believe there are people like Michael who are like radio receivers. By this I mean that they can pick up things the rest of us can't. These ghosts are attracted to people like Michael, but normally will leave the rest of us alone."

"So how come my bed shakes sometimes and we all see and hear things in the house?" Crystal spoke up. She had been sitting quietly, taking all of this in.

Steve ignored her. "Michael seems to have a pretty amazing psychic ability and the spirits...," he continued. Then he turned to Michael. "Why do they want you?" Steve asked him, echoing the same question that Bruce and I had asked my son so many times before. As always, Michael refused or couldn't answer. He simply shook his head, avoided making eye contact with anyone and quickly left the room. I heard the downstairs bathroom door shut.

"What happens now?" I asked Paul and Steve.

Steve spoke first. "With the data that we collected before, plus the footage of the tests, we have just about enough evidence to show that the house is genuinely..."

"—and without question—," Paul added.

"Haunted," Steve finished, glaring at his partner. "I propose that we come back one more time and conduct another investigation. At that point, we should have gathered enough information to move forward with the cleansing. Hopefully, we can bring an end to all of this at that point."

"Thank God," Crystal cried out before anyone else could speak. "I can tell you that I'm ready for it to end!"

Not wanting to waste time, I told them to come back on Sunday. By then, John and Paul, who had been hard at work repairing and replacing the broken equipment, would be ready. Accordingly, late in the afternoon on Sunday, the group arrived. Once more, they set up their cameras and equipment, using the family room as their base of operations.

I noticed, however, that this time, the investigation seemed much more haphazard and disorganized. The investigators weren't as careful with the placement of the cameras and equipment as before. In addition, little discussion took place among the members of the group. I got the impression that something had been done or said which had altered the relationships between them. I noticed this especially in regard to Paul and Kirsten, who kept to themselves and largely ignored Steve except to ask specific questions.

What is going on? I wondered.

Paul once again set up his monitoring equipment on the portable tables, and the computer system was again arranged on the dining room table. I saw that Paul had only three cameras with him this time, the fourth one not having been replaced. Three monitors and recording systems were placed on the table and lines were run upstairs to Michael's room.

Tonight, Steve planned to focus the entire investigation on Michael's bedroom. He wanted to maintain distance from it with the operations base downstairs, but all of the equipment would be set up in Michael's room. He planned to have three of the investigators inside the room as well. All of them were given cameras and portable instruments to record and document whatever activity took place.

I went upstairs to see the preparations which had been made in the bedroom. The three researchers who would stay in the room were John, Lisa and Kirsten. Amanda would have the job of maintaining the computer system while Paul and Steve would be observing as they had before.

The sensor equipment stood in the center of the room. Two small tables and three chairs were nearby. Here, the investigators would place their equipment and report their findings. I saw that Lisa's laptop computer was already here, as were several cameras and detection devices.

Three digital thermometers on small tripods had been placed around the bedroom so the team could record any temperature changes in different parts of the room. A stereo deck had been put together with several microphones to record the proceedings and, this time, Steve had installed an intercom system so that two-way communication could take place between the on-scene investigators and the observers.

It seemed like a very competent set-up, but I couldn't shake the feeling that they were going through the motions. Perhaps it was the attitude they all seemed to have, as if they didn't really want to be there. There was obvious tension and stress between them, but there seemed to be an undercurrent of something else, too. Watching them, I had a feeling that it was fear. I remembered the first time that Paul had come to the house alone and experienced the strange incident with his recorder in Michael's room. I recalled the look that he had in his eyes that day. I saw that same look in the eyes of the people around me now. They were all scared, I realized, which unsettled me.

Having lived in fear for so long, it had become second nature to me. I was constantly watching over my shoulder for what was going to happen next. What these investigators had experienced in my home had completely unnerved them. They had been fascinated with chasing paranormal phenomena, at least until those phenomena were given a chance to chase them back! I wondered what they expected to happen in Michael's room tonight, but I was betting that these people were wondering it even more. Scenes of Michael's visions passed through my mind as I remembered what the psychic Tim Sutherland had told me. "You can't be afraid, because the ghosts will use that fear against you."

I had a feeling the investigators in the bedroom were going to have a long night ahead of them.

Going back downstairs, I checked on Crystal. I had asked my parents to keep the boys at their house overnight. Even though Michael wanted to stay at home and observe the investigators, I wasn't about to expose him to a scene like the last time. Kenny, on the other hand, was more than happy to be gone. Bruce was, unfortunately for me, gone also, out of town on business again. Thankfully, Crystal had bravely volunteered to stay and keep me company.

By the time I took a position to the right of the monitor table and out of the way, the investigators were ready to begin. Steve gave curt last minute instructions to Kirsten, John and Lisa and then sent them upstairs. There was to be no door sealing or motion detectors in the hallway this time. Steve seemed very eager to get things underway, so I assumed he didn't want to waste time with these extra precautions.

I turned to look at the monitors. With all of the lights upstairs and most of the downstairs lamps turned off, the house was once again quite dark. The cameras had, as the first time, been equipped with night vision filters and the three television screens gave off that same eerie green light. The glow gave Paul's face a deathly pallor.

On the screen, I could see the investigators walk into Michael's bedroom and take their places at the small tables. Even though the microphones were open and picked up the sounds of the investigators' entrance, no voices were heard. The team members were not talking to one another. I couldn't help but notice how stiffly they sat in their respective chairs. Their discomfort managed to come through even the camera lens.

I felt someone move up beside me. It was Crystal. She wanted to watch, too. I put my arm around her and she smiled.

"How is the system doing?" Steve asked Amanda. He was standing just over Paul's left shoulder. He turned in her direction as he spoke.

Amanda was busy tapping the computer keyboard. "We have seismic activity caused by the team entering the room," she said, speaking around the pencil that she had gripped in her teeth. "I'm adjusting for that and setting levels for their locations now."

"Fine. Just keep me updated on any changes."

Amanda gave him a mock salute and went back to the computer.

Steve held what looked like a radio receiver up to his mouth and spoke into it. We could hear his voice echo from the stereo speakers that had been set up nearby. They were patched into the recording devices in the bedroom. "Can you hear me okay up there?" he asked. "You can just speak clearly to answer."

"Yes, we hear you fine," Kirsten replied. Her voice sounded strained through the speakers. I wasn't sure if that was because of the equipment or because of her own uneasiness.

"That's good. You can speak at normal levels. We seem to be hearing and seeing you just fine," Steve told them. He put down the radio and leaned against the back of the couch. He glanced around and found his coffee. "Now we wait," he said.

There was little conversation, save for that between Crystal and me, over the course of the next two hours. Despite this, I did get the feeling that the investigators were starting to relax. Whatever had been going on before they arrived at our house was forgotten, at least temporarily. The group members upstairs were now interacting with each other. The low murmur of conversation filtered through the speakers. They did several checks of the surrounding area with their portable equipment. but nothing out of the ordinary was apparently detected.

It was close to ten o'clock when we heard Lisa's voice emerge loudly from the speakers. "It's getting really cold up here," she said.

We turned our attention to the monitors. The three investigators were still seated at the tables, but Lisa now had her arms wrapped around her body. She was looking into one of the cameras.

"Anything on the sensors?" Steve called, directing his question to Amanda.

She shook her head. "Nothing yet," she replied, watching the screen in front of her.

Steve raised the radio back to his mouth. "What's going on up there?" he asked.

Kirsten shifted slightly in her chair and looked at the camera. "We can all feel a temperature change starting to take place, although it's not really significant yet," she replied and inclined her head to the closest tripod bearing a thermometer. "The gauges have registered about a seven-degree drop."

"Keep a close eye on…," Steve started to tell her, but his voice trailed off as, almost simultaneously both Lisa and Amanda called out. One voice came from inside the room and the other over the speaker from upstairs. "We're picking up a change in the static and electromagnetic fields," Amanda called. "There's definitely a disruption taking place."

"We're picking up readings on our EMF meters," Lisa spoke up at the same moment.

Steve hurried over to get a better look at the computer system as the rest of us moved closer to the monitors. Through the speakers we could hear the whine of the alarm on Lisa's field-strength detector. I had learned before that the alarm would sound when a change took place in the current field of the location. Apparently, something was starting to happen in Michael's bedroom.

Suddenly, a hard slamming sound echoed through the speakers! The door to Michael's bedroom, which had been closed, swung open, slammed shut and then continued to open and close with deafening force. The air was soon filled with the same rapping and tapping sounds which we had heard during the investigators' last visit. The noise grew so loud that we had trouble hearing each other speak. I couldn't imagine how loudly it must have sounded upstairs in the room.

The flurry of activity had started so suddenly that the equipment sensors had not had time to catch up. Alarms began to sound and the computer screen Amanda was tending flashed a variety of bright colors and blinking lights. The house was plunged into chaos in a matter of moments!

It quickly grew worse. The cameras sent pictures to us of objects flying around Michael's room. As they had done before, toys, clothing and books began to sweep across the room, banging into furniture, equipment and the investigators themselves. A tripod went over with a crash. One of the monitors went dark.

"We've lost camera three!" Paul shouted above the din. He was frantically flipping switches, trying to get a picture again.

"Amanda! Give me some information here!" Steve hollered. He was standing over Paul's shoulder and turned toward Amanda as he spoke.

I followed his gaze and saw that Amanda was not faring well in the excitement. She looked absolutely frazzled and terrified. Tears streamed down her face as she looked back and forth between the computer in front of her and the monitors that showed the strange activity in Michael's room. Amanda had been too afraid to go into the room herself, which was why John had volunteered, leaving his fiancée to watch over the computer system.

"Something horrible is going to happen," she shouted.

"Amanda!" Steve barked at her.

She stared at the television monitor, her eyes unfocused and round with fear. Her mouth opened to speak again and then she looked back at the computer screen. Her voice quavered. "There...there are...there is significant activity in every field. They...," she faltered, seemingly trying to get hold of herself. Steve interrupted her.

"Give me some numbers, Amanda!" he yelled. His voice was impatient and hostile, even harsher than the incredible noise around us required it to be.

"Leave her alone, Steve," Paul said. "Can't you see she's terrified?"

"I don't have time for this," Steve snarled in reply. He pounded over to the dining room table and spun the laptop computer away from Amanda. He studied the screen, his face a mask of anger and concentration. He made some hasty notes on a legal pad.

Upstairs, the activity had gotten worse. Paul's third camera still refused to transmit, but the other monitors continued to show objects being hurled violently around the room. All of the investigators had gotten up from their chairs. Kirsten and John were attempting to take readings with their equipment, but Lisa was looking for a chance to escape from the room. To her dismay, the door continued to bang open and shut. She ran the risk of being injured if she got too close to it. I could see her breath puffing out in a frosty cloud as she wept with fear and desperation.

Another crash sounded. The computer screen went dark as the sensors were broken or destroyed by the activity in the bedroom. Steve swore loudly. Kirsten's voice and face came over one of the monitors.

She held up a broken plastic box with wires hanging off it. "One of the EMF sensors has been destroyed," she said. Her breath fogged up the camera lens and she backed away from it. "One of the temperature gauges in the bedroom now reads only sixteen degrees."

"And it looks like the sensor array is out of commission," John added.

As he spoke, the sound of shattering and crunching glass came through the radio. Another television monitor went black. We were now down to one active camera. We heard someone yell, but we couldn't see where it came from as the camera was pointed toward Lisa and the door. A moment later, the door slammed shut. Lisa ran to it, grabbed the doorknob and twisted. I wasn't surprised to see that it wouldn't open. She slumped against the door. We could hear her sobbing incoherently over the speakers.

The pounding noise, which seemed to come from within the walls, abruptly ceased and all of a sudden the house quieted. In the silence, no one spoke. I peered at the monitor and saw that the activity in the room had stopped, too. John had picked up the video camera and held it in his hands, dragging the monitor cables behind him. As he turned, we got a blurry image of Kirsten's face. She was glancing around anxiously. The objects were no longer flying about, but the room remained at the same arctic temperature. As Kirsten exhaled, her breath formed a cloud in the darkness.

The entire house was now deathly still. Steve looked up from the remaining television monitor and Paul sat back. "The computer system is lost," Paul said. Amanda wept silently, curled on the edge of the couch. Crystal stood very close to me. We all watched each other warily.

What happened next began softly.

I heard it coming from the basement first. It was the sound of voices. They came to us as rustling, hissing, sighing voices. Then the sound intensified as if hundreds of people had suddenly started speaking at once. Each voice was hushed, but combined, the voices became thunderous. The volume of it climbed in rushing waves. Suddenly, the basement door flung open, and Amanda began to scream.

Thunder rumbled through the house. An invisible form filled with energy like a tornado roared out of the basement and entered the kitchen. Dishes rattled in the cabinets; silverware jangled in the drawers. The water in the kitchen taps turned on and gushed into the sink.

Amanda began to scream louder, wailing over and over again as if she could sense something none of the rest of us could see. In spite of all that I had already experienced, I was terrified, too. The situation was made even more fearful by Amanda's hysterical crying. I grabbed for Crystal, who was the closest to me, and was not surprised to find her hands grasping at mine. Steve was nowhere to be found. A few seconds later, I saw that he had scrambled for cover behind a chair.

Our eyes turned toward the kitchen.

The sensation of the force which had come into the room was, at this point, monumental. The entire room literally trembled, causing the pictures on the walls to shake and sway. The incredible sound of the voices continued and the rapping from inside the walls resumed. The noise was inconceivable! I felt the energy pass through the room as doors began to open and slam shut all over the first floor of the house. Moments later, framed photographs that hung on the walls of stairway began to shake and crack. Glass shattered to the floor. Lamps toppled and ornaments on the table flew by. The force was moving upstairs!

Stunned by the chaos around us, Paul and I stared numbly at the remaining monitor. Kirsten was now operating the video camera, because John was holding onto Lisa, who had collapsed into his arms. Her shoulders shook as she wept. John was barely able to keep her standing upright. She had slumped over and no longer seemed in control of her legs.

Amanda managed to drag herself from the couch and came over to where we were standing. "Do something!" she groaned to Paul. "Tell them upstairs something's wrong! Warn them it's coming for them!"

Paul shoved papers out of the way, looking for the radio that Steve had used to operate the intercom. He found it and switched the radio on, starting to call out a warning to the investigators upstairs. It was too late.

As he flicked the radio on, the door to the bedroom was struck so hard that it blew off one hinge. The door swung wildly into the room, yawning at an impossible angle. The three investigators began to scream. Suddenly, the final camera went dark.

We all stood there gaping at the now blank monitor, too surprised to even react. Amanda was the first to break the spell we all seemed to be under. Her face wild with fear, she began to wail John's name and then, surprisingly, given the state of hysteria she was in, ran for the stairs!

"Wait a moment!" I called after her, but she was already running up the staircase. I went after her, followed by Paul. Steve was still missing.

Amanda was three or four steps ahead of us when she reached the second floor landing and went straight for Michael's door. In the dim light of the room, the disembodied voices had now reached a fever pitch. The air around us was frigid with cold and filled with the riotous sounds. We could hear crashing and splintering noises coming from Michael's bedroom as we got closer. Amanda's feet became tangled in the equipment cables and she went down, floundering in the dark hallway. She managed to get back to her feet and pressed on.

She lunged for the knob of the wooden door leaning into the dark room, hoping to pull it out of her way. "John!" she screamed. Her hand wrapped around the edge of the door. Before anyone could see what happened, the door inexplicably leapt upwards and twisted back in her direction. The heavy wood crashed into her, hitting her in the head and knocking her back across the hallway. I heard a solid thump as Amanda's skull connected with the opposite wall. She slipped down to the floor in a motionless heap.

With one last thunderous roar, the voices and the rappings came to an inexplicable sudden halt. Eerie silence once again descended on the house.

With a strength I didn't know I had, I pushed the bedroom door out of the way and knelt beside Amanda. When I saw with relief that she was more stunned than injured, I steeled myself to whatever I might find next, got up and ran into the shadows outside Michael's bedroom. I heard a sound behind me as Paul came hurrying down the corridor. He caught up with me and we went into the room together. It was even colder and darker here than in the hallway. As we inched our way, our feet and legs collided with broken equipment and Michael's damaged possessions.

There was the soft moan of a voice ahead of us. I saw Kirsten in the murky darkness sprawled out on the floor. We got some light into the room. Blood trickled down Kirsten's forehead from a cut near her hairline. John and Lisa were sitting nearby, looking shaken and scared.

Paul took Kirsten in his arms. "We're okay," Kirsten said softly. "We're all okay." But when we looked closer at her forehead, we saw that around the wound appeared the imprint of a hand.

When we returned downstairs, we discovered Steve had fled the house, taking with him the laptop computer and the recording tapes from the video and audio monitors. He had left everything else behind. The rest of the group went outside and piled into Paul's work van. Amanda was dazed and battered after her encounter with the door and the others weren't much better off. They drove away with hardly a word to us, abandoning all of their equipment and leaving our home in shambles.

Disheartened, I shut the door after them. The house was quiet and cold. My nerves were shot and my mind was in an uproar. Crystal was shaking like a leaf. I knew I had to try to calm her. I made us cups of tea and we sipped them. As I sat there at the kitchen table, the whole evening flashed in front of me and, once again, what we had seen left me trembling. One thing was sure though, the investigators had certainly seen enough to be able to say with certainty that our house was haunted!

Such a revelation would plunge most people into a pit of despair. But somehow, I felt it a blessing. Not because I was glad the house was infested with ghosts, but because people outside my immediate family now were aware of it. All they needed, Steve had explained, was some concrete evidence. Well, they had it. Now they would be able to get us some help.

Crystal and I spent the rest of the evening cleaning up the house and gathering the broken and scattered equipment. We packed the stuff back into their cases as best we could and what didn't fit we carefully wrapped in newspaper and placed in cardboard boxes. Then we stacked all of it near the front door, sure that Steve would return to get his equipment very soon.

Two days passed with no word from the investigators. By the end of the third day, I wasn't concerned. I called Steve's number, but there was no answer. I left several messages on his answering machine. He never called back. Finally, as the weekend began to approach, I gathered all of the equipment into my car and took it to Dr. Holt's office to give to Janice, his receptionist. I wanted her to take it to Steve. She agreed, but told me, "I haven't spoken to him for over a week myself. I don't know where he is."

What is going on? I agonized. Surely, they wouldn't desert us. I remembered Steve's promises, his seeming dedication and professionalism. I couldn't believe that he would fail to contact us after all that we had witnessed. *I'll wait for his call,* I told myself. I knew it would come soon.

But more days went by and still I heard nothing.

Then early Friday afternoon of the following week, while I was in the kitchen making myself some soup, there was a knock at the back door. When I went to answer it, I was surprised to find Paul and Kirsten standing there. The two investigators looked a little sheepish. Their investigative team had simply, like so many others who said they would help my family, vanished without a trace. Now, here two of them were, standing on my doorstep.

"Hi, Denice," Paul said. He smiled nervously. "I know that we haven't been in touch since that evening with Steve, but we wondered if we could see you for a few minutes."

I greeted them, although not warmly, and invited them inside. Politely, I offered them something to drink, but they refused. I noticed that Paul was carrying a cardboard box under his arm. He placed it on the kitchen table.

"Would you like to sit down?" I asked.

"Let us first say how sorry we are that we haven't gotten in touch with you," Kirsten said. "There has been a lot going on that you don't know about."

"I'm not surprised," I answered, "considering that I have been calling Steve all this week and he has never called me back. I had all of the equipment that you left here on that last night and finally brought it to Janice at Dr. Holt's to take to Steve. The only thing is, she can't find him either." I didn't try to keep the icy tone out of my voice.

"You've got every right to be angry...," Paul started to say.

I cut him off; I wasn't quite finished yet. "Thanks," I snapped. "You're right, I do have every right. You all promised to help us. You said that you would determine if the house was haunted and if you did, you would put us in touch with someone who could help us. I would say that after what you saw you can be pretty sure the place is haunted, wouldn't you agree? So, what happened to you and your promises after that?"

Paul took a deep breath, let it out and said, "I guess that you should know that Steve deceived you. Really, he deceived us all." Paul slowly shook his head. "I have known the guy for quite a few years and trusted him, but he really stabbed everyone in the back."

"He got greedy and then it was lie after lie with him," Kirsten added.

"To be honest," Paul continued, "we had no business getting involved in a case like yours. None of the cases we've worked on in the past were as intense as what you have going on. I mean, sure, we investigated some places that were supposed to be haunted by ghosts, but minor stuff, nothing like you described. Steve thought you were going to be the big case that we were looking for, the one that would really get us known in the field. We allowed Steve to let you think we were a lot more qualified for this than we actually were. That's where we messed up."

"We just went along with it," Kirsten said. "We did until after the first big investigation anyway. After what we saw that night, Paul and I knew we were in way over our heads. We wanted Steve to put a stop to it and to contact someone who was really qualified to deal with your problems. He refused and we had a big blow-up over it."

I nodded. That explained the tension among the investigators when they came to the house that second night. It wasn't just fear, it also was the fight with Steve, combined with the fact that they knew they were way out of their league.

"And it gets worse," Kirsten told me.

Paul continued, "On our way back that night, Steve informed us that he had made a deal with a television show to purchase the footage we had already recorded at your house, plus his story of the investigation."

"He what?" I demanded, stunned.

"Obviously, he did it without your knowledge or ours for that matter," Paul said. "Apparently, some producer offered him a lot of money. That night all Steve wanted was some more footage of the events in your house. Then he was going to get out. He never intended to go any further in the case."

"When did he make this deal?" I asked.

"Apparently, it was after the first visit. After we reviewed the photos we showed you and the audio recordings. I guess Steve knew he had something the media would jump at and he contacted the producer." Paul frowned. "I seem to remember this television show fishing around for leads and video footage last year. I didn't even know that Steve remembered that, but I guess he did."

"So that was why he pushed so hard to get me to put Michael alone in his room that night?"

"Probably," Kirsten answered. "But we had no idea what was going on then. We still thought that he was honestly trying to help."

"I know that," I told them. "I'm not blaming you two. What about the others? Did they know anything about this?"

"No." Kirsten shook her head. "None of us knew but Steve. When he finally told us, Paul and I started talking about how we were going to stop him. We wanted to tell you, but things got so chaotic and then Steve told us to get out."

"The others didn't know anything about the television stuff either," Paul continued. "The only reason they aren't here with us right now is because they're just too scared to come back. They really are decent people and they only wanted to help you. They weren't in on this thing with Steve at all."

"They don't even know about our coming here," added Kirsten. "We were all just so embarrassed about this thing with Steve…and then, well, what Paul did."

"What did you do?" I asked him.

Paul stood up from his seat and pulled open the flaps on the cardboard box. He pulled out a dozen or more video and audiotapes, a thick packet of photographs and several envelopes of notes and reports. "That's everything," he said, making a pile of it all on the table. "This is all of the stuff that we recorded here. This is the material Steve was planning to send to that producer in California."

"How did you get all this?" I asked, more than a little amazed. I picked up one of the tapes and saw the date written on the label. It was the date when the investigators were present in our house.

"Paul broke into Steve's office and took the box before he could mail it to California," Kirsten told me. Paul's facial expression was a mixture of pride and guilt. "As far as we know, this is everything. We don't think he had time to make any copies."

"Can you get in trouble for this?" I questioned him.

"Well, yes and no," Paul replied. "Technically, I think this belongs to you, since it was recorded at your house and you never were asked or gave permission for it to be used. Also, most of it was recorded on equipment that belonged to me, or at least it did before Steve disappeared with it, but…."

"But what?" I demanded.

"Well, again technically, I did break into Steve's office," Paul conceded. "Yes, I did have a key to it…at least before he changed the locks…but legally, I'm not sure that I didn't bend a few laws. I think the best thing is for you to just put this stuff away somewhere and don't show it to anyone. It's better if you just forget you even have it."

"Do you think Steve will cause a problem?"

"He might," said Kirsten, "but I doubt that he will. Can you imagine how this would look for him? Not only would it destroy any reputation he might have, but also you could probably sue him if he sold this stuff to the television show without your permission. He told them that he had a release from you. Obviously, he didn't."

"Well, all I can say is thanks, I guess," I told them. "I really appreciate your getting all this and I know that you did try and help us in the first place."

"I'm sorry for what we didn't do, Denice," Paul insisted. "Please believe that we want to help you. Have you decided what to do next?"

"I don't know." I shook my head.

"We'll keep you in our thoughts, but please," Paul told me, "if there is anything that we can do, get in touch with us."

We stood up from the table and Kirsten hugged me. "Just remember," she said to me, "we may not have the resources that we had when we were working with Steve, but if there is a way that we can help you, we will." She paused. "And I want to give you this." She handed me a slip of paper. "It's the name of our bishop," she said. "He's a friend of my father's. I've heard he will, in extreme cases, do an exorcism. Maybe it would help."

I didn't want to tell her I had already tried the church route and failed, so I was silent.

"You two have helped already," I assured her. I gestured to the pile of tapes and envelopes on the table. "If it hadn't been for you, who knows, but something worse might have happened."

"Thanks for saying that," Paul said. "We know terrible things are happening in your house and, although I hate to even think it, I have an awful feeling that it may get worse before it gets better."

I sighed. "I hope you're wrong, Paul, I really do."

"So do I," the young man answered. "So do I. But, Denice, I want to tell you something more." He looked me in the eye. "I don't think you're just being haunted by ghosts. I'm afraid these are demonic entities."

"Oh my God," I said.

Kirsten looked at me. "Remember when Steve said there were earthbound ghosts here? Those ghosts are people who've lived and died, but haven't passed over." She paused and bit her lip.

"And the other...." I prodded.

"Well," she said soberly. "Demonic entities have never lived. They are fallen angels who do the Devil's work. In many cases you will see only one, but there are always three and they can take any form."

I shook my head. Was she mad or was I?

After they left, I played the tapes, but there was nothing on them. I sat dumbfounded on the family room couch. What had happened to the tapes?

I walked upstairs in a shocked daze with Kirsten's words tumbling through my mind. *Ghosts are bad enough. But demons! Does Michael know? Is that why Michael is so afraid?* I stumbled, grasped the rail and looked up. That's when I saw it etched on the ceiling in blood red, lurid letters as if carved by a knife. A large number three atop an eye and the words MICHAEL WE'RE COMING TO GET YOU VERY SOON. I ran to a phone and called Bruce, begging him to come home. As soon as he arrived, I rushed him upstairs to show him the ceiling, but the words had vanished.

❦ 14 ❧

THE MOVE

"We have to get out of this house," I said, explaining what I'd seen to Bruce.

"But...."

"No. Please. There are no more buts," I cried.

Bruce and I had talked of moving before, but our conversations had gone nowhere. I knew Bruce had sunk all his savings into our home and we'd both spent a lot of time and effort fixing it up. Still, in my mind we had no choice, especially after what Kirsten had said about demonic entities here and the words I had found scrawled on the ceiling.

"We'll just have to rent something until we can sell it. I can't live here any longer."

Bruce nodded, looking weary and beaten.

"I'll start looking tomorrow," I added.

And I did. Bruce left early that next morning. As soon as I got the kids off to school, I stopped at a realtor I passed en route. I didn't want to go to the one who had sold us our home, because I would have had to come up with an explanation.

Instead, I told Elspeth Harris, the new realtor, who was tall, black-haired and so slim she could have slipped under doors, "Our family needs to raise cash so we want to sell our home and rent another one, preferably in the same school district."

Obviously thinking of her double commission, she enthusiastically said, "I'll be by at eleven-thirty this morning. We'll go through your house and you can sign a contract."

She was as good as her word, appearing before noon. We went through the house on which Bruce and I had lavished so many dreams. She was favorably impressed, saying, "You've done great things here. Right now, this is a seller's market. I think we'll find you a buyer almost immediately." She smiled confidently. "And I think I have the perfect rental for you. Would you like to see it?"

I agreed to see the house. After signing the listing contract and watching her tack up the For Sale sign, I followed Elspeth in my car, thinking what an oddly old-fashioned name she had for a modern, high-profile business woman. We stopped at a lovely, old, well-kept home on the same side of town. The owners, an aged couple who answered the door, looked like they emerged from Grant Wood's painting, *American Gothic*. The wife was dressed in a long blue calico dress with a blue kerchief on her white hair and the husband wore a black, almost formal suit and a string tie. They were moving South that Monday or so they said.

"We need something right away," I said. "Could I come back with my husband this afternoon around four?" I asked.

Elspeth frowned. "I've got another appointment at that time, but I guess you could show the house to him if it's all right with the Gorings."

The old couple nodded in unison. "We're always here," they said, "and we'll be most pleased to have visitors."

I thought that a strange way to put it, but shrugged the thought off in my haste. As soon as I got home, I called Bruce at the office and explained, "I've found something perfect. Can you meet me at the Gorings' house at Thirty-three Elm around four?"

He agreed. After hanging up, I called my mom, who volunteered to pick up the kids and keep them at her place until after dinner.

Bruce and I arrived at almost the same time at the Gorings' house. I was glad Elspeth couldn't be there. I wanted to ask the owners some questions about their house.

As soon as I introduced Bruce, I blurted out, "Has there ever been any talk about ghosts in your home?" I suddenly realized how silly I must have sounded. Fearing they would think they were renting to some nuts, I quickly explained that our son Michael had a too fertile imagination and since their house was quite old, I didn't want him latching onto any stories.

The odd old couple told me no, answering together in unison, and quickly changed the subject. Perhaps too quickly, I thought. *Is something not right?* Then I told myself my imagination was getting the best of me.

Bruce seemed to like the house as well as I did. By the time we left, we'd agreed to a one-year lease.

That night, Bruce and I had an early dinner at a local restaurant to celebrate. "Now maybe we can all get some peace," he said wearily. I felt the same way. We had finally found an answer, not the solution I had hoped for, but a way to make all of the horror we had been experiencing stop. We were going to escape.

The following week, we moved into our new home with positive attitudes. "Let's put the past behind us," I said as we unloaded our suitcases and boxes and showed the kids around. They were happy they were out of the "spook" house, as they called it. I felt particularly glad for Michael that, though the distance was longer, his friend Justin would still be able to bicycle here to visit him.

That day, for the first time in months, each of the kids took baths alone with no sentry standing guard outside the door. And Bruce didn't even quibble about all the hot water that was being used.

At dinnertime, though we just ordered in pizza, we had a festive meal. The children insisted on using a lace tablecloth and lighting candles, though we couldn't locate our good china and had to settle for paper plates. The talk at the table was so upbeat that I had to keep reassuring myself that this was my family, that the terror we'd lived through was over and we all had somehow come through it unscathed.

It seemed almost too good to be true.

❧ 15 ❧

JUSTIN

Despite my fears, as days passed, our lives became normal again. The only thing lacking was time alone with my new husband. I longed for some so Bruce and I could rekindle our relationship.

As usual, my mother sensed my needs without my expressing them and the next Friday she invited the kids over to her and Dad's house for the night. The boys excitedly packed their clothes into duffel bags and ran about the house until Mom came to get them. Crystal had opted out of the grandparents' visit and instead was spending the night with a friend. Bruce had taken the night off work and we decided to order take-out food and spend the night at home. We would be alone, with no kids or ringing phones to disturb us. It all felt wonderfully romantic.

An hour or so after Mom had taken Michael and Kenny, there came a tapping on the back door. I opened it to find Justin standing there. I was surprised that the air had gotten suddenly cold and I shivered. "Justin," I said, surprised. He carried a gym bag in his hand and had a broad smile on his face, his bright red hair windswept from the bike ride over.

"Hi, Denice," he said, grinning at me. "I have arrived."

I laughed at him. The kid could always manage to make me chuckle. "That's great," I teased him, "but can I ask why?"

"Very funny," he answered and strode into the kitchen. He placed his gym bag on the table and looked around. The house was quiet and he looked at me questioningly. "Where's Michael?"

"Honey, he's not here," I replied and closed the door. "He's spending the night with his grandma and grandpa."

"Great. Why didn't he tell me that when he asked me to come over tonight?"

"I don't know. He's had plans to go over there since yesterday morning."

"But I just talked to him late this afternoon. Just a little while ago." Justin frowned. "He asked me if I wanted to come over to hang out. We were supposed to ride our bikes around the neighborhood until dark and then play some video games. Plus there is a cool movie on TV we were supposed to watch."

"Are you sure it was tonight, Justin?" I asked him. This was certainly strange. It wasn't like Justin to make things up, especially about something like this. However, I was sure Michael had already left with my mother when Justin claimed to have talked to him. I asked him about that again. "Are you sure that you talked to him today?"

He nodded his head. "Yeah. It was just twenty minutes ago," he told me, although I knew it couldn't have been. Michael had been gone for well over an hour.

"Did he call you or did you call him?"

"Michael left a message for me. He told me to ask my mom if I could come over to ride bikes and hang out and then spend the night."

This was the oddest thing. *Why had Michael told Justin to come to our house tonight?*

"Well, sweetie, I'm not sure what to tell you. Michael must have been mixed up," I said, still unsure what to think about

Justin's story. "He's staying with his grandma and grandpa tonight, but I'll tell you what. Why don't you come over tomorrow night instead? Would that be okay?"

Justin shrugged. "Sure. I guess so," he said. "I just don't get why Michael would invite me over if he wasn't going to be home."

"Like I said, maybe he mixed up the days or forgot."

"Yeah. That's probably it." Justin opened his gym bag and pulled out a package. Handing it to me he said, "This is for Michael. It's a cross my dad and I made. I want to give it to him."

Justin looked discouraged as he zipped his gym bag closed and headed for the door. I gave him a quick hug. The boys were rapidly getting to the age when hugs and kisses on the cheek were considered pretty gross, especially from a mom. So I took advantage of every opportunity.

He nodded. Surprisingly, he gave me a hug of his own.

"See you tomorrow," he said. I opened the door. The cold again accosted me and when I looked at Justin I realized he wasn't wearing a jacket.

"Wait, Justin. Put this on," I said, grabbing Michael's jacket from the peg. "It's suddenly gotten unseasonably cold." He obeyed and as I pulled the hood up, I was startled. "You look just like Michael with your hair covered," I told him, giving him a last hug.

I watched as Justin picked up his bicycle from the driveway and mounted it. His legs pumped as he rode out to the sidewalk and into the street. He made the turn at the corner. I watched him until he vanished out of sight. I closed the door behind me and returned to the kitchen, still amazed by what a good kid he was. I sometimes wondered if Michael realized how lucky he was to have a friend like Justin.

Afterward, I finished straightening up a few things in the kitchen and then, about a half hour later, called in an order to our favorite Chinese restaurant. I decided to swing by there and pick the order up, then stop at the video store for a movie or two and get back home in time to meet Bruce when he returned from work. Grabbing my car keys, I headed out the door. Slowly, I backed the car out of the driveway and started up the street.

A few blocks away, as I turned a corner, I saw the flashing lights of some police cars and what looked to be an ambulance and a fire truck in the block ahead. *I wonder what's going on?* I thought to myself. I took a detour and thought nothing more about it.

"That was a really good movie," Bruce remarked as the end credits began to scroll down the television screen. We had been blessed with a remarkably quiet and wonderfully romantic evening. No kids, no telephone and, especially, no unseen visitors. We had just finished watching the last of the movies that I had rented and Bruce flipped from the VCR to the television to watch the local news.

The opening titles flashed across the screen and two news anchors came on. The lead story involved an accident that had occurred early this evening, not far from our house. Bruce remarked at the location and I shushed him. "That must have been the accident that I saw on my way to pick up our Chinese food."

The sonorous voice of the anchor cut in. "The hit-and-run driver of a black sedan struck and killed a young boy on a bicycle in the northwest section of town. The child was taken to a nearby hospital and pronounced dead on arrival."

"Man, that's terrible," Bruce said, sadly shaking his head. "That's only a few blocks from our house. Think about that. It could have been one of our...."

Bruce's voice dropped off as a picture of the accident victim came on the screen. I looked up to see the smiling image of a very familiar face. "My God, it's Justin! That dear, sweet boy had been here looking for Michael, just before it happened!"

The blood drained out of my face and I suddenly began to weep. I choked for breath as my cries came in great wrenching sobs. "Justin! Not this!" I struggled to draw air into my lungs, but

I couldn't. Each choking breath sounded like hoarse, braying gasps.

A thousand thoughts and images flashed through my mind. *Why Justin?* Perhaps if I had asked him to stay longer? Perhaps if I had taken him home? Perhaps if he had not come over? *Oh God, could this be my fault?*

I continued to wail and cry. Bruce held me. Tears streamed down his face as well. He had loved the boy as much as I had. I think we both felt like one of our own children had been lost. How must his own parents feel? Why did this have to happen....

My thoughts suddenly broke off as I envisioned Michael finding out about Justin when my father watched the ten o'clock news. I suddenly pushed away from Bruce.

"Michael!" I shouted. "We can't let him find out this way!" I ran for the telephone in the kitchen. Snatching the receiver off the hook, I quickly dialed my parents' number. I was still weeping when Mom answered the phone.

"Mom, please don't turn on the television news!" I screamed at her.

"My goodness, Denice, what's wrong with you?"

"Just don't turn it on. And don't let Michael see anything that might be on."

"Will you please answer me?" my mother demanded.

"Mom, it's Michael's friend, Justin. He got killed in a car accident this afternoon. I don't want Michael to find out by seeing it on the news. I need to tell him about it myself." I tried to explain to her. I was still having trouble breathing and my words came out in short, broken sentences.

My mother gasped and I heard her choke back her own tears. "How terrible!" she groaned. "I heard about the accident on the radio this evening, but they didn't give the child's name. I never dreamed it could be.... Oh my goodness."

Mom began to cry, weeping into the receiver.

"Mom, please don't let Michael know you're upset," I begged her. "And please don't let him see the news."

"The boys are watching a movie with your dad," she sniffed. "I'll make sure that he sends them to bed when it's over. Oh, Denice, this is so terrible."

"I know, Mom, I know." I began sobbing all over again. "I'll tell Michael about it when he gets home tomorrow."

My mother struggled to compose herself and I could hear her sniffing on the other end of the line. She blew her nose and came back on the phone. "I won't say anything to him," she promised me. "I'm not sure how he's going to take it. This will just break his heart."

"Mine, too," I mumbled as we said our goodbyes. After we hung up, I tried to call Justin's parents, but the line was busy and when I asked the operator to check it, she said the receiver was off the hook. They probably didn't want to talk to anyone now, I reasoned and hung up.

Feeling faint, I slumped against the wall. Bruce was there to catch me and take me into his arms again. I continued to cry. Eventually, Bruce took me upstairs and literally put me to bed.

"Why Justin?" I kept asking him, but he had no answer for me.

Exhausted, I finally fell asleep.

The shrill screaming of the telephone jarred me awake in the middle of the night. Bleary-eyed, I looked around the dark bedroom and tried to focus. The telephone was directly beside me on the night stand next to the alarm clock which showed glowing numerals that read 2:43 A.M.

I fumbled for the receiver.

"Who is it?" Bruce groaned.

I ignored him, too worn out to think. "Hello?" I managed to say.

I could hear gulping sounds on the other end of the line.

Then, a small voice choked out, "Mommy? It's me." It was Michael. His voice cut through the fog surrounding my mind and I came fully awake.

"Michael, honey. What's wrong?" I asked him gently, dreading his reply.

"How come you didn't tell me? How come Justin got killed, Mom?" he cried.

"Oh, Michael. I wanted to tell you when you got home tomorrow," I replied. Tears began seeping from my eyes once again. I didn't know how I managed to cry anymore. Apparently though, tears come in an endless supply.

"He's just a little boy. How could that happen?" he asked me.

"I don't know, sweetie. Sometimes things are unexplainable. It was an accident."

"No, it wasn't!" Michael cut me off, his voice sharp and filled with both anger and pain. He began to sob uncontrollably, as though his heart had been broken. I realized that it had.

"What do you mean? Of course it was. Someone accidentally ran into him with a car, because they weren't being careful. Nobody meant for it to happen, honey. It just did. Sometimes things happen that we can't understand and…. How did you find out?"

He was crying so hard his words ran together. "The shadow man and the bad people. They came to tell me. They were laughing."

"What? Who laughed?" I demanded. I was crying hard myself and I had to repeat the question again to make him understand me.

"They said Justin was wearing my jacket. God and the Devil are fighting over me. The bad people said it was supposed to be me that died," he managed to say through his sobs. A chill ran down my spine.

"Was he wearing my jacket?" my son demanded.

"Yes," I murmured. "I gave it to him because of the cold."

"What cold?" Michael asked. "It was hot like summer today."

I shuddered. That eerie temperature change which some said indicated spirits were around—was that what I had felt?

What could the bad people have to do with Justin? Wasn't his death a tragic accident? *Surely this has nothing to do with Michael,* I thought. Then I remembered Tim Sutherland, the psychic who had tried to help us when everything first started. Hadn't he been injured in a car accident as well? And hadn't his mother said it was a mysterious black car?

"What else did they say?"

Michael groaned. "They laughed and told me he was dead! And I would be soon, too. And, well, I just knew it was true, Mom."

"That isn't true, Michael. Nothing will happen to you. Oh, Michael, I'm so sorry. I was waiting to tell you about Justin when I saw you tomorrow. I didn't want you to feel bad all night." I tried to apologize to him, but I couldn't shake the gut-wrenching guilt that I felt about everything, from the threat to Michael, to not telling Michael, to the fact that I didn't do something to save Justin. What could I have done? I didn't know, but I just wished that I had done something—anything.

"Mom, I know you're sorry about Justin. It's not your fault either," he told me, as if he knew what I was thinking. "Can you please come and get me? I don't want to sleep here tonight. I want to be home with you."

"Yes, sweetie, I'll come and get you right now. Wake up Grandma and tell her that I'm coming, okay? I'll see you as soon as I can get there." I said goodbye and hung up. I sat on the edge of the bed and grabbed the pants and shirt I had worn earlier. Bruce was still sleeping and had an early morning appointment. I scribbled a note.

Oh God, I thought to myself. I began to weep once more as I looked for my car keys. *How are we going to get through this?*

During the next few days a blankness, a sort of numbness settled over us as Justin's death affected each one of us in turn. Bruce lost himself in his work. The kids fell asleep in class. Our lives seemed to be coming apart even more ominously than in the old house. I managed to drive the kids back and forth, fix their meals and do the laundry, but little else. I was barely functioning, wandering aimlessly in a fog even at the funeral service for Justin that we attended.

I spent that time in a cloud of grief and fear, almost unaware of what was going on around me. Days passed, and I wandered the house like a zombie. On the weekend, I didn't bother to get dressed or even to shower until late in the afternoon. Justin's death and this new threat to Michael were the final straws.

Bruce was incapable of handling my depression. He had always dealt with things in his own way, his usual method being to bury himself in his work. Nothing had changed. He seemed to vanish each morning and magically reappear during the late evening.

Of course, the person most dramatically affected by Justin's death and burial was Michael. While I was drowning in my own despair, Michael slowly fell apart. It happened right in front of me. If I had been alert, I never would have abandoned my son to my own self-pity, but now he slipped away. When it finally penetrated my own fog-bound mind, guilt and frustration overwhelmed me.

Michael's anger and grief over the death of his friend spiraled him into a deep depression eerily like my own. He refused to leave his room except to go to school and almost totally refused to speak. I roused myself and tried everything I could to get my son to open up. I talked to him, hugged him, pleaded with him and even brought Dr. Holt to the house to try and get him to talk. Michael was barely able to mumble a few words to the doctor before he fell once more into silence.

Michael barely ate anything. His body took on the wasted appearance of one who has gone without food for much longer than Michael actually had. Mentally, he was causing his body to collapse. Dark circles formed beneath his eyes, and he grudgingly admitted to me that he was afraid to go to sleep. Each night, every light in Michael's room could be seen blazing from the crack beneath the door. To sleep would be to dream of Justin, and

Michael was simply not prepared to handle that yet. Until late each night I stayed on the chair in his room, but could do little except be there. And, when exhaustion was so great that Michael could no longer fight sleep, he would be impossible to wake the next morning. It sometimes took twenty minutes just to rouse him. I chalked it up to sleep deprivation.

Banging and hammering sounds within the walls sounded all night long, waking everyone from whatever sleep we had managed to steal. Voices and strange laughter echoed from every corner. Doors opened and closed by themselves and everyone, including Bruce, complained of hearing footsteps pacing up and down the second floor hallway. Now we were all pinched, poked and scratched by spirits we could not see. Blankets were pulled from the beds and one night Michael's blanket was on the floor twisted like rope into the form of a noose.

It was impossible to ignore the fact that the "bad people" had returned. They had followed us to the rented house. They wanted Michael and they preyed on the rest of us as well.

One night, Bruce started shouting at the unseen visitors and, surprisingly, the strange activity abruptly ceased. However, a few hours later it began again. This time it was even worse. We tried ignoring the things that were happening, but, needless to say, this was impossible.

I felt the bad spirits had not only returned, but were now dangerous.

One night several hours before dawn, there came a rapid banging on my bedroom door. This was not the spectral knocking of the spirits but a human hand. Who could it be? I looked over for Bruce then remembered he was away again on a business trip. I roused myself and slipped on my robe as Kenny walked in.

I knew as soon as I saw his face that something was terribly wrong.

"It's Michael," Kenny told me, his hands clutching at my robe. He pulled me into the hallway. "He's gone!"

"What? Gone?"

I stumbled after him, trying to become fully conscious. *Did Kenny just tell me that Michael was gone? Where could he be?* Confused, I looked at Kenny in a daze. "Gone? Isn't he in his room?"

"No, Mom, he's not in his room," Kenny replied impatiently. I ran to Michael's bedroom with Kenny right behind me and was accosted by a new but even worse smell than the one in our old house.

"Ugh," Kenny said. "It smells like blood."

When he said it I realized he was right and nodded my agreement. "It's awful." The bright lights made me blink. The ceiling fixture was on, along with two side lamps.

"Why are all the lights on? Where is he?" I wondered aloud.

"He does this every night," Kenny reminded me. "He always turns on every light in the room, but he's never disappeared before."

I quickly looked around. Michael's bed was unmade, but empty. The covers had been pulled back and dropped on the floor. I bent down and peered beneath the bed, but Michael was not there. I quickly crossed the room to the closet and pulled open the door.

"What could have happened?" I asked dazedly.

Suddenly, I remembered what Michael had said about the bad people confusing Justin with him because of the jacket and hood Justin wore. *Had they led Michael out? Did they still want to kill him after the mistake with Justin?*

Michael needed me. *How could I have allowed myself to wallow in my own grief?* I had to pull myself together. I spun around.

"Look at this," Kenny said. "Do you see what he's done?" His small hand pointed to a row of toys, mostly trucks, some small cars and a few video games. Each of these items had been carefully wrapped in clear plastic food wrap. Next to them was a bar of hand soap. It had also been wrapped in the plastic wrap.

"I don't understand," I murmured.

Kenny snatched one of the trucks from the shelf and thrust it toward me. "Do you know where Michael got this?" he asked. "Justin gave it to him for his last birthday." He reached for another toy. "And this one? Justin gave this to him, too!"

"Why are they wrapped up like that?" I asked.

"Michael has decided that he is going to wrap up everything that Justin ever gave him so that it will be preserved forever," Kenny said. He picked up the bar of soap and showed me some small indentations on its surface. "He wrapped up this soap, because Justin was the last person to use it at our house. These are his finger marks."

"Oh my God," I gasped. Tears sprang to my eyes and began to fall down my face. I may have imagined it, but at that moment I felt Justin's hand on my shoulder communing with me, comforting me. Suddenly I realized the depth of Michael's depression. I had been so buried in my own despair that I had not been able to see how bad it really was. I knew now that my love for my son had to be the catalyst I needed to snap out of my own grief-induced fog.

"Where can he be? Where should we start looking for him?" I asked Kenny, but he shook his head. "How long has he been gone?"

"I don't know. He locked himself in his room after dinner," Kenny told me.

"I'm going to get some clothes on and we'll see if we can find him. I'll be right back!"

I ran out of the room and hurried into my bedroom. Michael needed me. I forced myself to move quickly. The cobwebs were starting to clear from my brain. I knew I had to act. I slipped into a pair of jeans and grabbed a shirt from my closet. As I was leaving the room, I collided with Crystal. Awakened by the activity, she had come out to see what was going on. She was groggy until I told her that Michael was missing.

"What?" she screamed. "Where did he go?"

"That's what we don't know," I replied. "You stay here in case he returns. Kenny and I are going to go out and see if we can find him."

She nodded her head, still in shock. I moved past her into the hallway.

"Mom, take a look at this," Kenny called to me. I joined him in the downstairs hallway that led to the front door. The door was standing open about two feet. The cool night air blew in.

"Let's get in the car," I said to him. "Any ideas where he might have gone?"

"No." He shook his head.

I grabbed my keys from the hook in the kitchen and was stepping onto the porch when a small figure emerged from the shadows. The ghostlike form appeared from the trees at the side of the house and came slowly toward us. As it drew closer, I saw that it was Michael. He was wearing a pair of pale-colored shorts and a white T-shirt, thus creating the spectral image.

"Michael!" I cried and ran down the steps with Kenny behind me. As we got closer, I saw that Michael's eyes were vacant and unfocused. He wavered back and forth as he walked and his clothes looked torn and tattered. Then he collapsed onto the damp grass. What was wrong with him? What had happened? Was he having some sort of seizure? I crouched beside him.

Michael looked dazed and frightened. "I thought I heard Justin. He was calling me, asking for help, telling me to come down to the cemetery. He said he needed me."

"But Justin is dead," I said, staring at my son.

"I know you all say that, but I thought I heard him," he replied. "And I have to help him if he needs me."

"So you went there?" I asked. "It's a long way from here."

He nodded. "I went on my bicycle." I looked around for his bicycle, but didn't see it. Michael paused, his face so pale it scared me even more. "Just as I got to the gate of the cemetery, a big, black car came speeding toward me. I jumped off the bicycle and scrambled up the gate just as the car rammed my bike." He was tearful now. "It's ruined. It's all my fault."

I was so glad he was safe. I couldn't have cared less about the bicycle. "It's okay, Michael, and it's not your fault."

I took him in my arms and picked him up. With all the weight he had lost, he was not very heavy. I wanted to hold him close, like I did when he was a baby. "Michael, it's all right, but you must never do anything like that again. You must never go out at night alone. Come get Bruce or me if something like this happens in the future."

"I know I should have," he said, his eyes wide. "But I miss Justin so much. I was hoping it all was a mistake—that he was just lost, and I could find him."

"Oh, Michael, we all wish that was so, but Justin is gone."

He sighed. "I just wish I'd been able to say goodbye," he said tearfully.

There was nothing more to say right then. I held my son and when he calmed down, I put his feet down on the grass and led him back into the house.

I dozed fitfully for the remaining few hours of that night, curled into a pile of blankets I'd placed on the floor of Michael's room. I dreamed of a black car which already had claimed two victims and had narrowly missed its main objective: Michael. I thought of Kirsten saying that demonic entities could take any form and wondered if it had been demons, not Justin, that Michael had heard. My son slept soundly that night, completely oblivious to the lamps he insisted on brightly lighting the bedroom. For me, escape was impossible from that light, even with my eyes tightly shut.

When dawn began to appear reassuringly in the sky, streaking the clouds with a pale gold, I gave up my vigil and went downstairs.

As I went from making coffee to flipping pancakes for the kids' breakfast, I had some more time to think. I pondered what was happening in this house, a house as strange as the one we'd fled. I thought about Justin's death and the new threat to Michael. The "bad people" were becoming bloodthirsty. The move had seemed to work for a while, but the angry spirits had come back with a vengeance. Was there anything we could do to stop them? Would we lose Michael as well as Justin?

Stop it, I told myself, *this isn't over! We aren't going to lose him! There has to be something else that we can do, but what?* I didn't know, not yet anyway, but I was determined now to fight with everything I had left.

After breakfast I called a taxi to take Kenny and Crystal to school. Michael was still sleeping and I had decided to keep him home. I went upstairs to wake him and, not surprisingly, I couldn't get him to budge for several minutes. This was not new, but as more time passed I began to get nervous. He was so limp and unresponsive that I checked his pulse and listened for his breath. When I was sure he was okay, I continued calling his name and shaking him. Finally, after almost an hour, Michael's eyes slowly fluttered open.

"Are you okay, sweetie?" I asked anxiously.

"Yeah," he answered groggily. "I heard you calling me but the spirits wouldn't let me wake up."

I was stunned by this new assault on my son. All along I just thought he was suffering from sleep deprivation. "Is this why you've been having trouble waking up lately?" I asked.

"Yeah. They bother me in my sleep a lot now."

I tried not to let him see the horror I felt. Today was about helping Michael heal. I wanted to take his mind off his problems, not upset him more, so I quickly changed the subject. "Come on down when you're ready. I'm making pancakes," I announced brightly.

Michael gave me a vague nod as he dragged himself to the bathroom.

I went downstairs and busied myself making pancake batter. As I poured it onto the griddle and then flipped the pancakes, my thoughts returned to Michael's new problem. *Maybe he just needs more sleep*, I thought hopefully knowing deep down this was not the case. Just then, a pajama-clad Michael shuffled in and sat at the kitchen table. His hair was unkempt and tangled and the circles under his eyes looked even darker by the harsh kitchen lights. The first thing on my agenda was to get him cleaned up. Then I was determined to get some food into him. I would buy him anything he wanted, if he would only eat.

"Michael, I'm going to keep you home today." I set a plate of pancakes in front of him and sat down across from him at the table. I watched as he toyed with a small piece of pancake.

He shrugged and said nothing. He dipped the pancake into a pool of sticky syrup I had poured on the plate, but never raised it to his mouth to eat it.

"You're going to have to go back tomorrow," I told him. "You're missing too much work, but today will be our special day. You can play hookie with my permission."

Instead of being elated, Michael shrugged again and put the pancake back onto his plate. He stabbed at another piece and dipped that into the maple syrup as well. I watched him as he swirled it around, then put it back onto the plate.

"Aren't you going to eat any of that?" I asked him.

He looked up at me, his eyes like bottomless pools of sadness. "Just not hungry," he grumbled. He laid the fork down next to his plate and picked up his glass of juice. He took a sip and put it down again.

"Michael, you have to eat something," I told him.

He shrugged once more and tapped his finger against the side of the juice glass.

"I've got an idea," I said to him, trying to keep my tone light and upbeat. "How about if you get cleaned up and get dressed and we go down to the supermarket together? You can pick out anything you like for supper tonight. You can pick your favorite things. I won't even check to see if you're having a balanced meal. Then, we'll go to the video store and rent some movies to watch and we can get a hamburger for lunch somewhere. How's that sound?"

Finally, his expression changed and a glimmer of a smile appeared on his face. "I'd like that a lot," he told me.

At the moment he spoke, a sharp crack sounded in the kitchen. The breakfast plate in front of Michael suddenly snapped in two. The two sides with sharpened edges flipped over backward towards Michael and scattered pancakes, butter and syrup in all directions. Michael reeled back from the table. Suddenly his chair tipped up and back, balancing on only one of the legs. It spun around and pitched him hard onto the floor. The orange juice glass sprang from the table and shattered against one of the cabinets. His fork vibrated and shot off the table. It came to rest imbedded in the wall.

I jumped out of my chair and grabbed for Michael. I was too slow. I didn't reach him until he was already sprawled on the floor. Kneeling down I quickly gathering him up in my arms; I held onto him for dear life, refusing to let the spirits get to him again. If I had to shelter him with my own body, I would do so. I had finally seen a glimmer of hope on the boy's face and I didn't dare lose that again. We held each other in fear and love until the kitchen finally became silent. Then I helped Michael get to his feet. He was shaken, but not crying.

I brushed him off and straightened his pajamas. "Are you okay?" I asked. He simply nodded. I had to get him talking again. The best place to do this, I thought, would be out of the house.

"Come on, Michael," I said, leading him to the stairs. "Let's get you a quick shower and some clean clothes. I'll stand guard. Then we'll both get out of here for a while."

We left the house about thirty minutes later, happy to be away from the place, although no further incidents occurred while we were getting ready. I took Michael to the grocery store where we bought the ingredients for the spaghetti dinner, complete with garlic bread and salad that he requested. This had always been one of Michael's favorite meals. I allowed him to add a chocolate cake for dessert. After that, we picked out some movies at the video store and stopped at his favorite fast food place for lunch. Even though I have always found the food in these places about as appetizing as hunks of plastic, I endured it with a smile for Michael's sake.

I was rewarded. His mood seemed to brighten. Although hardly his former self, he began to talk a little and I even caught him smiling a time or two. However, right before we finished, he suddenly burst into tears. This crying jag lasted for three or four minutes. He had been thinking of Justin, he explained to me.

We were driving home from the restaurant on one of the side streets roughly a mile from our house. As we drove, we passed the cemetery where he'd gone the night before. Michael, buckled into the front seat, suddenly jolted forward against his seat belt. Stunned, I looked over at him and saw that his face had turned very pale and his eyes were round with fear. He began to pant in short, hoarse breaths.

"Michael, what's wrong?" I shouted at him.

"Over there!" he cried.

Suddenly, a dark car, which I hadn't noticed, cut us off. I hit the brakes and swerved my own car wildly trying to avoid a collision. Michael continued to buck against the seatbelt harness. He began to wail like an animal, pointing to something. Terrified that he was having a seizure, I braked harder and quickly steered the car safely to the side of the road along the cemetery fence. I looked down the street, and that's when I finally got a good look at the dark car that had tried to cut us off—a long, black car with dark-tinted windows—speeding away.

❦ 16 ❦

UNDER SIEGE

M ore terror followed. Each night, Bruce and I took turns
sleeping on a cot we had set up in Michael's room.
Neither of us got much sleep, whether it was our turn to stand
guard or not. During the night, objects flew about the room,
sometimes finding their targets. Unfortunately, these targets
seemed to be us! The blankets were pulled off Michael's bed and
off the cot. The closet door banged open and closed continuously, as did the dresser drawers.

On the sixth night of our vigil, I was exhausted and
Bruce had to go out of town again. My mother agreed to come
over and stay with us for the night. "Go to bed. You look
exhausted," she said. "Let me take over."

After making sure that Michael was in bed and asleep,
she turned off most of the lights, keeping a small night light on,
and lay down on the cot. I followed her into the room and, after
helping her get settled, I left, closing the door behind me. I had
gone no more than a few steps down the hallway when I heard a
tremendous thud in Michael's room.

I ran back and threw open the door. My mother was sprawled on the floor at the foot of the cot crying loudly. I went to her. Michael sat up in bed, rubbing his eyes sleepily, confused about all the noise.

Through her tears, Mom quickly explained that she had just lain down when the covers were jerked off her. She had reached down to pull them back up, only to have them once again yanked away. This time, she managed to hold onto them as they were whisked off her body. Her hands gripped the ends, and she held on as hard as she could. Suddenly, the tugging stopped and she managed to regain control of the covers once more. However, before she could savor this small victory, she felt what she described as "ice cold hands" grabbing her ankles. The invisible hands yanked hard and dragged her from the cot. As Mom landed hard on the floor, she felt the hands let go.

"Just moments before you came back into the room, I heard a low, menacing growl from the shadows," she said. Like us, she learned her lesson about trying to win a battle with Michael's "bad people."

On the eighth night of our vigil, they decided to try and get to Michael again.

We had all been up late that evening, attempting to have a normal night together. Bruce and I and the kids had ordered pizza and rented a movie. After the movie, we played several rounds of board games, simply enjoying a distraction from the edgy atmosphere of the house. Even Michael began to show a spark of life and we were able to coax a few smiles out of him. I put the kids to bed that night with a feeling that perhaps everything was going to be alright after all. We still planned to maintain our watch in Michael's room, but we figured that he would be okay for a few hours while the adults stayed downstairs to talk.

We were mistaken.

About forty minutes after the kids went to bed, Bruce and I were sitting in the living room drinking coffee. The television set was on, but we weren't really watching it. Instead, we were talking about anything other than the disturbing problems we had with Michael. Although he was our son and a common bond, his plight was something we needed to stop discussing at least for a few moments.

Bruce was in the middle of a sentence when suddenly the television snapped off and the room was plunged into silence. Neither of us spoke as, one by one, the lights in the house began to go out. A banging sound began. "It sounds like it's coming from the basement," I whispered.

At the pounding on the stairs, we started.

Someone in heavy boots seemed to be coming up the wooden steps. The overhead fixture in the kitchen snapped off. The small light over the stove began to flicker off and then on again, like a lantern flame in a wind storm. The banging sound grew louder. It turned into a knocking noise. This time, it seemed to come from the other side of the basement door.

Bruce swore. He got up from his chair and angrily marched into the kitchen. He grabbed hold of the basement door knob. "I'm going down there to confront the spirits at their own game," he shouted angrily. He twisted the knob and jerked the door. I watched as some unseen force pushed against him, shoving him back two steps and against the wall. A cold wind whipped around him, causing his hair to fly back and his trousers to whip about his legs.

All around him the kitchen seemed to vibrate. Dishes and pots and pans rattled and trembled. Cabinet doors swung slowly outward as if they were being pulled by some magnetic force. A staccato tapping came from the room and the chairs around the kitchen table quivered backward several feet, pulsating to a rhythm we could not hear. The atmosphere literally seemed alive with energy. The kitchen was plunged into darkness and an arctic chill permeated the air in the room. Bruce's breath clouded around him as he looked around in angry bewilderment.

The family room went dark. As on the night of the final investigation with the ghost hunters, an invisible but overpowering presence emerged from the lower regions of the house and was coming close to us.

Suddenly, picture frames and knickknacks began to rattle and shake as though a small earthquake had attacked our house. Bruce ran into the family room. As I followed, I watched a photo frame sail off a table and skitter along the top of his head. He cried out and ducked, narrowly missed by the frame's sharp corners. A small ceramic figure vaulted in Bruce's direction, connecting solidly with his forehead. He yelped in pain and put his hand to his head. When he pulled it away, it was coated with blood.

The air around us was thick and heavy with moisture. It was like being in a humid swamp, although piercingly cold. The frigid blast was now chillingly familiar to all of us. "We have to get upstairs!" I yelled. We had to get to Michael before these things could menace him. I vividly remembered what had happened to the luckless researchers who had been in Michael's room that night.

Terrified and shocked, I felt myself thrown forward and went sprawling onto the floor. Bruce grabbed my arm and helped me up. We had to get upstairs!

The knocking sounds had turned into a thrumming noise that now reverberated throughout the house. I thought wearily of how many times we had cleaned up and repaired the places we lived in since all this had begun. As we ran, pictures that hung along the stairway wall to the second floor were shaking and vibrating with a horrible urgency. The banging from upstairs could only be the sound of bedroom doors opening and closing along the hallway. We mounted the stairs and collided with Crystal and Kenny, who were on their way down. Bruce grabbed both of them and wrapped his arms around them. I ran to Michael's room, calling back to Crystal to take Kenny down to the family room. They were trembling and terrified. I had seen that too many times in my children not to recognize that panic would quickly set in if we couldn't get this new situation under control. How we were going to do that, however, was beyond my reasoning.

I stumbled toward Michael's room. The thundering in the house was growing louder. Just as we reached for Michael's door, it slammed shut in front of us. Bruce threw the full weight of his body against the wooden panel. The doorframe shook and cracked, but wouldn't budge. Bruce was not about to surrender and hurled his weight against the door once more. This time, the wood splintered and cracked and came away from the frame. The door spun out of the way and we rushed into the room.

Chaos greeted us. The dark room was eerily shadowed by light from a lamp that had been thrown into the corner. Its lampshade lay a dozen feet away. Clothing and toys were scattered everywhere in haphazard piles. Michael's bed was empty. His covers had been thrown off the bed and lay twisted along the floor, again in the shape of a noose. The rapping sounds were even louder here, ringing inside the walls and the ceiling on which was scrawled: HA-HA. WE'VE FOUND YOU. It was signed with the familiar 3 and an eye dripping red tears.

I heard muffled sobbing sounds coming from the closet. Opening the door, I saw Michael and screamed. He wore angry red marks as if someone had raked their fingernails down his face.

"Oh my God," I cried out.

Michael nodded and through his tears wailed, "I've been trying to tell you this house is worse than the old one."

Michael's words about the place we'd rented stayed in my mind all night.

The next morning, after I'd taken Michael and the other kids to school, I decided to stop at the town hall and pull up the records of the Goring's house to see who in the past had owned it. I knew it was public information.

At the front desk I was told to go to the basement where they kept the records. Walking down a creaky stairway, I nervously entered a long room filled with musty documents. The dim light added to the gloom. I asked a very nice elderly woman who smelled of flowery perfume how to trace a house's ownership. She showed me how.

Luckily, I was sitting down as I delved into the record book. I found that the house had been sold back and forth by the Goring family most times for only a dollar, since the early eighteen hundreds. The family members were undertakers. The house had served as a funeral home for many generations.

I ran out of the town hall. I now agreed with Michael. The place into which we had moved was worse than our old house. Out of all the houses I could have rented, I'd picked one belonging to the dead.

"I want to move again," I told Bruce as soon as he got home that evening.

"What's the use, Denice," he said wearily. "They followed us here. They'll follow us everywhere."

And I knew he was right.

It wasn't this or any house that was our main problem.

It was my son. And I was now sure that Kirsten had been right. Those who stalked him were not earthbound ghosts but demons. But why did they want Michael and when would they attack next? How could we keep him safe?

The following day, terror reigned. That afternoon, Michael was going upstairs to do his homework in Kenny's room because he felt so uncomfortable in his own. As he reached the top stair, he called out, "Something is behind me," and when he looked back, he screamed, "The shadow man says he's going to kill me."

As I ran up towards him, he began to topple backward. Somehow, I climbed the steps two at a time and was able to grab him as he fell.

"Michael, calm down," I said, holding him tightly in my arms. "I will protect you."

"No, Mom, you can't," he said. "He will kill me just like he said."

Chills went down my spine. "I won't let it kill you. I promise," I stated.

As soon as Michael had calmed down a bit, I said, "Let's call Grandma and Grandpa to come over. We'll talk about our problem. Remember how they helped you when you first saw the ghost of Grandpa Pierce?" Michael nodded but was silent.

After I called my parents, we went out to the car and waited for their arrival. I honestly did not know if I could stop this thing from harming my baby, but it would have to take me first.

I prayed to God for guidance.

When my parents got there, we waved so they'd see us and then we all went back into the house together.

Sitting in the living room, I explained to my mother with a heavy heart that things were worsening. "They want to get Michael," I said.

"They?" she said questioningly.

"Mom, we don't think they're ghosts. We think they're demons who want to kill Michael."

"But why Michael?" she asked, voicing the question I had asked myself so many times.

I shook my head. "I don't know. I wish I did."

Suddenly, Michael who was sitting next to me started to scream. He thrashed about on the couch. We all watched in horror as a slash as if from a knife appeared on Michael's right arm. The other children froze in fear and started to cry. Michael was screaming, "Help me!" as I tried to push away invisible hands from his arm.

In my fear, my religious training flooded back. I heard myself yell, "In the name of Jesus Christ, I command you to leave my son alone!" I repeated this admonishment three times.

As fast as it had happened, whatever had been there was gone. I held Michael until he calmed down.

"Crystal," I finally said. "Bring some antiseptic and Band-Aids from the bathroom."

Still crying, she returned with them as my mother and the rest of us stared in horror at Michael's arm.

As I cleaned the wound, my mother shook her head. "It's like Michael draws them to him, as if he's some kind of light in the darkness," she said, musing. "But what is that light? And why does he have it?" Her voice shook as she spoke.

"And now they're drawing blood," I said, more afraid than I had ever been.

❧ 17 ❧

No Recess

Not only was Michael besieged at home as he had been in our old house, but now the demons accosted him in other places.

On Wednesday of the week following Michael's cutting, the sound of the telephone ringing startled me. I was sitting on the living room couch poring through some books on the paranormal that I had just brought home from the library.

"Hello?" I answered cautiously.

"Denice?" the voice on the other end of the line queried. "Hi, this is Kathy Ackerman, the social worker from Michael's school."

"Oh hi, Kathy," I replied. "How are you?" Then the thought crossed my mind, *why is she calling me?* "What's wrong? Is there something wrong with the boys?"

"Well, we do have a bit of a problem here," she replied sympathetically. "I was wondering if you could come down to the school now."

"Is Michael hurt?" I asked anxiously.

"No, it's nothing like that. Michael's fine, but I'm afraid that, well, um, Michael's here in my office with me and...." She paused.

"You can't really talk, right?"

"Exactly," Kathy said. "I don't want you to worry all the way down here though. It's not that serious. It's just a problem with Michael's teacher, and, well, things got a little strange. Do you understand what I mean?"

"Yes, I do," I assured her. She was trying her best not to upset Michael, but apparently this had something to do with the supernatural activity surrounding him. I was terrified. Whatever was happening at home seemed to have followed him to school.

"I'll be down there as soon as I can."

I hung up the telephone and ran upstairs to change my clothes. In a few minutes, I was on my way to the school. I parked in the visitor's spot and rushed through the front doors and straight to the social worker's office. The door was partially open, but I tapped on it anyway. Kathy opened it all the way and invited me in. Michael was sitting on a small couch on the left side of the room reading a book. He looked up and gave me a faint smile as I walked in.

"Hi, sweetie," I said to him, then turned to Kathy. She smiled at me and shook my hand.

"How are you, Denice?" she asked me.

"I'm not sure. I'll let you know after I hear what you have to say."

She smiled. "I don't think it's that bad, but you may want to think about keeping Michael home for a couple of days," she told me.

"That sounds bad already."

"Well, let's just say that it was a little upsetting, especially to Susan Leonard," she replied, meaning Michael's reading teacher. We had gone through some difficulties with her in the past. She had been rather impatient with Michael, mostly during the early days with the spirits when we were all trying to understand what was going on in our house. At that point, no one in the family was getting much sleep, especially Michael. Not surprisingly, his schoolwork had suffered badly and he had fallen asleep in class a few times. If not for Kathy Ackerman's understanding and intervention, things probably would have been a lot worse.

"What happened?" I asked her. We moved to the far side of the room and sat down at a small table by the window. It was cluttered with papers, coffee mugs and a laptop computer. Kathy moved the things out of the way and we sat facing each other.

"Well, I had to sort of piece things together from what Michael and Ms. Leonard told me. I really wasn't sure what to think about it at first, but with all of the things you've communicated to me about Michael and, well, the strange incidents—perhaps it will all make sense to you," she said and paused.

What had happened? I wondered. Michael's reading teacher, Ms. Leonard, did not seem to like him much, as he was not "on task" as she called it. She said his mind was never on school. But what could one expect, I wanted to say when she first phoned me about it. He was being emotionally and physically attacked by demons.

"This morning," Kathy began, "Ms. Leonard was in the front of the class when Michael started getting nervous. When she asked him what was wrong, Michael said he saw the shadow demon standing behind Ms. Leonard. There was also a white ball of light, he told her, and the demon then chased the ball of light out of the window. 'Michael, come here,' she told the boy." Kathy paused as if gathering her thoughts. "Well, Michael very slowly walked up to her desk. As he stood next to her, she told me she couldn't shake the feeling that his attention was directed toward someone else who, it seemed, was standing just beyond her left shoulder. Ms. Leonard began to talk to Michael and explained that he needed to pay attention to what was going on in class. 'Do your homework or at least read a book.' Could he do that, she asked him.

"Michael apparently looked at her strangely and then he leaned toward her. 'The Devil and God are fighting over me. The Devil wants to kill me and anyone who gets in his way, you know,' he whispered.

"'What are you talking about?' she asked.

"He repeated his words.

"Unsure of what was happening, but terrified," Kathy continued, "Susan Leonard began to cry and told Michael to leave. Michael knew I was in my office and he ran to me crying about what had happened. I then brought him to the principal's office, and we all sat down to talk about how 'it' had followed him to school.

"The principal, Mrs. Price, as you know, is a very nice person with an open mind. We came to the conclusion that if Michael was scared at anything he was seeing in school, Mrs. Price would give him an open pass allowing him to leave class to go to the office at any time. Mrs. Price said she would inform the teachers about the pass and also walk Michael back to Ms. Leonard's class. She said to reassure Michael that he was not going to be banished from the school as long as she was the principal."

After the meeting, as I drove home, I thought back to what Kirsten had said about demonic entities. I decided to speak with her about Michael and left a message with her service. She called back almost instantly. I was happy about that since I was feeling terribly frightened.

"Why is it following him to school?" I asked.

"Denice, I'm glad you called. Paul and I have thought about your family a lot. As I told you the last time we met, you are dealing almost certainly with a demonic entity. It has no time constraints, it can travel anywhere and it can take any form. I think Michael is beginning to be under possession," she said.

"What does it come from?" I asked.

"It wants to destroy your family and take Michael's soul," she told me, without really answering my question.

"Why Michael?" I asked.

"As I said before, we really don't know why. We cannot see the big picture, but I think Michael is like a torch," Kirsten stated.

"Funny, that's what my mother said." I sighed. "What do we do now?" I asked.

"I think you need to get help. Michael needs an exorcism and as I told you, my father's friend is a bishop. How do you feel about that?" she asked.

"What will happen to Michael during an exorcism?"

"Well, the result of the ritual hopefully will make these things stop coming after him. If you want to do it, you have to discuss this with Bruce and Michael," she said.

"Well, if it will help, I'm all for it, and I know they will be, too," I said.

Kirsten told me, "Gather all of Michael's medical records, psychiatric records and school records and any photos or other documentation you have. Then call me if you want me to approach the bishop."

I paged Bruce right away and told him what had happened at school and Kirsten's recommendations. To my surprise, he said, "Well, let's do it."

"I just want to talk to Michael about it so that he feels he is part of the decision," I said. "After that, I'll call Kirsten and ask her to make the phone call."

That afternoon, when I went back to pick up Michael from school, he had a note from Mrs. Price asking me to come in and see her if I had a minute. I asked Michael if everything had been okay the rest of the day and he said yes. I went into the school and upstairs to the principal's office where the secretary ushered me in immediately.

Mrs. Price said she just wanted me to know that she had spoken with Susan Leonard and her response was that she wanted Michael out of her classroom, because she did not want "it" near her.

I said angrily, "These things don't want her. They want my son. They are not going to just leave us and attach to Ms. Leonard or anyone else or we would not have been going through this for so long." At that moment I wanted to find her and tell her she did not deserve to be a teacher as she had no compassion. You just don't give up on a student when he is having troubles. I understood that Michael's situation was not like the trouble children ordinarily go through, but just the same, you cannot pick and choose whom you will teach. If she could, Ms. Leonard would have only a select few in her classroom.

Michael's principal assured me, "Don't worry. Michael is staying where he belongs. I informed Ms. Leonard the same. I just wanted you to be aware of the situation." I thanked her and left the school, hurting for Michael.

When we got home, I sat Michael down and explained to him what Kirsten had suggested.

He immediately said yes. "Does that mean I will be normal?"

I held him tight. "You are normal. We are just dealing with a terrible thing, something most people won't talk about, but we know it's real."

"Please. Let's do it in a hurry, Mom," he pleaded.

But we had to wait until Kirsten talked to the bishop.

I prayed she would be successful.

❧ 18 ❧

THE EXORCISM

Kirsten came over the next day to say she had talked to the bishop and given him all the evidence I had collected. After viewing it, he had told her he felt Satan was trying to possess Michael and he agreed to perform an exorcism.

Kirsten went on, "The bishop is busy on another matter, but will schedule this for a week from Monday."

She then pulled out five sets of rosary beads. "The bishop wants each family member to have one and to say the rosary together at night."

We took them from her. She also gave us a large bottle of holy water blessed by the bishop and said, "This will help until you can see him."

When she left, questions churned in my mind. Was it possible Michael was possessed by demons? How could this be? Why Michael? Why had he been chosen? He was such a gentle, loving child. Maybe that was the kind of person demons wanted, or maybe it was something else, something no one could figure out. It all seemed so impossible. In fact, our lives seemed impossible to live.

Still, I prayed that Kirsten was right and that the bishop could end our agony.

Bruce and I decided to take the children out for dinner to a neighborhood restaurant and discuss the exorcism in a setting away from the house. As we sat around the table, I explained what was going to happen. "Well, Mikey, what do you think?" I asked, using a name he had long outgrown. "Still want to give it a try?"

"I don't think so," he said with his serious face.

"What?" I burst out.

And then Michael started to laugh. "I was only teasing, Mom."

I got up, went over to his chair and started to tickle him. "Say no, huh?"

We all laughed. It was such a natural, unforced moment that my laughter almost turned to tears. It was so nice to see my family so relaxed, so hopeful again.

Bruce took advantage of the pleasant atmosphere to say, "I'm really glad you can laugh about it, that we all can, but we all know this is a serious matter. We're all suffering, but it's especially hard on you, Michael, so we need to know your feelings."

"If this will make it go away, you don't even have to ask," Michael replied earnestly. "When are we going to do it?"

"Next Monday," I said.

"Good. Now, let's eat." Michael smiled.

What a wonderful way, I thought, children have of adapting to circumstances no matter how stressful and inexplicable. We adults could learn much from them.

We tried to emulate Michael's mood. We ordered a light dinner. We chattered away about what we were going to wear to the bishop's service. Soon it was time for dessert. We ordered ice cream for everyone and Crystal excused herself to go to the ladies room.

Before she returned, we were served the dessert and the boys began spooning it down. Suddenly, Michael let out a piercing scream, jumped out of his seat and ran over to me, brandishing his arm. "They're hurting me again," he yelled. As we all watched, an angry red mark appeared on Michael's arm as if inflicted by unseen hands.

By now I did not care who in the restaurant was watching us. I was angry and scared for my son. "Look what they are doing to him! Why? Why?" I cried.

Bruce shook his head. "Maybe they are angry because of the exorcism. Maybe this is the demon retaliating. We just don't know."

Everyone in that restaurant, many of whom we knew, who had any doubts about our predicament were made believers that night as they witnessed one of the horrible events our family was suffering. Everyone just stared. Two old women came over and touched Michael and asked to see the wound, as if he had some magical powers or bore the stigmata of Christ.

Crystal, who had been standing off to one side, afraid to return, finally came back to the table. As she walked by Michael, she bent to kiss his cheek.

Our family togetherness gave me comfort, but I felt like we were a sideshow. "Please," I said to Bruce. "Let's go."

Bruce quietly paid the check and we all went home.

The next two days went by very slowly as we waited fearfully for more incidents, but things were strangely quiet. On Thursday morning, Bruce decided I needed to relax and he took the children to school. I made myself a cup of tea and picked up the community newspaper. I like the small paper because it is so friendly. There were announcements of events like garden and pet shows and people placed messages for others. As I read through the messages in the Speak Out column, I saw something that shocked me. It was about us.

The Exorcist

Please pray for the Jones family in Manchester. They have negative spirits in their home. They are to have an exorcism next Monday. I'm a neighbor of theirs and this is no joke. Please, everyone, pray for them.

I was concerned who would write in and say this, as I didn't want the bishop to have second thoughts about helping us. *Could they have been witnesses of the scene at the restaurant,* I wondered. *My God, I hope nobody bothers us. That would be too much for Michael,* I thought.

The next day was going fine until I picked up that day's town paper. In it were more messages about my family. The first one said:

The Paranormal

In response to the exorcist, do you mean to tell me at this late stage of human progress that some people still believe in exorcism, Satan and other foolishness? Come on. This is 1998, not 1198. Disregard those childish, superstitious myths.

I felt very upset reading this. I was afraid the kids would see the paper. I did not want to hurt them more. They'd gone through pure hell. I knew there were people who had never experienced this phenomena and didn't believe in it. I hoped that they would always feel that way, because if they changed, that would mean they too were attacked by demons.

On Saturday I read another letter for us:

Exorcism is still an authorized ritual of the Catholic Church. In fact, it's been reported that Pope John Paul II performed an exorcism himself, right in the Vatican in the

1980s. Our prayers are for the family in Manchester. And yes, this is no joke. The people who wrote in don't know what it's like dealing with demons. Their skepticism only feeds the fire and promotes the fear. Many families and individuals have been in your shoes, including ourselves. The bottom line is, you can call in the pope or the marines but the answer to this paranormal phenomena is within yourselves. Only you can take control back from the demons. Fear is not the answer— it only serves as a feeding ground. Let Christ's white light surround your family.

On Sunday, we went to church with my mother, because my father was in the hospital preparing to have a catheter test on his heart. My dad, whose health was deteriorating, told me if he died even for a second during the test he would pass over to my house, kick the hell out of the demons and make them leave. He was being funny, but I knew if he could do something like that, he would. With all her worry about Dad's health, my mother really needed a few extra prayers. I also wanted to tell the priest that the bishop was going to give us the help we needed.

However, as we all walked into the church, the priest looked at us strangely, almost as if he did not want us near him, so I never approached him. On the way home from church, Michael and I were talking.

"Mom," he said, "can we move from our house again?"

"Michael, you know if we move they will only follow us again," I replied.

"No," he said. "When the exorcism is over and they are gone, can we move? I want to be able to go into my room and feel safe again."

It was then I turned away and started to cry silently so Michael would not see my tears. I prayed the bishop would be able to stop my child's pain. Somehow, we all got through the remaining hours and went to bed. Now we had only a matter of hours left to wait....

Finally it was here, the day for which we had all been waiting. Everyone was very nervous. Michael had on his white dress shirt with an angel pin my mother had given him specially for the occasion. Hung around his neck was one of the rosaries the Bishop had given us. He looked young, innocent and fearful as he said to me, "Maybe *they* are gone since nothing happened last night." Then he shook his head and laughed. "Yeah, right." I laughed, too, glad to see that in spite of everything Michael still had a sense of humor.

In the car, as we began the journey to the church, our spirits were high although we said little. All was quiet; each one of us lost in his or her own thoughts. Most of mine were prayers for my son and our future.

The trip went uneventfully until we were about ten miles from our destination. A large, black sedan tried to cut us off, almost forcing our car off the road. I shuddered as Bruce swerved just in time.

"What was that?" Michael called out from the back seat where his brother and stepsister were dozing.

"Nothing," I shushed him. "It's going to be a long day. You ought to take a nap, too." I threw a frightened glance at Bruce, who had taken his eyes off the road for a moment and nodded at me. I nodded back and saw his lips tighten as he turned his eyes back to the road.

The feeling of tension mounted during the remainder of the trip.

Finally, we entered Lynn, Connecticut, a quaint old town, the kind you see in photographs of New England in the early twentieth century. I had always wished to live in that picturesque era and here I was entering it, but unable to enjoy the scenery.

It was exactly ten o'clock when we began climbing the steps of the large, old white church. A cemetery filled with headstones and flower offerings was off to the right and a large statue of the Virgin Mary, her arms outstretched, stood on the front lawn.

We were greeted at the door by Bishop Carey, a small man with snow white hair dressed in purple vestments. He looked wan as he had to fast for three days prior to performing an exorcism. With him was Father Tom, a young dark-haired priest who obviously lifted weights or had been a football player. Yet even in the bishop's frailness, the quiet man had a calm, soothing presence and an inner strength that made me feel loved just by talking to him.

However, when he asked Michael, "What is happening to you, son?" Michael clammed up. The boy was now petrified.

"It's alright," the bishop assured Michael, patting his shoulder. "I already know. I just want to make you comfortable. I have heard you are being besieged by demons, but Michael," he inclined his head toward the boy, "whether they are within or without, God can repel them. You know that, don't you?" Michael nodded, his face solemn, his eyes wide.

But I felt my child's fear and pain. Michael was such a gentle, innocent, loving child. Why would demons attack him? It was a question I had wrestled with since the beginning. Then again, perhaps that was the exact kind of child they chose to target and corrupt if they could. I prayed that God wouldn't let that happen and that the bishop could end the terror we, but especially Michael, had been going through once and for all. After all, if we believed there could be demonic intervention then we had to believe there could be divine intervention as well.

Next the bishop instructed us as to our places during the ceremony. "Michael, you sit in the front pew with your mother on your left and your stepfather on your right." The other children and my mother were to sit in the row behind us. Then Bishop Carey draped a purple surplice around his neck and he and the other priest, Father Tom, knelt in front of the church with their backs to us. Afterward, the bishop blessed Michael with holy water, making the sign of the cross over my son as he prayed in Latin. Next, both priests prayed over Michael and the bishop wrapped Michael's head with his purple robes as he continued to pray. "Be gone now," the bishop admonished and sliced the air with his hand, once again making the sign of the cross. "Be gone, thou seducer. Thy place is in solitude, thy dwelling in the serpent. Humble thyself and fall prostrate! The matter brooks no delay. For behold, the Lord, the Ruler comes quickly."

After a half hour or so I saw that Michael's eyes glistened with unshed tears and that he was trembling. The bishop must have seen it also as he paused several times to ask Michael if he was okay. My son gave a small nod each time, but maintained the same silence that had gripped him since we entered the church. I sensed something was wrong. Bishop Carey told us that he prayed the ritual would give Michael the strength to fight back against the demons and drive away their evil influences.

Michael solemnly nodded. Then the bishop began the most powerful part of the ritual.

"I cast thee out, thou unclean spirit," the bishop entoned in Latin. "Along with the last encroachment of the wicked enemy and every phantom and diabolical legion."

He leaned close to Michael and once again made the sign of a cross over him. "Depart and vanish from this creature of God," the bishop continued. "For it is He who commands thee. He who ordered thee cast down from the heights of heaven and into the nethermost pit of the earth."

Then the bishop reached forward and placed his thumb against Michael's forehead tracing the sign of the cross three times—once for God the Father, once for God the Son and once for the Holy Spirit. "Wherefore get thee gone in the name of the Father, Son and the Holy Spirit. Make way for God the Holy Spirit through this sign of the Holy Cross of our Lord Jesus Christ, who liveth the self same Holy Spirit, God, forever and ever."

"Amen," entoned Father Tom.

"Amen," we echoed.

"O Lord, hear my prayer," the bishop prayed.

And Father Tom responded again, "And let my cry come unto thee." Then Father Tom, standing in front of Michael, said, "The Lord be with you."

And the bishop ended, "And with thy spirit."

Tears fell from my eyes the whole time the ritual was going on. I was scared, excited and very much grateful to this man of God who was helping my son. I watched Michael closely as the bishop finished his prayers. Michael looked scared and for some reason, kept looking toward the far left corner of the church. I leaned toward my son. "Is everything alright, honey?"

He shook his head. "No Mom, the shadow man is over there watching us and he looks very angry," he whispered. Then he added, "My stomach is burning. I think I am going to be sick."

The bishop, who had heard Michael's last words, sent Father Tom to get a cup of holy water. When Father Tom returned, the bishop said to Michael gently, "Michael, please drink this."

As Michael was drinking the holy water, I felt a breeze brush by my face and with it I was surprised to feel an overwhelming sense of calm and love.

The bishop then talked to us and said, "I hope that it worked. Sometimes people need two or even three exorcisms. Remember, the closer you get to God, the harder the demons will try."

I nodded and asked the bishop, "May I kiss your ring?"

"Yes," he said and I did, feeling honored. Then the bishop told us three to kneel by him as he recited the Lord's prayer.

Afterward I asked if we could give him a check for the church.

"Your love is all I need," he replied.

I assured him he had that.

We left the church feeling elated. Even Michael looked happy and somehow, despite the shadow man's appearance, peaceful.

In the car on the way home, I asked Michael how he was feeling and he said, "Mom, it was funny. Not ha-ha funny. Strange funny. I felt this really good wind cleaning my face." I smiled at him. *So he had felt it, too.*

Michael smiled back. "And..."

"And what?"

"I know now."

"What do you know?" I asked, still not understanding.

"Even if the demons come, I am not alone." Suddenly he gazed at me and spoke with a wisdom beyond his years. "None of us are ever alone."

❦ 19 ❧

FRENZY

After the exorcism, tranquility settled over the house. We all got comfortable going upstairs alone and even sleeping in our own beds. Was it permanent or would it be like the other times, a short interlude followed by an avalanche of violence? I could not be sure, but I tried to believe in our blessing while still remaining vigilant.

One night, while the boys were in the family room quietly playing a boardgame, Crystal came running downstairs. "Guess what's on 104 FM, my favorite station," she said. "Us!"

"Us?" I asked.

"Yeah. They're reading these Speak Out columns about us and talking about the paranormal."

I felt my face turning red. I wondered if our neighbors would be listening and talking about us more than they already were.

What I hadn't contemplated, however, began the next morning when the publicity started a media frenzy. Reporters from the local newspapers were gathered at my door. One of the reporters, Katie Roberts, asked me if I wanted to let other people who might have suffered as we had know that there is help out there and not to be afraid. I thought of the bishop and his help and what it had meant to us and I agreed to be interviewed. Once the column came out in the local papers, other newspapers began calling. We heard from the *Hartford Courant*, *New York Post* and the Associated Press all in one day.

I was devastated, however, when the papers came out and I saw that they had done a hatchet job on the bishop and disputed the exorcism he had performed on Michael. According to the reports, whatever ritual was performed on Michael was not sanctioned by the Church because Bishop Carey, who told reporters he had been a priest for forty years and had been made a bishop in France, had been ostracized by much of the Church's hierarchy for resisting the Vatican II reforms of the 1960s. He was best known, said one article, for performing perhaps hundreds of exorcisms. Bishop Carey told the newspapers he performed the rituals because the establishment "shies away from them, leaving people nowhere to turn." I bit my lip and read on. Most of those criticizing the bishop weren't acquainted with him or they would have been praising the pious, caring priest instead of calling him a defrocked rebel. Not only did they put down the bishop who took his time and love to help us, they were going against what the Bible says. I went to get mine and reread Mark 9:38-40:

> *And John answered him, saying, Master, we saw one casting out devils in thy name, and he followeth not us: and we forbad him, because he followeth not us.*

> *But Jesus said, Forbid him not: for there is no man which shall do a miracle in my name, that can lightly speak evil of me.*

> *For he that is not against us is on our part.*

I felt very angry and hurt and wondered if I should ever talk to the press again. Nevertheless, by the next morning, even more reporters appeared at my door. I decided I had to try to clear the bishop's good name and forcefully gave them my opinion on his goodness. The reporters wanted to talk to the bishop again, but he now refused to comment, having learned the secret I did not yet know: that most reporters have their own angle and will write what they want and cut out the rest. All my sticking up for the bishop and the quote I gave from the Bible was never put in any of the articles. I was saddened that so wonderful a man was so woefully portrayed. As I watched my son and saw his newfound confidence that whatever he had to face his family and God were with him, I knew it was the bishop's exorcism which had brought Michael this good news.

Even when the principal of Michael's school called to let me know that a lot of parents who knew about the situation were having their children wear crosses to school and demanding that Michael not be allowed to go anywhere near them, I was upset but Michael assured me he would be fine. And, strangely enough, he was.

As national television offers and the news barrage escalated, my mind was occupied elsewhere. I was waiting to see if the demons would return. It was a week later that I got my answer.

That Friday evening, Bruce was still at work when I brought the children home from visiting my parents, where we had an early dinner. I decided to sit down with the children and say the rosary as the bishop had asked. Since the exorcism, the children wanted to get as close to God as they could. It was a nice thing, I thought, to have the children aware of His help. It was the bishop's message to us.

"I'll start," Michael said and began to pray, his sweet voice almost musical. We all chimed in, then took turns. We were about halfway done when we heard a strange groan come from Michael's throat. We all looked at him and saw his face changing. Before our eyes, his color became a dark gray and his eyes seemed to sink in their sockets and become an even darker gray. I tried not to show my fear. I had the holy water that the bishop had given us close by.

"Please go on, Mom," Michael begged as I dipped my fingers in the water and splashed him. I then prayed in a stronger voice, but after a few more Hail Marys, Michael started to cry. Tears rolled down his cheeks. I stopped. "Are you alright, Michael?"

He shook his head. "The shadow man is walking around us calling my name."

Suddenly I heard a smacking sound and saw Michael's cheek turn red. He screamed the words he had learned from the bishop. "In the name of Jesus Christ, I command you to leave me alone!"

I grabbed the holy water, splashed him again and screamed with him for *it* to leave. I was so proud of Michael for his bravery.

"Please Mom, keep praying," Michael said, his voice rising. We continued saying the rosary, our voices getting louder and louder. We were now at the end, screaming the prayers when Michael cried out, "I feel dizzy and weak." As soon as he said that, he fell to the floor on his knees. He looked like death. Suddenly he cried out again, "Mom, the shadow man is throwing something in my eyes." A few seconds later he cried, "I'm blind. I can't see!"

Kenny and Crystal began to panic. Michael's hands were frantically searching for the chair in front of him. I threw holy water on his face and his sight came back. A few moments later he screamed again that he was blind and cried out, "The demon is real mad. He says he's coming and he will kill me this time." I bathed his face in the holy water and his sight returned for good.

But that night there was no peace. The bad spirits returned angrier than ever. I ran back and forth between Crystal and Kenny, who insisted on sleeping downstairs, to Michael's room, where he insisted on sleeping. "I won't let them win," he said. Indeed, when I got there, Michael had fallen asleep with his day clothes on. I decided not to wake him. Exhausted, I finally fell asleep on the floor in the corner of Michael's room. I don't know how long I slept when I heard a blood-curdling scream. "They're trying to smother me," Michael yelled out.

I shook myself awake and rushed to his side. "What? Who?" I asked.

"The shadow man was here with all his ghosts. One had blood dripping from his head. The shadow man was flying over me. He tried to lay on top of me and smother me. He kept yelling, 'Die!'"

I lay down beside my son watching for what seemed like hours. Sometime before dawn I must have dozed off as Michael woke me up crying again that there was something in the room. He described it as red with a black lining that look like muscles without skin. "And in the corner there's hissing smoke. Over there near the lamp," he pointed, "See?"

I got up to check and saw with shock that the electrical socket in the room was blackened with soot. I checked the others. They were all the same—as though they had been on fire.

Then I realized I had forgotten one thing the bishop had told us. It came flooding back to me now: when you get closer to God, the demons will retaliate—and that is exactly what they did.

During the next week I agonized over what to do next as the attacks not only continued, but escalated.

Kenny stayed home from school that Friday as his class was taking a field trip that he just didn't want to go on. He was helping me straighten the kitchen. I was happy he was home so I could do laundry. In this house, the washer and dryer were in the basement and since Mary's attack in the previous house, I refused go down to even this cellar on my own. I asked Kenny to go to his room and get me his dirty laundry. As he passed the open cellar door, I heard "Oh my God" and then I heard nothing. I spun around and ran across the kitchen towards Kenny's voice. As I got close to him, Kenny slammed the cellar door closed and grabbed me saying, "We have to get out, Mom, we have to get out!"

I was trying to get him to stop pulling at me. "Calm down. What is the matter?"

"GET OUT! MOVE!" he screamed. I grabbed my purse off the counter and ran outside with him. There was no way he would tell me what was wrong while we were still inside the house.

As we stood on the porch, he explained, "There was a very tall shadow in the shape of a man walking up the cellar stairs towards me. Mom, they want me too now. I can't go back in." I was frantic, but I had to stay calm for Kenny's sake. Yet I could not calm Kenny enough to get him to go back into the house until the other children were home from school.

That night, there was again no peace. This time, however, it was Crystal who saw horrible things, huge balls of light and ghosts.

The next night was no better. Michael went up to his room early saying he was too tired to watch his favorite television show with us. Not even a half hour went by when he cried out. As I ran upstairs he screamed again, then the scream broke and there was silence as if he had stopped breathing. I rushed into his room and Michael was gulping for air. Going over to the bed, I clasped him in my arms. "What happened?"

"The shadow man tried to strangle me," he gasped, pointing to his neck. I looked closer and on either side was the mark of a hand.

"But how did you get away?" I asked, stunned.

Michael looked at me. "Grandpa and Justin came and made him leave."

As I held him I asked myself, *what really happened in this room? Had the spirit of Michael's dead friend and my grandfather appeared and stopped the attack?* I had learned long ago in our haunting that anything was possible. I just wasn't sure I was ready for this.

One thing I was sure about was that Michael had almost been strangled and something had made the attackers stop. I was also sure that whatever it was had a positive effect on my son, who went back to sleep. Though all was quiet, I stayed by his side the rest of the night. But I knew as I lay there and agonized that though this time the demons had gone, they would surely return to try to accomplish the task at which they had thus far failed— killing my son.

❧ 20 ❧

HELP FROM BEYOND

The next morning, confused and tired, I called my parents. I felt I had to be the one to tell them that though the exorcism had taught Michael, and through him all of us, that God was with us, it had not banished the demons.

I also wanted to go over with them what Michael had said about Justin and his great grandfather stopping the attack on him. "Mom and Dad, could you come over? I really need support." They said they would come immediately.

An hour later, my parents and I sat on deck chairs on the back patio discussing the strange and alarming events of the night before.

"I feel like something heavy is crushing my heart," I said. "What has Michael done? What have we all done to deserve this torment? Were we bad in another life? Why us? Why us?" I kept asking.

"Denice, you and the boys are wonderful caring people. It's nothing you've done. I'm sure of that," my mom said and shook her head as we watched Kenny and Michael quietly playing in the yard. I marveled again at the children's resilience.

While I felt tired and discouraged, they seemed to have returned to their child's world with few ill effects.

"Perhaps," my dad said, "Michael is being tried."

"But why," I said. "Why?"

"That is the question, isn't it," my dad mused.

"And what about what Michael said about Justin and Grandpa stopping the attack? Do you think that could be true?"

My mother looked searchingly at me and then off in the distance as if her thoughts were far away.

Minutes passed in silence. Then my mother said, "Denice, I know this is going to sound crazy," she spread out her hands, "but then this whole thing is..." She paused and shook her head.

"Please," I said, "go on. I'm willing to try anything."

"Well," she continued, "do you remember when Michael was born? He was so ill and you asked for your grandfather's help..."

"Yes," I responded, "I've thought of that often."

"What if we call on Justin and your grandfather to come to your aid now?"

"Ourselves? But how?" I asked.

"We'll hold a kind of séance and ask them to come to us."

My father looked shocked at Mom's suggestion, but he didn't disagree.

"Let's go to the library. There must be some book on what we need."

"When should we do it?" I murmured.

"Today," my mom broke in. "The sooner the better."

I nodded.

Dad agreed to watch the kids and Mom and I headed to the library. Indeed, she was right. We found a book titled *Spirit Summoning,* which had a wealth of information.

"We'll pick up what we need on the way home," I suggested. Scanning the pages, I made a list. We were able to buy the candles and sea salt, which the book said was for purification, at the grocery store. I already had the holy water, breadcrumbs and prayer book and we bought the silver and metal crosses at a religious store in the area.

When we got home, I told the kids about our plans and called Bruce at work. Then Mom convinced me to try to take a nap. "You look so tired and we could have a long night ahead." I nodded and lay down on the couch in the living room. Soon Michael, who had come in to keep me company, was peacefully sleeping. I tried to relax. My body was like a live wire, anxious and excited, yet frightened of the events to come. For a long while, I drifted in and out of sleep worrying over Michael and the rest of my family.

A clap of thunder startled me. A storm had begun to settle in over the area. A glance at the clock told me that it was almost 7:00 in the evening. Michael had switched the television and a nearby lamp on. He was sitting on the floor eating dinner from a tray my mother had brought him and watching a cartoon. As I was sitting up, the television and lamp both flickered, then went out. A moment later they came back on again.

Michael turned and looked at me. He gave a weak grin. "The storm's getting bad. The lights keep going out and there's lots of thunder and lightening outside."

"Come here," I told him with a smile and patted the couch cushion beside me.

He hopped up onto the couch. He snuggled close to me and as I hugged him I inhaled the scent of his hair. *I won't be able to do this much longer*, I thought. *It won't be long until he's too old to cuddle with his mom on the couch.* I held him a little apart and looked into his face. "Are you nervous about the séance?" I asked, watching him.

"Maybe a little," he said, "but I'll be glad to talk to Justin and Grandpa."

"They might not come," I said.

"I think they will," he said firmly.

I stood up and went over to the table where I'd put the bag with the items we bought. Reaching inside, I took two of the silver crosses on chains I'd brought home. "I want you to put one on and I will, too."

He nodded as we both hung crosses around our necks. "I have something, too. I'll get it and show you," he said and left.

A few minutes later, Michael ran back into the room. In his hands he held a crooked wooden crucifix. I had seen it before. Justin had given it to me to give to Michael the afternoon Justin had died. Justin had made it to protect his friend.

"I thought you had that all wrapped up with the other things," I said. I recalled seeing it in the drawer in Michael's desk. Nearby on his shelf were the toys which had all been gifts from Justin. Michael had wrapped them all in clear plastic to preserve them in the condition they were when his friend had last handled them.

"I did, but Justin told me last night to unwrap everything and keep his things around me. He said that would make him happy."

"I'm sure that's so, Michael," I said and then I remembered the tasks I needed to complete. "Would you like to help prepare the house for the séance?"

Michael nodded. We began in the basement, where I hated to go. I steeled myself spreading the sea salt in the corners of the room and placing candles as the book instructed.

"This is where the bad people come in," Michael told me.

I winced. "What makes you say that?"

"I just know, that's all."

I crossed my arms in front of my chest as a chill rippled through my body. When we finished spreading the salt and placing candles in the basement, we did the same thing in the other rooms of the house.

Bruce arrived home from work and helped us gather the others. I placed more candles in a circle on the dining room table. Nearby I put three metal crosses, a crucifix, the bottle of holy water, my prayer book and the rest of the sea salt. I turned off the phone and stopped the clock that chimed. We all stood around the table. "Please place both your hands on the tabletop. Let us meditate silently for a few minutes." Now we were ready to begin…or at least as ready as we would ever be.

I looked at Michael whose face was stoic, and was proud once again of his bravery. Bruce handed me a box of kitchen matches and I began to light the candles. Then I picked up the prayer book.

"In the name of the Father, and of the Son, and of the Holy Ghost. Amen," I read and took the bottle of holy water splashing it in front and around me so it touched us all. We all bowed our heads. "We ask that Your Divine Spirit be present and watch over our work tonight."

I went on. "I call upon Thee and I suppliantly invoke Thy holy name and the compassion of Thy radiant majesty that would lend my family aid against the spirit of iniquity, that wherever He may be when Thy name is spoken He may at once give place and give flight—"

From the corner of the room came a hissing sound. We all looked up and at each other. I shuddered, but continued.

"—and the spirits of thy faithful departed, Justin Kelly and Grandpa Alan Collier Pierce come to us so that they may tell us why the demons beset us and especially my son, Michael."

The wind that had been blowing outside the house became a mighty roar resonating in my ears. As I continued, the storm outside intensified. "Let us pause as we let our consciousness expand so we are open to their surrounding vibration and energies." Silence filled the room.

"Thou are bidden in the name of our Lord, Jesus Christ, who will come to judge the living and the dead."

As these last words left my lips, the floor beneath our feet began to shake and Michael stepped closer to me. Never had I seen his face so intense and determined. He stood there solid as a rock, his eyes squeezed tight, his knuckles whitening around the edges of Justin's crucifix. "Come," he called out.

At that same moment, I was startled by a sudden flash of lightning outside. It was followed by a crack of thunder so intense it must have been directly above us. The entire house shook from its power.

A heartbeat later...the lights went out. I was suddenly very dizzy, but felt a rush of adrenaline course through me. Within seconds in the darkened room in which only the candles shone, an aura of white light appeared. Looking around, I saw it did not come from any natural or electrical source. It came instead from two forms which now began to materialize in front of us. It was almost too bright for me to make out their features, but slowly I saw them take shape. Then I realized the shimmering figures were my grandfather and Justin.

I rubbed my eyes almost not, despite my prayers, believing they were standing there in front of us. I was shocked, not sure what to do or say. The luminous form that was Justin spoke first.

"Remember when you needed to comfort Michael about my death and you felt a hand upon your shoulder? That was me." He smiled.

No one else knew what I had felt that night. Suddenly, I knew it was true. This was Justin and my Grandfather. I found my own voice. "If you can hear me, please help Michael," I beseeched them. "Please help us all to understand what we can do and why evil spirits want my son."

My grandfather stepped forward and once again the scent of his minty aftershave filled the air.

"Denice, Michael has a gift. It is the gift of the Third Eye."

I inclined my head not really understanding. It was as if he immediately sensed my puzzlement. He explained.

"According to this theory, originally there was a special organ in human beings which brought them past the material world and into the realm of ethers. The third eye was originally the only eye used in the Cyclops. Then man gained two physical eyes and the original one was spread over the nervous system. In Egypt, once the Pharoahs were trained to use it, a knob was placed on their statues or a serpent's head was carved above the pharoah's head. In China, the mandarin wore a peacock's feather in his headdress to show the third eye reborn.

"Though the third eye is now dormant, it can be reawakened and in a few, it already is. The person who has the eye is able to 'see' vibrations invisible to others, the creatures and activities of the realm of ethers. Thus he will, when mature, understand the causes and realities of life—he will see truth. And since truth is the essence of purity, only a special being pure in motive and heart will be able to contact this realm. Since the function quality of the heart is love—it is this which holds life together and the person who possesses such a heart will have direct access to the divine spirit of love and truth. He will understand the past and see the future.

"All of us are at differing stages on this path, but those born with pure hearts may reach the destination through the purity of their love. Michael is such a being and with the right training and development, his third eye will open wide and he will see in ways those who are blind to all but the physical world cannot."

But how is this possible? I wondered.

As if hearing my unspoken question, once again he explained: "The first step is to put his mind in order so it works clearly, dispassionately and gives the true perspective on life. Michael must eliminate the poisons of hate, fear, anger, greed and envy and attain absolute faith. To do so, he must fight the demons. With these experiences and the trials of his suffering, through his free choice he will be able to grow, to learn and to choose wisely.

"Without resisting Satan's temptations and experiences, choice would mean nothing. Remember, once, Satan was God's angel. He was in charge of Karma and numbers. He gave out the lawful effects of unbalance. But Satan fell from grace when he desired to be a law unto himself and gathered his staff of demons to do his bidding.

"Since then, as Michael has told you, God and the Devil have been warring and he is quite right that they now war over him."

I nodded, remembering Michael saying that.

Grandfather went on: "From the day of Satan's original treachery until now, elements of the world have been racked by fanaticism, oppression and dictatorship. However, a higher form of learning and teaching will bring regeneration and renaissance which will vanquish the illusion of division and unite people into one Whole.

But how and when will that happen? I asked myself thinking about our world today.

Grandpa spoke again: "This will come about when the Third Eye is reborn and linked with the highest creative force in the universe. That is why Satan must, if he is to triumph, stop those to whom it is given. For he wishes the gift of cosmic consciousness only for himself. If he can capture Michael and possess the Third Eye, he will not only know the whys and wherefore of the universe but be able to predict the future and turn it to his own use. He will achieve his ultimate aim to be master of the universe and its beings will do his bidding and be his slaves for eternity."

Is that why Michael is being attacked?

Once again, Grandpa picked up the thread of my thought.

"For this reason Michael is besieged by Satan's demons. To gain the full vision of his third eye he must tread a path on which there are many pitfalls, dangers and illusions. And on this journey, not only now but in the future, he will be cunningly assailed. Nevertheless, if he remains pure of heart, his honesty and faith will enable him to reach and recognize Truth. He must learn to be 'wise as a serpent and harmless as a dove,' a reservoir of love and a creative constructor. After he comes to maturity at age fourteen, he must retain pure motives and not desire power over others, but understand the Great Law which stipulates free will to all. Remember, if Michael is completely honest and wholeheartedly trusts in the power of Good, no demons, no evil force or astral horror can— in the ultimate battle—overcome him. For as the Bible says, 'according to thy faith be it done unto thee.'"

What does he have to do? I asked so softly none of the others heard me.

"To ward off the demons' attacks, Michael needs only to cleanse his own heart of fear, doubt or ulterior motives. If he does this, God's grace can and will protect him. I promise you, the power to do battle, to overcome and to master his own stars lies within him. 'Resist the Devil and he will flee from you.'"

I prayed he was right, for we, especially Michael, were being attacked unmercifully. I silently pleaded, *Please help us. Michael needs you. Our family needs you.*

Michael looked at me. "It's alright Mom, you don't have to speak with your mouth if you don't want to. All you have to do is think what you want to say and they will answer you through your head."

I nodded. *So that is how Grandpa understood my earlier questions.*

"But how are they going to help us? Help you?" I asked, unable to stop myself from crying.

"I don't know, but they say they will," Michael nodded.

"And Mom, in answer to your other question—the one you didn't ask—Justin says I will live to be very old, because I have much work to do."

I smiled. "Tell him I love him and I love Grandpa, too."

"They know Mom. They know."

Michael smiled back at me as the shimmering figures faded. It was over.

A short while later, Michael asked if he could go to his room. I nodded and asked if he wanted me or one of his siblings to go with him. He shook his head. "No. I need to be alone. First, I want to write a letter to Justin's mother and tell her he's okay and that he loves her."

I was surprised that he didn't want to be accompanied, but agreed and said, "I'll stop in later just to see that you're alright."

"You don't have to do that," he insisted. "I am fine now. Remember, I have a lot of work to do."

He looked so serious, so grown up, that I had to smile.

I brought out cookies and milk for the other children and tea for the adults. After the snack, my parents went home and somehow we all settled down. Before I went to my room, I checked on Michael who was sitting at his desk writing. "Mom, I'm fine," he repeated. "Please get some sleep."

After the excitement of the evening, I thought it best to let him unwind in his own way and didn't admonish him about the lateness of the hour. Tomorrow would be Sunday anyway and he could sleep in. I gave him a last kiss and went to my own room. Bruce was there, already asleep. I quietly undressed and went to the window to see how the storm was progressing. I was surprised to see it had apparently ended. All was calm. Climbing into bed, I fell into a deep, exhausted sleep, never imagining that the quiet outside was merely the lull before the full brunt of the tempest unleashed its fury.

How long my sleep swirling with dreams lasted, I am not sure, but I awakened to find myself being shaken. "What's the matter?" I asked groggily as my eyes focused and I saw it was Kenny.

"It's Michael," Kenny said. "He's gone."

I bolted upright. "Gone? But where? When?"

Kenny, who had begun crying, shook his head. "I don't know. I heard a noise from his room and I went to see what was wrong. He wasn't there."

Getting out of bed, I stumbled to Michael's room. His bed was empty, the covers thrown back. I looked around. Nothing seemed disturbed except the desk drawer, which had been sticking lately. It lay on the chair. The contents had fallen on the floor. Without thinking, I walked over to pick them up and noticed that Justin's crucifix was missing. Then I saw a note on the desk:

Justin needs me. I'll be back soon.
M

I began to cry. What did it mean? Where was Michael? A horrible thought struck me. Could the note not be from him? Suddenly, I heard the crack of thunder and the screech of devilish laughter. *Oh my God, the demons!* Trembling, I went back to my room and woke Bruce and then Crystal. We all began to frantically search the house. When we didn't find Michael, Bruce said, "I'm going to search the neighborhood."

"But the storm's starting again."

"I have to go anyway," Bruce said soberly and grabbed his raincoat. "We have to find Michael."

"I'll go with you."

"No. You stay here. He may come back or the police or hospital may call. I'll take the truck so you'll have the car if you need it." With that, he dashed out the door.

I sat at the kitchen table racking my brain. Where was Michael? Was he hurt? Then I remembered the last time Michael had thought Justin wanted his help. That time it had been the demons assuming Justin's form and voice. They were capable of changing form; they could be anything, anywhere, Kirsten had told me. Was it the demons now or really Justin? And could Michael have gone to the cemetery as he had the last time?

I couldn't be sure, but I had to find out. I told Kenny and Crystal to stay in the house and wait for Bruce. Then, quickly running to my room and getting dressed, I got my keys, ran out of the house and jumped in the car. I tried to calm myself as I drove to the cemetery. With the wind and rain so heavy, I could barely see.

Finally there, I brought the car to a stop and unhooked my seat belt. Getting out, I was immediately pelted by chunks of hail as I ran the short distance to the cemetery gate.

To my surprise, it was unlocked and swung open at my touch. Inside, barely able to see between the rain and the darkness, I began calling Michael's name as I ran up and down the paths. I was soaked now and shivering but I couldn't, wouldn't stop.

And then from somewhere behind me, I heard the roar of a car engine. I turned around and mouthed a silent scream. It was a black sedan, its windows darkened. *It must have gotten in through the open gate*, I thought. I cursed myself for forgetting, in my haste, to close it. The car moved up a nearby path and something which felt like an intense wind of supernatural energy hit me in the face. I spiraled backward. I thought I heard a voice call, "Denice, you'll be first! Then Michael!" I ran to a crypt and hid behind it shaking. Once more I heard the same devilish laughter that I'd earlier heard outside Michael's room. Frightened, I tried to search my surroundings for more cover, but all I saw were rows of old tombstones and some trees thick with foliage. It was dangerous to make my way between them in a lightning storm. Still, though I knew I should stay hidden, I had to keep going.

"Michael," I murmured. *I must find Michael before they do.* Moving in and out of the shadows, I ran through the cemetery, up and down the paths with the car, gunning its engine, still behind me and the rain beating down. *Whatever this...this ghost car is, it seems to be following me to get to Michael!* In fits and starts, I ran a short distance and then hid behind tombstones, my heart pounding, terror rising in my chest. Finally, there was a clearing. I had to cross it to get to the site of the newer graves, some of which had flowers upon them. *This is where Justin's grave is!* I looked to see if the car was behind me. When I didn't see it, I darted out, but somehow the car was now in front of me. Heading towards me, it sped up. Desperately, I jumped out of the way and ran into a wooded area. I was trembling with fear. I winced with pain and realized I had twisted my ankle. I got down on the ground and crawled. My breaths were coming harder and harder and my clothes clung to me soaked with mud and rain. Behind me I heard an inhuman screech of pure rage mixed with mad delight. Despite myself, I cried out, but luckily the sound was drowned out by a clap of thunder. I knew now the demons were playing a monstrous game with me as the prey.

A few moments later, I fought off a wave of nausea as the lights of the black car passed so close to me I had to hold my breath. Looking inside, I could see no one behind the wheel, only dark shadows. I ran, limping, inside a mausoleum. I prayed I had not been seen. "Please let me have gotten away," I softly pleaded, "so I can find my son."

All was suddenly silent. The rain had stopped. *Are they springing a trap?* I didn't know. Slowly, I stood up. I hobbled out, took a few steps, stopped and began then to make my way down each row with fresh churned earth mounded up. Suddenly, I felt a burst of cold air rush past me, the feel of hands on my back and then a powerful shove threw me forward. I fell into the soft, squishy mud piled high on a fresh grave. The taste of blood and earth mixed in my mouth. I willed myself to get back up.

Gagging and coughing as I dragged myself forward, I saw a small figure about ten feet ahead on the path. I edged closer. It was Michael kneeling at Justin's tombstone, praying. I called out, "I'm here, Michael. Stay there. I'm coming."

At that moment, I felt myself knocked to the side as the black car, coming out of nowhere, zoomed forward, grazing my hip and shoulder and heading straight for my son.

I opened my mouth to scream 'get out of the way' when I saw something I will never forget. As Michael stood up and the car continued to bear down on him, he was suddenly surrounded by a white light in which Justin and Grandpa Pierce appeared, each moving to either side of Michael. Then, just as the car was about to strike him down, Justin and Grandpa Pierce stepped in front of Michael. The white light intensified, throwing off red hot heat as if it was a fire. I shielded my face and my tearing eyes squeezed shut against the heat and blinding light. When I could open them again, I saw that both the light and the black car had vanished. Where the car had been a trail of thick black smoke dissipated into the atmosphere. Only my son stood there, unharmed. I limped to his side and saw in his hands the crude, wooden crucifix Justin had made him. He looked at me and smiled that wonderful, cherub's smile.

"See," Michael said, "I told you we are not alone."

EPILOGUE

The events that took place on that night in the cemetery were not really the end for us. Even today, as I sit and write these final words, strange incidents, mostly centering around Michael, continue. As well as angels and ghosts, he still sees demonic entities which, at times, besiege and try to attack him. No matter where we live, and we have moved several times, it isn't unusual to hear unfamiliar footsteps in the hallways at night, for objects to appear and disappear or to walk through an area or a room which suddenly has a noxious odor or becomes inexplicably icy cold.

These things still happen, but they are not the same as before. The terror is gone and we are no longer living in fear. Nevertheless, there is no denying that every member of our family still has moments when he or she is unnerved by some unexplainable event. The spirits still come...perhaps they always will. But we now know why, and that we must fight them with all our hearts and souls. Most of all, we know we can triumph, because God is with us.

Each of us has learned to cope in his or her own way. For some, it has been easier than others.

Except for Michael, I think I have been the most changed by our torment. For the first time in my life, I have discovered independence and the ability to stand on my own in the face of fear. Perhaps it is my destiny in this life to walk a path on which I am forced to learn courage. Before our besiegement by the negative spirits, I had always leaned on others and waited for someone to help, whether it was my parents, my husband, an authority figure, my church or my Maker. I have learned that though God is with us, we must help ourselves.

I have spent much time researching the paranormal. After our plight gained the public's attention, others from around the world contacted me for help. Because I know how much agony can be inflicted by paranormal forces, I have turned to assisting people who find themselves in similar situations. I formed a non-profit organization called the L.I.F.E. (Living in Fear Ends) Foundation. Our goal is to aid families and individuals who are experiencing paranormal phenomena and to put them in touch with trained specialists and investigators who can bring them some relief. Thanks to my wonderful friend and attorney, Stuart Rothenberg, we have been able to provide contact information and assistance to hundreds of people.

I never would have dreamed that my family's frightening experiences could inspire me to change my life in the way that I have. Always, I try to remember the Biblical words Grandpa Pierce repeated: 'Resist the devil and he will flee from you.' This I have found to be true.

However, I disagree with much information that is out there. I do not believe those who have psychic powers or see spirits should or can shut off their abilities. Nor do I believe those who say individuals who are attacked by demons in some way invite them into their lives.

What about, I want to ask such erudite authorities, the plaguing of innocent children? I will never accept that Michael or other innocents, through any act of their own volition, have motivated or warranted being persecuted by the devil. Instead, I have come to believe that evil of all kinds, whether it be: deadly illnesses, war, famine, holocausts, criminal assaults, bigotry, treachery or other undeserved pain comes unbidden.

Evil roams the world, scheming to destroy, attacking the good and the kind, and most of all, the innocent, trying to make them lose or give up their faith. Much as Christ, the ultimate innocent, was tempted and tried by Satan, the only answer as the Bible reveals and Grandpa repeated is to resist. This is the path we have chosen.

For my husband, Bruce, such things as ghosts and spirits had not existed in his philosophy prior to entering Michael's and my life. The horrible events we experienced in the past and still experience have become a permanent reminder for him that rationality cannot explain everything in our universe as well as how strange and unpredictable life can become in a matter of moments. Perhaps this is his life lesson. I value beyond words the ongoing loyal support and love he gives me and the children so unstintingly.

As for my parents, who also have loved and supported us through our pain and trials, these events have not destroyed their trust in God and his ultimate plan. Their faith has been tested, ennobled and helped sustain our own.

Kenny and Crystal, who continue to face eerie, frightening incidents that still occur today, who still sometimes are awakened in the night to see objects fly about or hear the groans of their brother being plagued, still fly to Michael's side to help. Through our trials they have come to understand the value of unity, courage and family love. And I have been amazed at their becoming, despite it all, caring, well-adjusted teenagers.

None of us has been so affected by the strange events in our lives as has Michael. Yet with love, grace and magnanimity, he has learned to turn his initial terror into acceptance and cope with his powers, a gift some perceive as a curse.

I now am sure that Michael is a beacon of light in the darkness. For this reason, I also believe he may never be free of the spirits, good and evil, which come to him until his journey is over. Sometimes I wonder, despite his seeming acceptance of his gift, does he ever look with foreboding at the long years (if Justin's prophecy is right) that stretch ahead of him? Does he ever wonder what it would be like to be able to shut off the supernatural forces and forms that come to him and be like everyone else?

If he does, he does not say. I'm not sure how I would deal with it, but Michael, despite the trials he endures, is amazingly optimistic and filled with the joys, as well as moved by the sorrows, of life. Perhaps that is why he was chosen.

I have no idea what Michael will become, but he is a very special person. I have a strong feeling that Grandpa was right: that in some way, Michael will touch many people's lives before his time here on earth is through.

If you are in need of paranormal assistance, contact us at:
The L.I.F.E Foundation
P.O. Box 1112
Manchester, CT 06045-1112